Robert Coles

Twayne's United States Authors Series

Frank Day, Editor
Clemson University

TUSAS 681

ROBERT COLES
Photo by Micah Marty

Robert Coles

Susan Hilligoss

Clemson University

Twayne Publishers
An Imprint of Simon & Schuster Macmillan
New York

Prentice Hall International
London • Mexico City • New Delhi • Singapore • Sydney • Toronto

#36225890

Twayne's United States Authors Series No. 681

Robert Coles
Susan Hilligoss

Twayne Publishers
An Imprint of Simon & Schuster Macmillan
1633 Broadway
New York, NY 10019

Library of Congress Cataloging-in-Publication Data

Hilligoss, Susan, 1948–
    Robert Coles / Susan Hilligoss.
        p.   cm.—(Twayne's United States authors series : TUSAS 681)
    Includes bibliographical references and index.
    ISBN 0-8057-4014-7 (alk. paper)
    1. Coles, Robert—Criticism and interpretation.   2. Poor—United
States—Historiography.   3. Afro-Americans—Historiography.   4. Afro-
Americans in literature.   5. Poor in literature.
    6. Psychoanalysis.   I. Title.   II. Series.
PS3553.O47456Z675   1997
808'.0092—dc21   96-54699
                                                                                    CIP

The paper used in this publication meets the minimum requirements of American
National Standard for Information Sciences—Permanence of Paper for Printed Library
Materials. ANSI Z39.48-1984. ⊚ ™

10 9 8 7 6 5 4 3

Printed in the United States of America

For my parents, Don and Peg Hilligoss

Contents

Preface

Robert Coles has written more than 50 works of nonfiction, including two that were awarded a Pulitzer Prize and one best-seller. A medical doctor and child psychiatrist with roots in literature, art, philosophy, theology, and civil rights, he has always written for the general reader as well as the specialist. In a prolific career he has published major studies of the socialization of children—the five-volume *Children of Crisis*, on race and class in America, and a three-volume collection on children's moral, political, and spiritual lives—as well as literary appreciations of James Agee, William Carlos Williams, Flannery O'Connor, and Walker Percy, essays on the documentary photographers Dorothea Lange and Doris Ulmann, and biographies of Erik Erikson, Dorothy Day, Simone Weil, and Anna Freud. Although he has extended his research around the world, he first applied his naturalistic methods of observation in the American South. His writing blends ethical, literary, psychoanalytic, sociological, and activist concerns.

Coles has labored to show the connections between his many interests, which blur genres and purposes as well as subjects. Indeed, a major question about his writing is how to characterize it. He places his work in an eclectic space bounded by scientific case study, nineteenth-century realist fiction, mid-twentieth-century documentary writing and photography, and existential theology. Commentators have agreed that his work has a unique moral tone and a self-deprecating persona. Most also agree that Coles is an extraordinarily sensitive interpreter of literature, conversations, and children's expressions about themselves and their culture, especially their drawings. The one book-length study of Coles to date, Bruce A. Ronda's *Robert Coles: Intellect and Spirit*, posits an autobiographical impulse as central to his writing and traces Coles's major influences to Søren Kierkegaard, Ralph Waldo Emerson, and American transcendentalism. The question of genre remains moot.

In this study I examine 38 of Coles's works, grouping them by subject: psychoanalysis, social psychological studies of children and adults, photography, literature, and spirituality. I propose that the quest is a major theme in Coles's writing, offering a variant on Walker Percy's solitary wayfarer, since to glimpse transcendence Coles's searcher needs to engage an other in sustained conversation. I have also proposed that an additional major theme in his works on intellectual subjects is the tension among three aspects of the searching mind, which I have called the scientist, the artist, and the pilgrim. These aspects of mind figure in the development of Coles's aesthetic, as he has struggled to maintain the respect of readers with different expectations of genre as well as to find integrating threads for himself. This study also blends his interests in visual art, which are usually treated separately, with his literary and psychiatric concerns. Although Coles has written well over a thousand articles, essays, and reviews, I focus here on his major book-length works.

To engage Coles's breadth of interests I have drawn on many experiences, chiefly my graduate studies in medieval literature, my teaching of literature, scientific and technical writing, and visual communication, and my humble status as a Northerner living for 16 years in the South. I learned of Robert Coles in 1966 when my introductory sociology instructor at the University of Michigan approvingly noted Coles's new synthesis of methods, then called social psychology. Much later, having moved to the Carolinas, I began to read magazine excerpts from *Children of Crisis* as well as his book reviews. I undertook this study in the late 1980s, during a period of extraordinary output for Coles following his five-year tenure as a MacArthur Fellow, a period that has been most rewarding to observe.

Acknowledgments

I wish to thank the Twayne editors, especially Frank Day, Mark Zadrozny, Patricia Mulrane, and Anne Davidson, for their assistance in bringing this project to print. Graduate assistants Teresa Fishman, Sarah Del Collo, and Beth Lyons helped with research and bibliography. Susan Walker volunteered her knowledge of editing and publishing. Mary Ray Worley and the staff of Impressions capably oversaw production, and Carol Hoke lucidly copyedited the manuscript. The research was supported by a Clemson University Provost research award and the Idol-South fund of the Department of English. Dixie Goswami has been an inspiration as the best example I know of Robert Coles's kind of scholarship and service. And, as always, I am grateful to Margaret Duggan for her patience and good advice.

The following publishers have kindly granted permission to quote from copyrighted material: Houghton Mifflin Co. for excerpts from *The Spiritual Life of Children*, © 1990 by Robert Coles; *Their Eyes Meeting the World*, © 1992 by Robert Coles; *The Call of Stories*, © 1993 by Robert Coles; *The Call of Service*, © 1990 by Robert Coles. The University of Iowa Press for excerpts from *That Red Wheelbarrow: Selected Literary Essays* and *Times of Surrender: Selected Essays* by Robert Coles, © 1988 by University of Iowa Press; and from *A Piece of Work: Five Writers Discuss Their Revisions*, edited by Jay Woodruff, © 1993 by University of Iowa Press. Addison-Wesley Publishing Company, Inc., for excerpts from Robert Coles, *Anna Freud: The Dream of Psychoanalysis*, © 1992 Robert Coles, M.D.; *Simone Weil: A Modern Pilgrimage*, © 1987 Robert Coles, M.D.; *Dorothy Day: A Radical Devotion*, © 1987 Robert Coles, M.D. Little, Brown and Company for excerpts from *Children of Crisis* volumes 1–5 by Robert Coles, © 1967, 1971, 1971, 1977, 1977 by Robert Coles; *Walker Percy: An American Search* by Robert Coles, © 1978 by Robert Coles; *The Mind's Fate: Ways of Seeing Psychiatry and Psychoanalysis* by Robert Coles, © 1975, 1995 by Robert Coles; *Erik H. Erikson: The Growth of His Work* by Robert Coles, © 1970 by Robert Coles; *The Middle Americans: Proud and Uncertain* by Robert Coles, © 1971 by Robert Coles, photographs © 1971 by Jon Erikson. Grove/Atlantic, Inc., for excerpts from *The Moral Life of Children* and *The Political Life of Children* by Robert Coles, © 1986 by Robert Coles.

Chronology

1929   Robert Martin Coles born 12 October in Boston to Philip and Sandra Coles.

1946   Graduates from Boston Latin School.

1950   Graduates from Harvard College with an A.B. in English. Enrolls in the College of Physicians and Surgeons at Columbia University.

1952   Meets Dorothy Day during a period of despair at becoming a physician.

1953   Makes several visits to William Carlos Williams in New Jersey and accompanies him on house calls.

1954   Receives M.D. from Columbia. Attends classes at Union Theological Seminary and hears Reinhold Niebuhr. Interns at the University of Chicago Clinics. Hears Paul Tillich lecture; reads Erikson's *Childhood and Society* and Freud's "A General Introduction to Psychoanalysis." Returns to Boston for psychiatric residencies, Massachusetts General Hospital and McLean Hospital.

1956   Attends Paul Tillich's seminar on systematic theology. Reads Georges Bernanos and Walker Percy's essay "The Man on the Train."

1957   Residency in child psychiatry, Children's Hospital in Boston.

1958   Drafted into Air Force, serving as captain in charge of a neuropsychiatric unit in Biloxi. Undergoes analysis at New Orleans Psychoanalytic Institute. Witnesses swim-in at a segregated beach.

1960   Marries Jane Hallowell 4 July in Boston. The couple moves to Vinings, Georgia, to aid Robert's study of children desegregating Southern schools. Robert witnesses mob protests when Ruby Bridges enters Frantz Elementary School, New Orleans.

1961 "A Young Psychiatrist Looks at His Profession" appears in *Atlantic.*

1963 Meets with Martin Luther King.

1964 Serves as trainer for the Mississippi Summer Project in Oxford, Ohio, and accompanies students South. Son Robert Emmet is born 21 August. Family returns to Boston and Robert enrolls in Erikson's courses at Harvard. Begins visiting homes of Roxbury children who are being bused.

1965 Serves as consultant to Operation Head Start. Treats migrant and sharecropper children in a mobile public health clinic. Testifies before Senator Robert F. Kennedy's subcommittee on poverty.

1966 A second son, Daniel Agee, is born 15 August.

1967 *Children of Crisis: A Study of Courage and Fear* published. Testifies before Senate subcommittee on hunger and malnutrition. Meets Robert F. Kennedy.

1970 Meets with Daniel Berrigan. *Uprooted Children: The Early Lives of Migrant Farm Workers* and *Erik H. Erikson: The Growth of His Work* published. Third son, Michael Hallowell, is born 7 July.

1971 Conducts research in Rio Grande Valley, spending time in New Mexico. *Migrants, Sharecroppers, Mountaineers* and *The South Goes North* (volumes 2 and 3 of *Children of Crisis*) published. *The Geography of Faith: Conversations between Daniel Berrigan, When Underground, and Robert Coles* published with Daniel Berrigan. *The Middle Americans* published with Jon Erikson's photographs.

1972 Family moves to New Mexico. Robert makes first trip to Alaska, accompanied by son Bob. *Farewell to the South* published.

1973 Shares Pulitzer Prize for General Nonfiction with Frances FitzGerald. *The Old Ones of New Mexico* published with Alex Harris's photographs and *A Spectacle Unto the World* published with Jon Erikson's photographs.

1974   Family returns to Boston area. Delivers T. B. Davie Memorial Lecture at the University of Cape Town, South Africa. Visits Brazil. *Irony in the Mind's Life: Essays on Novels by James Agee, Elizabeth Bowen, and George Eliot* published.

1975   *The Mind's Fate: Ways of Seeing Psychiatry and Psychoanalysis* and *William Carlos Williams: The Knack of Survival in America* published. Wellesley symposium remarks appear in *Photography within the Humanities.*

1976   Delivers Yale University Trumbull lectures on Walker Percy.

1977   Family goes back to New Mexico. Robert and Jane begin interviewing children in Northern Ireland and South Africa. *Eskimos, Chicanos, Indians* and *Privileged Ones* published, completing the five volumes of *Children of Crisis.*

1978   Returns to Boston as professor of psychiatry and medical humanities, Harvard University. *Walker Percy: An American Search* and *A Festering Sweetness: Poems of American People* published. *Women of Crisis: Lives of Struggle and Hope* published with Jane Hallowell Coles. *The Last and First Eskimos* published with Alex Harris.

1979   Visits Rio de Janeiro.

1980   *Women of Crisis II: Lives of Work and Dreams* published with Jane Hallowell Coles. *Flannery O'Connor's South* published.

1981   Receives MacArthur Fellowship. Column, "Harvard Diary," begins appearing in *New Oxford Review.* Continues international research with children.

1982   *Dorothea Lange: Photographs of a Lifetime* published.

1985   Father, Philip, and mother, Sandra, die.

1986   *The Moral Life of Children* and *The Political Life of Children* published.

1987   *Dorothy Day: A Radical Devotion* and *Simone Weil: A Modern Pilgrimage* published.

1988   *That Red Wheelbarrow: Selected Literary Essays; Times of Surrender: Selected Literary Essays;* and *Harvard Diary: Reflections on the Sacred and the Secular* published.

1989 *The Call of Stories: Teaching and the Moral Imagination* and *Rumors of Separate Worlds* published.

1990 *The Spiritual Life of Children* published.

1992 *Anna Freud: The Dream of Psychoanalysis* and *Their Eyes Meeting the World* published.

1993 *The Call of Service* published.

1995 *DoubleTake,* a documentary magazine edited with Alex Harris, premieres.

Chapter One
"A Knowing and Searching Human Being"

Robert Coles does not easily or willingly fit into a category. Perhaps because of that defiance of classification, he has become adept at characterizing himself and his work. In 1971 he gave this epitome of himself:

> I am in my everyday work a social anthropologist, a pediatrician, a child psychiatrist, a teacher and a friend, a visitor and a welcome guest, a busybody and a nuisance somehow to be tolerated and endured and (at last!) sent off with a sigh of relief or worse; but in this book I am only an observer who is trying to make both himself and the people he has spent time with as intelligible as possible. My main hope is to convey directly and simply what I have heard and seen, and hope the reader will be able to understand what I am getting at—perhaps an obvious wish for any writer.[1]

Just as his livelihood spans the boundaries of several professions, Coles's works often defy genre. Although they are scholarly, they read like overheard conversations or the internal monologues we have with ourselves. His writing is filled with people of warmth, complexity, and moral feeling. Like the people he interviews, Coles is many faceted, but he strives for simplicity. Uneasy with the labels that divide experts from the rest of us, he would rather be considered, as he once called another humane psychiatrist, "a knowing and searching human being."[2]

Biography

Robert Martin Coles was born 12 October 1929 in Boston, Massachusetts.[3] His father, Philip, came from Leeds, in Yorkshire, England, and numbered lawyers, a rabbi, a writer, and a surgeon in his family tree.[4] Philip Coles was a chemical engineer at a large company, having come to the United States to study at the Massachusetts Institute of Technology ("End," 49), where he majored in the difficult subject of physical chemistry.[5] Robert's mother, Sandra, grew up in Sioux City, Iowa, with a minister father, and a grandfather and uncles who were farmers (Ronda 1989, 21; *South*, 43–44; "End," 47). She met Philip on a visit to Boston. Fond of art and literature, she was also devoutly religious, with "a mystical bent" ("End," 47). Philip, too, was widely read in Victorian and other authors.[6] However, as a scientist and a skeptic, he was uninterested in matters of faith and was casual about his Jewishness to the point of disavowing it ("End," 48).

Later Robert Coles would recall that this "somewhat unusual and confusing pair" had conflicts, but they agreed on how their two sons, Bob and his younger brother Bill, should conduct themselves ("End," 47). (William Coles later taught at the University of Virginia.[7]) The boys were to study hard—Robert attended Boston Latin School—and enter a profession but not become too intellectual ("End," 49). Sports tempered bookish pursuits. In the evening, while they listened to radio programs in the kitchen, their parents sat in the living room and read aloud to each other from American, British, and European novels (*Stories*, xiv). The boys went to church with their mother. Their scientist father stressed that answers were tentative, always being revised by new observations and analyses. Their mother watched her older son for signs of intellectual pride ("End," 49). With his background colored by his mother's religious idealism and his father's scientific skepticism, Coles learned that "one should not take this life, or the mind, or a particular century or idea or system of ideas too seriously" ("End," 48).

At Harvard College, young Coles studied literature and history, earning his A.B. degree in 1950 and being elected to Phi Beta Kappa (Ronda 1989, 22). He studied with Perry Miller, a scholar of Puritanism and adviser for his senior thesis, on the first book of William Carlos Williams's long poem, *Paterson*.[8] He even corresponded with the New Jersey physician-poet. However, this bright start in life was clouded by uncertainty about the direction he should take. For almost 10 years, from 1950 to 1960, he describes his choices as fitful and his aspirations as not matched by his talents or experiences. Coles's uncertainty during this period is chronicled throughout his essays and prefaces, especially "The End of the Affair" and "Shadowing Binx." On the surface, all appeared straightforward: medical school at Columbia University, a grueling internship at the University of Chicago Clinics, residencies in psychiatry at Massachusetts General Hospital and McLean Hospital, and then advanced training in child psychiatry at the Children's Hospital in Boston. But the longer he prepared, the more confused he became ("End," 52).

In 1950 a psychoanalyst who would become important in Coles's life had described such a prolonged adolescence as a "moratorium," or waiting period. Erik Erikson, writing in *Childhood and Society*, regarded this waiting as an interval of significance, in which experiences are accumulated and mulled over, to be drawn on much later.[9] These years, from 1950 to 1958, were just such a moratorium for Coles. As a college junior, he decided to pursue not literature or theology but medicine, inspired by the example of Dr. Williams ("End," 46). Nevertheless, he despaired of ever becoming a physician.[10] In the required undergraduate science courses, he did poorly. Medical school, which also emphasized laboratory science, was a constant struggle until the students began seeing patients.[11] Even then, his exhilaration at working on the pediatric ward was followed by appalling disappointment because he was too tenderhearted to draw blood from the tiny patients ("End," 46, 50–51; "Binx," 101). Psychiatry was his poorest clinical subject ("End," 50). Interning in Chicago gave him a vigorous respect for medicine and surgery but did nothing to resolve his uncertainty ("End," 46).

At the end of the internship in 1955, he faced a spiritual crisis ("End," 52). During these years of training, teachers and friends had come to his aid when he was plagued by doubts, and time and again he turned to theology for guidance. In New York, the dean of Columbia's College of Physicians and Surgeons put Coles in touch with a faculty member at Union Theological Seminary; there he audited courses and heard the philosopher Reinhold Niebuhr ("Niebuhr," 152). While an intern Coles fit in lectures by the theologian Paul Tillich, then visiting Chicago; at the same time he was becoming interested in psychoanalysis ("End," 53). On several occasions William Carlos Williams gave him "tactful" vocational advice.[12] Before he returned to the East Coast, he stopped briefly in Trappist, Kentucky, at the Abbey of Gethsemani— Thomas Merton's monastery ("End," 52). Back in Boston, one of Coles's psychoanalytic teachers encouraged him to join Tillich's seminar on systematic theology at Harvard (*Irony*, 5). There he read Georges Bernanos's novel *Diary of a Country Priest* and Walker Percy's essay "The Man on the Train," works that touched a chord in him. He also learned a theological perspective, liberal but at the same time critical, from which to view psychoanalysis (*Irony*, 5; *Diary*, 163). Another supervisor, Dr. Elizabeth Zetzel, suggested that Coles "read novels and learn from them a more intricate, a more subtle kind of, psychology" (*Irony*, 5). This sort of advice he could heed.

Moreover, he felt called to help others as a way to resolve his confusion and break through the intellectual shell of his academic courses. During college he tutored at a settlement house (*Day*, xvii). One afternoon in 1952, after leaving his lab courses, he first witnessed a woman die on the streets of New York and then found his way to "the Catholic Worker soup kitchen on the Lower East Side," where he met Dorothy Day, the legendary Catholic writer and activist (*Day*, xvi–xvii).

Impressed by the close relationship of a small-town doctor with his patients, Coles visited Dr. Williams several times in 1953 and accompanied the New Jersey doctor on house calls (*Stories*, 110). Williams obliged by raining contempt on academic doctors. After interning, Coles inquired about serving in one of Dr. Albert Schweitzer's hospitals in Africa or India, and during residency, he worked with skid-row drunks and delinquents in an alcoholism recovery clinic attached to one hospital ("End," 55).

None of these disclosed to the young doctor the direction he sought. As sometimes happens, events beyond his control lent a hand. In the 1950s, physicians were still subject to mandatory military service under the "doctors' draft." Coles had prolonged his medical studies in part to delay going into the service ("End," 52). But in 1958 these deferments came to an end, and Dr. Coles became Captain Coles, stationed at Keesler Air Force Base, Biloxi, Mississippi,[13] where he superintended the neuropsychiatric unit of the base hospital. The experience gave him both the confidence of seeing his knowledge "come alive" in practice and a sense of rakish freedom, as he drove his sports car into New Orleans to see his analyst, attend movies, and go out with women ("End," 56; also "Binx," 102–3). He continued reading; among the authors numbered the psychoanalysts "Erik Erikson, Anna Freud, Frieda Fromm-Reichmann, Allen Wheelis, Harold Searles, Charles Rycroft, D. W. Winnicott" ("End," 57). He read Walker Percy's novel *The Moviegoer* and likened himself to the novel's restless, entertainment-minded protagonist, Binx Bolling ("Binx," 105).

The long, wandering interlude came to an end one Sunday morning in 1958. Coles, riding a bicycle along the Gulf beach, witnessed what seemed a strange incident: Several black people crossed the short stretch of sand into the water and were immediately arrested by police. What he had seen was a "swim-in" to protest the segregation of the beach (*Courage*, 4–5). This dramatic demonstration of protest and racism in action precipitated a series of events that changed his life.[14] Bruce A. Ronda calls this event not only an "identity crisis" in Erikson's sense but also a spiritual awakening in the tradition of St. Augustine (Ronda 1989, 14–15). Pursuits that had once divided Coles's attention—practical service, theology, medicine, psychiatry, and literature—over several years were slowly gathered into focus through the lens of civil rights. He decided to stay in the South after his military discharge to work with the black children who had been chosen to desegregate New Orleans schools.[15] On 4 July 1960 in Boston, he and Jane Hallowell, a Radcliffe graduate, married and moved to Vinings, Georgia (*Authors,* 89; Ronda 1989, 37). They had little money and no certain means of support (Ronda 1989, 37). Still, Coles traveled thousands of miles visiting children in New Orleans and Atlanta. Jane taught high school English and history and began accompanying her husband on many of his visits to the children and their families (*Stories,* xix).

During his residency, just prior to the discovery and use of the Salk vaccine, Coles had researched the stress suffered by children with polio and published an article in a psychiatric journal (*Courage,* 17). Not entirely sure what this new research might be called or how it was to proceed, he proposed to study the children integrating the New Orleans schools for signs of psychiatric stress. The study would be conducted in the children's homes and at their schools. Foundations turned him down again and again, however. At last the New World Foundation agreed to fund his proposal, and over time others signed on (Ronda 1989, 37–38). The "field work," as he called it, was nebulous and uncertain; simply getting in touch with the children took some doing. Families naturally did not want their privacy intruded upon or their children exploited, even by so-called experts. That reluctance was magnified by the constant threat of violence. In New Orleans, the names of the four children chosen to begin desegregation were kept secret by the school board (*Courage,* 23). Dr. Kenneth Clark in New York City and Thurgood Marshall, then with the Legal Defense Fund of the National Association for the Advancement of Colored People (NAACP), put Coles in touch with black leaders in several Southern cities.[16] Through them he found trusted intermediaries who arranged for him to meet the families of children he might include in his fieldwork. Jane became a habitual companion on many of their visits. The appearance of husband and wife together tended to put people at ease, allaying suspicions that they were simply research subjects.

Gradually the couple earned the trust of the families and children, and adults were added to the study. In medical school Coles had been rebuked for chatting too much with patients; now that ability to reach across class, race, and suffering was an invaluable skill ("End," 50). In these first groups Coles found a number of remarkable people about whom he has often written. Chief among them is Ruby Bridges, who was six years old when, on his way to a medical conference, Coles first saw her walk through a mob at the William T. Frantz School in New Orleans.[17] Their encounters make up some of the most startling portions of his first book, *Children of Crisis: A Study of Courage and Fear*. Gradually, too, he started to work with young civil-rights activists through the Student Non-Violent Coordinating Committee—SNCC (*Farewell*, 221–22; 242–43). As their staff psychiatrist, he established relationships with 23 students between 1960 and 1964 (*Farewell*, 221–42).

Traveling constantly between cities, schools, families, meetings, and jails, Coles began writing occasional essays about his work and conditions in the South. The writing did not come easily; he recalls that several people had to push him hard for those first articles (Woodruff 119). Whitney Ellsworth at *Atlantic*, Margaret Long, a novelist and editor of *New South* magazine, and William Carlos Williams were among those who badgered, encouraged, and praised the reluctant writer (*Farewell*, 6; Woodruff 119). From the beginning of Coles's work in the South, Peter Davison, editor for *Atlantic*'s book imprint, served as his publishing guide (*Farewell*, 17).

The pattern of Coles's involvement with his subjects was repeated many times in the next 14 years and is documented in the prefaces and the "Method" sections of the five volumes that became the *Children of Crisis* series. To urban children were added rural children; to schools in the South were added schools in the North; to problems of the eastern United States were added those of the West; to civil rights was added poverty; to race was added class. Each time, according to Ronda, "Suddenly he [Coles] found himself, he reported to his wife, doing his same old work again, finding people on hunches, talking with them, listening to their stories" (Ronda 1989, 123).

The times were turbulent, the issues urgent. In 1963 Coles recalls talking with Dr. Martin Luther King in Atlanta.[18] The next year found Coles at Western College for Women, in Oxford, Ohio, serving as a trainer and psychiatric resource person for young civil-rights workers in the Mississippi Summer Project (*Courage*, 28–29; *Farewell*, 244). Soon after the two weeks of training began, project members Michael Schwerner, Andrew Goodman, and James E. Cheney left for Mississippi to make preparations but were murdered near the small town of Philadelphia, in Neshoba County. The news of their disappearance and the confirmation of their deaths at first appalled the students and staff, then gave them the conviction to continue (*Farewell*, 244; 247; 267–69; 340). Troubled by his own fears, Coles accompanied the main group to Mississippi where they joined freedom fighters to register black voters. He counseled the organizers and, after they were inevitably arrested, he visited them in jail (*Courage*, 28–29; *Farewell*, 231–32). Often lawyers and other students who feared for their friends' health and spirits requested these visits. During this time, Coles read Dorothy Day's *Long Loneliness* "in places like Humphrey or Leflore counties, Mississippi."[19] In Louisiana he read Erikson's *Young Man Luther* and found that Luther's plight resonated with that of the youthful civil-rights activists.[20] While in Mississippi, he got a telephone call from Erik Erikson, inviting him to contribute an essay on the activists to a collection entitled *Youth: Change and Challenge*.[21]

In the fall of 1964, Robert Coles moved back to Boston (*Erikson*, xv). He and Jane were now parents of a son, Robert Emmet (Hubbard 84). Two more, Daniel Agee and Michael Hallowell, would follow. Coles, now almost 35, enrolled in Erikson's undergraduate course at Harvard and his seminar in life history (*Erikson*, xv). In 1966 he served as one of Erikson's graduate teaching assistants. As Ronda has noted, a teaching assistantship was a lowly position for a man of 37, but Coles loved teaching nonetheless (94). Among Erikson's other assistants at this time was Carol Gilligan, the future feminist psychologist (94).

Pursuing his "old work," Coles began visiting black children in Roxbury, the site of Boston's turbulent school desegregation (*South*, 30). Now, and for years afterward, the Harvard University Health Services gave him a professional "home" when he had no other. At the clinic he served as research psychiatrist, seeing patients, but he was also out in the streets, observing and listening to children (*Authors*, 89). Jane's teaching and grants from the Field, New World, and Ford Foundations, among others, supported the family (*Farewell*, 17).

The mid-1960s were years of activism and service, as Coles's efforts came to the attention of a public and a government interested in doing better by its poorer citizens. He still visited children extensively in the South, not simply observing but also drawing on his doctor's training to treat migrant and sharecropper children in a mobile public health clinic (*Farewell*, 170). He teamed up with other physicians to study hunger, malnutrition, and disease among children in Mississippi and the Appalachians (*Farewell*, 170–71). Twice he testified before Senate subcommittees on the problems of rural children.[22] Robert F. Kennedy sat on one of these, and Coles accompanied him through the Appalachian region, documenting hunger and malnutrition in America (*Eskimos,* xi–xii). Later the writer would credit the senator as the inspiration for *Eskimos, Chicanos, Indians.* The story of Southern children desegregating schools, *Children of Crisis: A Study of Courage and Fear,* which Coles began writing in 1965, was finally published in 1967 and received several honors, including Phi Beta Kappa's Ralph Waldo Emerson Award (*Authors,* 32). Throughout this time he had been writing article after article for magazines, a number of them collected in *Farewell to the South* (1972), as well as reports to agencies concerned with poverty, chiefly the Southern Regional Council.

During late July of 1970, Coles met with Father Daniel Berrigan. Father Berrigan and his brother Philip, both Roman Catholic priests who opposed the Vietnam War, had been convicted of burning draft files in Catonsville, Maryland. Daniel Berrigan had refused to surrender to federal authorities and for several months in 1970 remained in hiding.[23] Ambivalent about the peace movement, Coles was only slightly involved in the resistance to the war. Like the civil-rights movement, the opposition was inspired by ethical responsibility, but it was almost exclusively a middle-class cause. In addition, the antiwar protesters sometimes condoned violence and were occasionally as intolerant of ordinary, struggling Americans as they were of "radicals" (*Geography,* 25). Indeed, by the mid-1960s the civil-rights movement had also changed, becoming more analytical, more organized, more militant— and less the inspired outpouring of individuals' longing for justice that had characterized the early days. Coles continued to write—about poor children, their schooling, and drugs. He completed as well a study of his mentor, Erik Erikson, and tried his hand at books for children.

The early 1970s witnessed the continuation of research for *Children of Crisis.* In 1971 Coles was living in New Mexico (as he did off and on during these years), interviewing children in the Rio Grande Valley.[24] In 1972 he made his first trip to Alaska, accompanied by eight-year-old, eldest son Bob (*Eskimos,* 47). In May of 1973, a month dominated by the growing scandal of Watergate, *Migrants, Sharecroppers and Mountaineers* and *The South Goes North,* the second and third volumes of *Children of Crisis,* were awarded the Pulitzer Prize for General Nonfiction. Coles shared the prize with Frances FitzGerald, author of *Fire in the Lake: The Vietnamese and the Americans in Vietnam.*

Always skillful at drawing on literature, philosophy, and theology in his writings on social issues, Coles began producing books on the writers themselves during this decade. First was a 1974 study of the psychological and theological ages of man, *Irony in the Mind's Life*, illustrated by three novels. That was followed in 1975 by a study of William Carlos Williams. Coles also published a book of poems, *A Rumor of Separate Worlds*.

In 1974, Coles was invited to South Africa to deliver the 15th T. B. Davie Memorial Lecture at the University of Cape Town (*Fate*, 225). For the first time he ventured outside the United States (*Political Life*, 11). The lecture series commemorates those who battle apartheid, and the students invite the lecturers. The tradition of student protest and the memory of American civil-rights advocates who had preceded him made Coles mindful of the honor bestowed on him. Robert F. Kennedy had delivered the 1966 lecture, and that same year Martin Luther King had been denied a visa to meet with South African students.[25] Coles chose to speak about a new subject: children and politics. This emotionally charged trip marked the formal beginning of his international research, which was fully underway between 1978 and 1985.[26] Various members of the family—by this time the three boys were adolescents—went to Northern Ireland, Poland, East Germany, Nicaragua, South Africa, Brazil, and Canada, and also conducted further interviews in New England (*Spiritual Life*, xiii; *Political Life*, 16).

As with his American travels, Coles kept in touch with a number of children for many years, visiting them whenever possible (*Political Life*, 17). Originally he and Jane did all the interviewing; Jane also typed and edited her husband's work for many years (Ronda 1989, 101). Later their sons joined them in the undertaking (*Political Life*, 16). In 1981, Coles was named a MacArthur Fellow. It was the first year that these five-year fellowships, popularly known as "genius" grants, were awarded. He was now able to afford assistance for the research that became known collectively as *The Inner Lives of Children* (Woodruff 99). The last volume in that series, *The Spiritual Life of Children*, published in 1990, declared an interest in faith and spirituality that had been growing since the 1970s, when Coles became interested in writing about Dorothy Day and the French philosopher and mystic Simone Weil. Jane Hallowell Coles had long urged him to take seriously the religious tone of children's conversations, and eventually he did. A persistent if unresolved theme even in Coles's early writing, spirituality emerged as a major direction starting in 1981. He agreed to write a column on psychoanalysis and religion for the conservative magazine *New Oxford Review*, a series of articles that were later gathered under the title of *Harvard Diary*.

In the late 1970s, yet another opportunity arose. At the request of a friend and administrator at Harvard College, Coles began teaching a freshman seminar entitled "A Literature of Social Reflection" (*Stories*, xvi). The following years found him teaching that course regularly, as well as others for students in education, divinity, politics, business, medicine, and law. He subsequently taught at Harvard, Duke University, the University of North Carolina at Chapel Hill, the University of Massachusetts medical school, and other colleges (*Stories*, xvii–ix). In 1978 Harvard University named him professor of psychiatry and medical humanities. Coles gave another longtime personal interest—documentary photography and writing—institutional recognition when he lent his support to the founding of Duke University's Center for Documentary Studies.[27] In 1995 he and photographer Alex Harris launched a quarterly magazine, *DoubleTake*, published by the center and dedicated to social awareness through the arts of documentary. The overall goal of the center, Coles has asserted, is " 'to reclaim both the humanities and the old tradition of social inquiry' " (Coughlin A12). The same goal describes most of Coles's writing. For over 20 years, in between travels, he and his wife have lived in an old farmhouse in Concord, Massachusetts (Woodruff 99; *Spiritual*, 37; Ronda 1989, 93; Hubbard 86). Both Philip and Sandra Coles died in late 1985, causing their elder son to reflect on his life and his own parenting (Woodruff 111). In addition to teaching university students, Coles has taught art history to elementary school students in Cambridge (*Spiritual*, 109–10). The author of more than 50 books and a contributor to many more, Coles continues to write, teach, and work with young people who are interested in the kind of ethical, literary, activist research that has engaged him for almost 40 years.

In 1980 he described his method of writing to David Hellerstein:

> I write on yellow lined legal pads. I write in the mornings, early, just after my children have gone to school. I think about what I'm going to write the night before. Then I sit down and by golly, I write. I write on a quota basis. I try to write three to four yellow pages a day, five days a week. And if you keep on doing that with some—almost a religious—dedication, the books mount up over the years. One of the reasons is some sort of a necessary feeling I have that I must do this fairly regularly. The only time I stop writing is when I'm out in the so-called field.[28]

After the draft is typed, he revises once. He does not usually "tinker repeatedly over a long period of time" with a piece (Woodruff 127). In 1986 he announced that he was giving his papers to the library of the

University of North Carolina at Chapel Hill, including three decades' worth of tapes, transcripts, and children's drawings (*Political Life*, 8; 311, n. 5).

Major Themes

For a long time the research and writing were lonely going. Not surprisingly, perhaps, the theme of journey runs quietly throughout Coles's work. The journey includes the exhaustive travel that lies behind the fieldwork, but it is also a spiritual pilgrimage, a quest, a search for answers about life's purpose. That inquiry is revealed and made significant by the actions of mind, in particular, through self-scrutiny, close observation, and long conversation with another mind. The extended conversations that characterize Coles's writing are shaped by many influences. Among these are Christian writers and existentialist philosophers, realistic novelists, and twentieth-century documenters of human suffering. Also important is Coles's long training in psychoanalysis, with its method of the patient, or analysand, talking at length to an analyst to reveal truths about a life. A set of themes runs through the five-volume series *Children of Crisis*, the three-volume international series (*The Moral Life of Children*, *The Political Life of Children*, and *The Spiritual Life of Children*), several books of similar research with adults, his collaborations with photographers, and his book-length works on psychiatry, literature, and religion.[29]

Coles is a searcher in the existential sense, and so are his subjects. The best of these live self-consciously, with a keen capacity for *"moral notice"* (*Moral Life*, 275; emphasis Coles's). They live in precarious, even dangerous, circumstances. More often than not they are poor and far from the centers of power. Certainly they are ordinary people. The real heroes also seem to live at a crossroads of history and culture, a time of crisis. They suffer greatly and often doubt themselves, but they have profound sources of strength and endurance. Ruby Bridges and Dietrich Bonhoeffer, who resisted the Nazis, are two whom Coles would call heroes. They are people "not only of high conscience . . . but of demanding conscience, a voice within that (at a minimum) said there is no pathway but *this* pathway" (*Diary*, 115–16). Their lives have achieved "a kind of transcendence" as humble "instruments of a cause, a nation's destiny, an ethical struggle, a people's needs" (*Diary*, 116).

Coles's purpose in writing about such lives is didactic, that is, to instill a lesson. Still, people do not always learn from moralistic preaching. Rather they respond to the emotion of another's choices: "And all the while the rest of us pay close attention, feel the awe, the curiosity, the wonder—and ask about ourselves: what might we do when and if this or that extraordinary, exigent moment falls upon us?" (*Diary*, 117). This question, like other existential questions, is never answered completely, nor can it be. But over time, through thousands of particulars, a mind and a life can be known to a degree and capture others' attention, perhaps directing them to a different, better, more ethical life. In 1991 Coles explained to interviewer Jay Woodruff: "You can't just write for aesthetics. You write for some kind of purpose, moral purpose" (Woodruff 121).

Most people do not have the opportunity to join historical awareness and spiritual aspiration as Ruby Bridges and Dietrich Bonhoeffer did. After the energy and achievements of the early civil-rights movement, Coles never found in any other cause the same compelling union of contemporary history and individual life. If there is any other site for transcendence, it is in the encounter of two people talking—listening deeply to and learning from one another. Whether its roots are in psychoanalysis or in the theological relationship of "I-Thou," which completely engages the participants, this exchange underlies most of Coles's writing.[30] Along with a persistent focus on class and the family, this philosophical or spiritual meeting ties together Coles's early work, with its unabashed liberalism, and his later writing, which in some respects is markedly conservative.

This exchange consists not of verbatim transcriptions of conversation but rather is a kind of monologue that places the narrator—Dr. Robert Coles—largely in the background and foregrounds his interlocutor. Each speaker's journey is rendered by his words, chosen from many conversations and interviews with Coles. Silences are noted, interestingly, as are gestures. The words themselves meander, as life does. Often a speaker returns to an idea or image, then reverses himself, recognizes his contradiction, and moves on. The arrangement is selective but mimics the randomness of life.

Coles's major writings focus on the words of these speakers, through which their thoughts and feelings become known: "The whole point of this work has been to put myself (body, mind, and, I pray but cannot at all be sure, heart and soul) in a position, with respect to a number of children, that offers them a chance to indicate a certain amount about themselves to me, and through me, to others. But each life, as we ought know, has its own history, its own authority, dignity, fragility, rock-bottom strength" (*Eskimos*, 57). The rendering suggests the interlocutor's life but is no substitute for it. Because the encounter is between minds, the main "speaker" may be a text rather than a person. Thus, in his study of authors like Flannery O'Connor or Simone Weil, Coles engages the writers' minds by readings—that is, empathetic interpretations—of their work. At times, as in *Walker Percy: An American Search*, the reading becomes a dialogue of sorts. Together Coles and his chosen writer, speaking through his or her work, tell stories from their experience.

Talking itself is not transcendent, but it can prepare one for a possible metaphysical experience. To transcend is "to rise above or go beyond the limits," from Latin *transcendere*, "to climb across."[31] In Coles's writing, it means climbing out of oneself. The possibility of this experience impels the wayfarer to keep searching out and talking with others. At times the spiritual traveler can forget pride, ego, class, education, and race in the presence of another ordinary person. One of Coles's favorite phrases for this unexpected moment is "being brought up short." Other images that describe the experience include "surrender" and being "refreshed" (*Times*, x; *Farewell*, 399); sometimes "redemption" and the elusive term "grace" are used ("End," 48).

Citing Gabriel Marcel, a French existentialist theologian and playwright, Coles defines transcendence: "[T]ranscendence has to do with man's capacity to see and be part of the world around him in a unique way, and ultimately, in a way that moves the person closer to God: each of us is not the sum of what the body urges, the environment demands; each of us is, or at least can be, *homo viator*, man en route, possessed of an active, responsive nature which fathoms, reaches out, defies those who would come near with the chains of the abstract, the categorical, the empirically measurable" (*Percy*, 104–5). In mundane terms, we prepare for transcendence by reaching out from ourselves. For Marcel, "[p]hilosophy begins not with *I am* but with *we are*."[32] That reaching or searching may not be directly toward God; it may simply be toward another person, who, if only we could see, is wholly worthy of our attention. For Coles, we learn *from* each other by attending closely *to* each other. This tenet closely follows Marcel, that we must "become spiritually available (*disponible*) to others" if we are to have "a foretaste of eternal realities" (Keen 155, 153).

Although the focus of the encounter is the "other"—a child, a weary sharecropper, a famous writer—Coles often appears as narrator. After all, Dr. Robert Coles, psychiatrist, is in effect sitting across from these speakers. Even if the narrator intrudes only briefly, that presence lends drama and a kind of honesty because he has his flaws, too. Certainly rendering both sides of the conversation helps to make the *encounter* as well as the person real for the reader. Unless the conversational experience itself is depicted, there is no possibility for the reader to recognize the fleeting, unpredictable points of transcendence that some conversations display. These moments stretch out across the boundaries of traditional narration and make the narrator, and perhaps the reader, aware of herself and her biases. Like the careful ordering that suggests randomness, the participation of the narrator is an artful technique that contributes to the apparent effortlessness of Coles's writing.

Closely related to the journey is another theme, prominent mainly in Coles's works about writers and thinkers. Bruce A. Ronda and others have remarked on the quixotic array of writers that Coles studies (Ronda 1989, 74, 88). They seem to have little in common except his admiration. Many of them, however, are judged by how well they balance the concerns of the scientist, the artist, and the pilgrim. These are not so much separate beings as three aspects of the single thoughtful person to which Coles often refers. The scientist, the artist, and the pilgrim are all searchers: "The mind is active and searching as well as passive and reflexic" (*Percy*, 110). At best these aspects harmonize. Of Erik Erikson, Coles noted: "And if it takes a sharp scientist to find them [truths], trace them back, and figure them out so that the mysterious and baffling becomes suddenly all too obvious, the artist is the one who puts them all together, gives believable coherence to rays of light which come from various directions, bounce, and collide, and often enough cause glitter and glare more than anything else. The search is for Gandhi, but also for more . . ." (*Erikson*, 318–19).

However, the scientist, the artist, and the pilgrim are in tension, too, always shifting toward and away from each other. They all search, but their investigations take somewhat different forms. The scientist seeks precision, demonstrable truths, and neat categories. He deplores ambiguity and "wants to have every possible 'variable' tracked down and fitted right in its place" (*Fate*, 188). The scientist usually has formidable analytical skills and is also a theorist, formulating generalizations from observations—in that sense sharing a great deal with the philosopher. The scientist also likes to apply knowledge to things, to practical everyday problems; this is the engineering side of the scientist (Woodruff 123). But the doctor and social scientist, who are researchers, too, also seek to improve human life directly; hence there is a point—an ethical awareness—where the scientist shades into the pilgrim.

As a physician, Coles himself is beholden to science. He long had the title of "research psychiatrist." He has sought acceptance of his work by the American community of academic social scientists. However, scientists—particularly social scientists, psychiatrists, and psychoanalysts—also receive his harshest criticism. In the quest for certainty, these professionals are vulnerable to making their methods and ideas into "a kind of creed."[33] Ambition contributes to this hardening of investigation into orthodoxy, as does the need to judge others by labeling them as "sick" or "abnormal." In contrast, real science is "open inquiry" (*Anna Freud*, 68). The best researcher is primarily the patient, cautious observer who constructs a view of the world only after painstaking examination of that world, as by clinical observation or fieldwork. Theory then generalizes from that observation. (There is almost no recognition of the notion that we can perceive only by having some ideas, or "theories," about what we are perceiving.) Hypotheses, however, must be flexible and tentative because the complexity of life cannot be pinned down in theories or words. Coles has claimed a "rampant anti-intellectualism" in his opposition to theory (Woodruff 115). Above all, analysis, the breaking down of something into pieces or categories, does not constitute knowledge of a person's life. Scientists and philosophers are constantly in danger of narrowing their vision, fixing life into secular creeds, abstractions, categories, and bureaucratic procedures.

The artist—who may be literary or visual—can lead the scientist away from the dangers of abstraction and false belief in a system or method. Writers of poetry and fiction qualify, as do painters and photographers. Realist fiction, with its close social and psychological observation, is especially important. Fiction improves on social scientific method because it can portray the infinite nuances of particular lives. Storytelling itself is a strong motif in Coles's writing. Certain kinds of knowledge about a life can be approached only by "resort to a story, with attendant use of metaphors or of a webbed collection of symbols" (*Irony*, 8). The language of literature can also purify and remedy the ills of science, at least up to a point: Literature can "help straighten things out—rescue us from sweeping generalization, from a myriad of statistics, from moralistic judgments concealed as factual assertion, and worst of all, from the heavy, murky jargon we have had to grow used to" (*Williams*, xiii). In writing philosophical fiction or poetry, the literary artist undertakes a journey. Of Walker Percy's shift from essays to fiction, Coles remarks: "The departure is from statements, interpretations—the fixed, static, asserted, and defined. The voyage is toward the ambiguous, the imaginary—the con-

crete, yet metaphorical and 'merely' entertaining or 'only' suggestive"
(*Percy*, 36). Indeed, fiction can approach the high status of science. Coles
had, after all, been encouraged to read novels by a supervisor who recog-
nized their psychological insight (*Irony*, 5). In his first book of literary
criticism, Coles longed for storytelling to be acknowledged as scientific
and honored with the vocabulary of science. Fiction would be known as
"*that* 'integrative process,' *that* 'synthesizing procedure,' *that* 'research
method' " (*Irony*, 61).

The visual artist is also a seeker. Children's drawings are a major
resource in Coles's work, and he sees in them a source of tremendous psychological energy and insight. These sketches and paintings are "efforts
to represent the distinctive psychological reality of a given life" (*Privileged
Ones*, 475). Visual art has a special place in the existential search. Children, like adults, engage in "the banal inquiries we never quite stop asking ourselves: who am I, why am I here, whence do I come, and where
am I going—the continuing preoccupations of philosophers, novelists,
and painters. Children prefer the painter's approach. They sometimes
don't pay much attention to the answers to their questions. After all too
verbal family meals they retire to a desk or table, draw pictures meant to
suggest what life is and will be about" (*Privileged Ones*, 385).

Because visual artists are concerned with space rather than time,
there is a sense of timelessness in their perception of the world. This
aspect of the mind tends to be concrete. Artists are not inclined to theory, prefer the open-ended to the categorical, and are reluctant to judge.
They are eager to experience and represent all sensations. Artists must
beware vagueness, mere craft or virtuosity, and anti-intellectualism,
which is a mark of the "pseudo-artist" (*Fate*, 90). In Coles's earlier work,
the artist is also associated with Søren Kierkegaard's "aesthetic" level of
existence, that is, a vain seeking of sensation for its own sake (*Percy*,
151). The artist not only aims to convey the complexity of life, in defiance of the scientist and pilgrim, but also is a crafter of words or paint or
photographic images. In fact, each aspect of the mind has a characteristic job to do. To wonder, then observe closely—that is the scientist, the
re-searcher. To wonder and craft—that is the artist. To wonder and
serve—that is the pilgrim.

The pilgrim is the quintessential solitary wanderer or seeker, a traveler through life on earth. The pilgrim is that aspect of ourselves concerned with the idealistic, the philosophical, the ethical, and the spiritual. For example, Simone Weil, the French philosopher and mystic, is
called "an extraordinary pilgrim of the twentieth century."[34] A wanderer

and an exile, she strove physically, intellectually, emotionally, and spiritually for a destination that she never reached.

Although not everyone is a scientist or an artist—those terms smack of modern, middle-class sensibility—everyone is a pilgrim. Everyone has the authority of a life lived: "We're all readers and we're all human beings in the sense that we're sojourners or pilgrims. . . ."[35] The search may be a patient spiritual examination of self more than an actual journey. This generic pilgrim may not have a particular destination in mind, but she does have a goal or vision of some sort, perhaps just to get through life somehow. The journey itself is at its best an act of devotion. She seeks but cannot be assured of redemption or transcendence, that momentary connection with the other and the forgetting of self. This forgetting may be our closest earthly experience of the divine.

However, the self-knowledge that derives from such moments also reminds us of our flaws, chiefly pride. Coles regularly draws on both psychoanalysis and religion—chiefly the Bible, St. Augustine, and the Danish philosopher Søren Kierkegaard—to describe human imperfection. Psychoanalysis views human nature as driven by selfish emotions, making insight a mixed revelation. In psychoanalysis the analysand combines the careful scientist and the searching pilgrim. Again, the encounter of one person talking with another is a key experience for the pilgrim. In talking she reaches toward the other, in the theological and philosophical sense of someone wholly different from oneself.

In that she is aware of the brevity of life, the pilgrim is concerned with time. She is concerned with people, not pieces of people or things, as the scientist might be. She is restless, striving, dynamic, ethical, uncertain, and full of the self-doubt that Augustine and Kierkegaard had. She is open to new persons and outlooks but not willy-nilly. Rather her thinking and feeling tend toward the apocalyptic and the teleological. That is, the seeker suspects but cannot confirm that there is a single answer or meaning to life. For example, Coles characterizes Mahatma Gandhi's autobiography as a purposeful journey. Gandhi writes "as if . . . he was trying to get someplace, figure something out, solve a predicament and puzzle whose psychological presence, in various forms, simply could not be ignored" (*Erikson*, 329). The pilgrim faces the dangers of mysticism and may reject the humble knowledge of the everyday world that scientists and artists accept. Like the scientist, the pilgrim can easily fall prey to rigid orthodoxy, polemics, and spiritual and psychological fads. Organized religion can be the pilgrim's bane because religion can substitute unexamined pieties for an honest, lonely search.

In talking with and reaching out to the other, the pilgrim also seeks
social justice. She acts in the world to help others. Caring for patients,
bringing up children, and teaching are acts of service, as are registering
people to vote, feeding and sheltering the homeless, and sitting in jail
for a moral cause.[36] Writing may also be service if it brings readers to
greater moral notice of their world. Here the artist and the pilgrim may
be joined. According to Ronda, "[a]s a teacher and a writer, Coles wants
to heal the split between thought and action, intellect and life. This
effort takes on added poignancy when one considers that Coles himself
is a fragmented, often alienated, man on the margins, 'a wounded
healer' in Henri Nouwen's phrase, working to heal a wounded culture"
(Ronda 1989, 175–76). However, good works are not the occasion for
smugness. In true acts of service—acts, really, of devotion—a person
receives the grace of learning from those he serves. Ultimately, the pilgrim's experience cannot be written, for it dissolves into the humble life
of action and self-scrutiny, on the one hand, and moments of transcendence, on the other. Through art, however, its outline can be rendered
for our examination.

There is no typical life that combines the scientist, the artist, and the
pilgrim. Each is individual. Sigmund Freud, for example, blended these
elements in a stellar but disturbing way. Although Coles has rarely written at length on Freud, he has often scrutinized the inventor of psychoanalysis in his writing about other subjects. Above all, Freud was a scientist who observed and reported what others had feared or ignored,
thus opening a whole new field of inquiry. But he employed art in his
science. In a daring move away from the mechanistic assumptions of
nineteenth-century neurology and psychiatry, he shifted to a study of
everyday dreams and stories, which he told in "a stark and compelling
mythological language" (*Irony*, 1). He used ancient Greek drama as
illustrations and evidence for his theories. He was a fine writer whose
work, laced with story after story, still appeals to a lay public as well as
to professionals (*Anna Freud*, 169). He was "a scientist searching for tan-
gible discoveries, but also . . . a man of artistic temperament, especially
sensitive to the opportunities and hazards that words present" (*Fate*,
188). Although not much interested in religion (which in one work he
called an illusion), Freud was a seeker. He pursued new knowledge to
help his patients. In this vein he "called himself a conquistador" (*Irony*,
1), an intriguing metaphor to which Coles returns throughout his writing about Freud. Being a conquistador meant being on a bold, lonely
journey of discovery, combining the scientist and the pilgrim (*Irony*, 3).

Ambition and pride also fueled Freud's search. The Viennese doctor had "a dash of the messianic explorer, determined at fifty-three to find an intellectual New Jerusalem" (*Fate*, 189). In later works, Coles is more willing to acknowledge the connotations of armed force in this image: ". . . like all conquistadors, there was just so much territory he could conquer" (*Fate*, 187; see also *Anna Freud*, 111). Over time the conquistador has become less attractive as an image for the searcher.

Like all theories, this triad of scientist, artist, and pilgrim oversimplifies. As the example of Freud illustrates, when presented as a system the images are full of contradictions and paradoxes. Some people—William Carlos Williams and Erik Erikson, for example—seem to fit Coles's idea of the scientist, the artist, and the pilgrim quite well. Others, like Freud, strain the categories. But as shifting aspects of the mind's life, the three elements trace some of the polarities and tensions that run through Coles's writing. Finally, the pilgrim subsumes the others. Coles remarked in 1991 that "ultimately what I am is a fellow human being, and a journeyman, a voyager who's stumbled and fallen down" (Woodruff 113). The play on *journeyman*—a man who journeys but also an ordinary workman—is typical of Coles's self-conscious use of images. He portrays himself as an Everyman, and his writing renders the course of his fitful voyage.

Chapter Two

"Every Limit Is a Beginning": Psychoanalytic Roots

By the time that Coles wrote his first book-length study of a psychoanalytic subject, he had already published his landmark study of racism, *Children of Crisis: A Study of Courage and Fear*, plus several other books about and for children. Still, his roots have always been in the fields of psychiatry and psychoanalysis, which disciplines have provided Coles with the beginnings of a philosophy of mind. At its best, he has considered psychoanalysis "at once a therapeutic contract, a conceptual design and a means of systematic self-analysis" (*Erikson*, 201). For Coles, as for many other educated Americans who came of age in the 1950s, psychoanalysis was an exciting alternative to the physiological psychology on which earlier psychiatry had been based. However, psychoanalysis has its limits, especially as a substitute for ethics or philosophy. Those limits have energized Robert Coles's thinking, as he has struggled to be true to the principles of psychoanalysis while trying to escape its bounds. His writing about psychiatry and psychoanalysis illustrates a favorite line of his, George Eliot's paradoxical "Every limit is a beginning."[1] The major books and essays on psychoanalysis emphasize two areas: first, the field's values and limitations, some of which have given rise to new perspectives in his research, and second, the lives and works of other investigators who have shared his concerns. Chief among the latter are Anna Freud and Erik Erikson, both innovators in the psychoanalytic study of children and Coles's mentors for over 20 years (*Moral Life*, 19). Anna Freud, in particular, was associated with ego psychology, a dominant influence on American psychoanalysis for many years. This chapter covers *Erik H. Erikson: The Growth of His Work* (1970), the essay collection *The Mind's Fate: Ways of Seeing Psychiatry and Psychoanalysis* (1975), and *Anna Freud: The Dream of Psychoanalysis* (1992).

Erik H. Erikson: The Growth of His Work

By the late 1960s, Coles had developed a long-standing professional association and personal friendship with Erikson and his family. When

William Shawn, editor of *The New Yorker*, encouraged Coles to write about his teacher, the eventual result was *Erik H. Erikson: The Growth of His Work* (1970). As Coles's first effort at biography, it established his style of writing about celebrated lives, a combination of empathetic life history and interpretive reading. *Erik H. Erikson* portrays Erikson as an artist in his youth, a scientist (in this case, a trained psychoanalyst and researcher) in his maturity, and a wanderer at several stages of his life. He exemplified the cosmopolitan European intellectual who, in the face of Hitler's persecutions, made a new life in the United States. Claiming both Jewish and Christian roots, Erikson was born in 1902 of Danish parents—with a German pediatrician as his stepfather—and grew up in solid upper-middle-class European fashion. *Erik H. Erikson* stresses the boy's artistic bent and youthful wandering about Europe, in the tradition of the *Kunstler*, which Coles defines as "a young student who had his doubts about things" (*Erikson*, 14). Erikson did not go to college but rather traveled, drew, and painted. In 1927, teaching children of Americans who were undergoing psychoanalysis, Erikson gradually was drawn into the Viennese intellectual colony around Sigmund Freud and his daughter Anna (22). Having studied with several outstanding analysts, he also received Montessori training, which would later be reflected in his style of research, wherein children arranged objects imaginatively (23). He graduated from the Vienna Psychoanalytic Society in 1933 without medical training (30). Soon he, his American wife, and two sons left the deteriorating political climate in Austria and ended up in the United States. Shortly afterward, Erikson procured positions in Boston at both Harvard Medical School and Massachusetts General Hospital, then at the University of California, eventually becoming a naturalized citizen (32). He undertook research, including cross-cultural studies of the Sioux Indians in South Dakota and the Yurok Indians of the Pacific Northwest. This research was "naturalistic," that is, it was conducted in the subjects' own surroundings, not in an office or otherwise contrived setting. With his other research, these studies also showed Erikson the importance of the relationship between the growing young individual and the world. These points would influence Coles's own inquiry into and outlook on psychiatry. Resigning his position at Berkeley in 1950 rather than sign a McCarthy-era contract that contained a loyalty clause, Erikson returned to Massachusetts and eventually, in 1960, obtained a professorship at Harvard Medical School. *Childhood and Society*, his first book, was published in 1950. During these years he also worked in clinics for poor families. Erikson made several extended visits to India, which resulted in *Gandhi's Truth*, his most recent book by the time Coles's study of him was published.

Erik H. Erikson is an intellectual biography that explicates the psychoanalyst/researcher's ideas (xvii). Bruce Ronda has observed that, like Coles's subsequent books on intellectual subjects, *Erikson* is more a set of close readings of Erikson's books and scholarly papers than a full-scale biography (Ronda 1989, 95). After all, Erikson was still alive and working. The biography's structure takes advantage of the life cycle that Erikson's *Childhood and Society*, made famous. Chapters on "Philosophical Roots" and "Personal and Professional Roots" laid the groundwork of Erikson's complex personal and intellectual journey. After making connections between the existentialist philosopher and theologian Søren Kierkegaard and the father of psychoanalysis, Sigmund Freud, these chapters describe the wandering and diffuse interests of Erikson's youth as a model for his later ideas of identity crisis and moratorium. Then, after fleeing Vienna to avoid the predations of Hitler, a more mature Erikson made a career across the Atlantic, described in chapters entitled "To America" and "To California." These were also the years of his cross-cultural research that helped him formulate a new theory.

Two chapters detail the thinking that became Erikson's first book on the life cycle, "Building a New Point of View" and "*Childhood and Society* Achieved." The years after the publication of *Childhood and Society* were a time of decision for Erikson, even a time of a "second" identity crisis, according to Coles (*Erikson*, 181). Using his clinical research, Erikson turned toward the study of the lives of historical figures, emphasizing their adolescence and early adulthood (151, 202). "Back East" focuses on several scholarly papers of this period that prepared the way for Erikson's extended study of Martin Luther, analyzed in the chapter "Luther and History." A section on further events in Erikson's life is followed by two chapters on Erikson's next major work, *Gandhi's Truth*. In a brief conclusion, "Epilogue, Interlude and Prologue," Coles himself appears alongside Erikson and his wife as they travel through Mississippi in 1970. In particular, Erikson's professional shifts of interest to different stages along the life cycle parallel his own progress toward middle and old age. Shortly, Coles would again use the broad outlines of the life cycle—childhood, youth, age—to organize his first literary study, *Irony in the Mind's Life*.

Erikson is portrayed as a wanderer and a seeker. The biography stresses his willingness to travel to new places, spurred by political and ethical concerns as well as by intellectual curiosity. Moreover, he explored ideas new to psychoanalysis, ideas that had social, political, and eventually ethical implications, certainly for Coles. Psychoanalysis had been evolving from a single-minded focus on "drives" and adult memories to more emphasis on the ego as well as direct observation of children, lines of thought that Anna Freud would help pioneer (44–48). Erikson derived his theories from observation of children and adolescents. His theory of the stages of the psychological and social "life cycle" widened the psychoanalytic perspective to include not only infancy and early childhood but also adolescence, maturity, and age (48–49). Erikson formulated the concepts of identity, identity crisis, and moratorium, all associated with adolescence and early adulthood. His clinical observations showed that the style and process by which children learn from their parents and community are far from superficial, but rather important elements of their development (59). By observing not only patients but also ordinary children, young people, and adults going about their daily business, he contributed to a psychology of everyday life.

After his studies of childhood and adolescence, Erikson developed the genre of biography that is known as "life history" or sometimes "psychohistory," in which, in the words of George Abbott White, "an individual's celebrated inner life makes continual transactions with his outer life or with history."[2] Coles's biography shows the ease, flexibility, and discipline in Erikson's intellectual work. That ease with himself, combined with thoroughness in probing a clinical case or a life situation, corresponds to his theories about human existence, which are both open-ended and cyclical. According to Coles, Erikson kept true to the original principles of psychoanalysis. Equally important was Erikson's strong ethical sensibility. He wrote about ethics, interpreting the Golden Rule as an "active sharing" or mutual influence that strengthens both giver and receiver (*Erikson*, 280). Although one of the cultural elite, he got to know Native Americans, GIs, and poor mothers and their children. Coles implies that Erikson's thought was part of a broad confluence of philosophy and psychology (8–11).

At times the style of the biography self-consciously imitates certain features of Erikson's style. This homage is an expression of mutual influence as an ethical act. According to Coles, Erikson found affinities in his subjects that were expressed in his style. For example, he "seems in places to enjoy himself writing" about Gandhi, "an amusing, daring, challenging man" (*Erikson*, 356). The implication is that Coles, in writing about Erikson, should do so in the same spirit in which his subject wrote, even if such efforts fail. Only by so writing will a biographer achieve that ethical give-and-take, that being acted on as well as acting. By 1970 this "I-Thou" approach to writing and life was already a part of Coles's style. At best it brings a subject startlingly to life. At worst, it idealizes the subject and parodies the distinctive notes of a well-known style. Psychiatrist David Elkind sympathetically reviewed *Erikson* but decried Coles's tendency to use "the same rhythms, cadences, strings of adjectives, and italics that are so characteristic of Erikson's unmistakable literary style."[3] In particular, Coles imitates a daring technique that Erikson employed in *Gandhi's Truth:* imagining what his subject thought. Coles creates several imaginary monologues in *Erik H. Erikson* when Erikson or another putative speaker is at a moral and intellectual crossroads. For example, Coles conjures up an inner dialogue that a troubled Erikson might have had while writing "The Dream Specimen of Psychoanalysis," an examination of Freud's so-called Irma Dream (*Erikson*, 184). Coles speculates that Erikson might have been asking permission from Freud, whom he had known in life, to criticize his work, and he has Erikson "speak" in first person: "I am moved by a spirit you knew so very well, an urge to explore new territory, not in defiance of you, or to 'revise' your ideas, but to honor you, a very creative man, by following suit the best I can, with whatever energy and originality I can summon" (183).

At another point Coles creates words for Gandhi (307). Certainly Coles was conscious of his task as a biographer and writer. He proclaims that in history and biography mere narrative skill is not enough; historians must also "be essayists of the first order, sensitive to the problems of exposition, possessed of a dramatic touch, desirous that their words have both clarity and life" (386). There is evidence in *Erik H. Erikson* that Coles attempted to reach that ideal. In addition to the imaginary monologues, he experiments with other literary techniques. For example, he places a statement from Erikson about his youth so that it was framed by Erikson's mature ideas (180).

Never again would Coles find such a congenial biographical subject. Bruce Ronda has noted the parallels between the two psychoanalysts, as have a number of reviewers.[4] Coles met Erikson when the younger man was in his thirties, and—to use Erikson's terms—fairly well along in the life cycle. Coles was already engaged in his major research and held firm ideas about many things. That is, he was at an age that Erikson had so well documented in his studies of Freud, Luther, and Gandhi: He was adult but not settled. He was innovating in the area of psychoanalytic research and so perhaps needed the support of a certain kind of mentor. Erikson showed the world how Wilhelm Fliess had supported Freud and how Rajchandra had inspired Gandhi. Although he claimed other, earlier mentors, especially Perry Miller and William Carlos Williams, Coles found a new guide for this time of his life, interestingly back at Harvard. With Erikson Coles could also humbly claim a mutuality of influence. Before meeting Coles, Erikson clearly appreciated his research, inviting him to contribute to *Youth: Change and Challenge.* In 1970 Erikson and his wife accompanied Coles to Mississippi, visiting the younger man's territory, as it were (409).

The mutuality was more than coincidence. Even though he has never achieved the sensuality or robustness of Erikson's best writing (or the scholastic dryness of his worst), Coles shared much with his teacher even before they met: an inductive, naturalistic, cross-cultural approach to psychoanalytic research; similar views on good writing; the ability to visualize as well as to intellectualize; deep concern with moral and political values; and an attraction to great minds and ideas while maintaining a sturdy, even stubborn, interest in ordinary people. Erikson's background differs substantially from Coles's, but it also has modest parallels. Rather like Coles, Erikson acknowledged a heritage that was both Jewish and Christian. His European education and training were inflected by living and practicing in the United States. He was artistic in temperament but professed science, that is, psychoanalysis. Above all, Erikson followed necessity and interest alike to new places, new people, and new ideas while holding fast to his roots. Coles appreciated that rootedness and that wanderlust, as shown in the chapter titles and the conclusion to *Erik H. Erikson.* One passage sums up the crucial qualities that Erikson possessed, all of them aspects of truthseeking: "And if it takes a sharp scientist to find them [truths], trace them back, and figure them out so that the mysterious and baffling becomes suddenly all too obvious, the artist is the one who puts them all together, gives believable coherence to rays of light which come from various directions, bounce, and collide, and often enough cause glitter and glare more than anything else. The search is for Gandhi, but also for more" (*Erikson,* 318–19). Coles's teacher was in all ways a scientist and an artist. By implication he is also a seeker and a pilgrim.

The Mind's Fate: Ways of Seeing Psychiatry and Psychoanalysis

In 1975, five years after *Erik H. Erikson* appeared, Coles's reputation was well established. The second and third volumes of *Children of Crisis* had won the Pulitzer Prize. His name was also on the title page of 21 other books, including 5 for children. *The Mind's Fate* gathers 28 pieces written between 1961 and 1975. With comparatively little psychiatric terminology, the various essays in *Fate* treat subjects from crime to film to painting and introduce general readers to Coles's outlook on specific topics in psychiatry and psychoanalysis. They also draw the reader into the United States of the early 1970s. The articles are mostly brief reviews and occasional pieces originally published in *The New Republic, The Atlantic, The New Yorker,* and elsewhere. A few lengthy "thought" pieces, which had appeared in *The New York Review of Books,* are included, the most noteworthy of which is the volume's concluding essay, "Children and Political Authority." This published version of Coles's 1974 lecture at the University of Cape Town, South Africa, was later incorporated into *The Political Life of Children.*

The Mind's Fate, containing four sections, is Coles's second anthology after 1972's *Farewell to the South.* The first presents a humane psychiatrist's commentary on American social problems, including essays on spree killers, war resisters, and life in prisons, asylums, and schools. On these issues Coles's positions are liberal but not rigidly so. For example, in "The Letter Killeth," Coles compares two documents, both examples of the misapplication of psychology to children's learning. The first is an obscure teachers' handbook used in Pittsburgh, designed to keep God and American moral values in the curriculum without violating the 1963 Supreme Court decision against prayer in the schools (*Fate,* 35). The second example is A. S. Neill's radical testament *Freedom—Not License!,* known to a generation of students of educational psychology. Coles lays bare the doctrinaire foundation of each text. Soon, in *Irony in the Mind's Life,* he would extend this criticism from Neill to other educators in the romantic tradition. This section also reprints "A Young Psychiatrist Looks at His Profession," one of Coles's earliest essays, appearing in the *Atlantic* in 1961. Already it expresses many of the views that would be his trademark: a sense of the noble, rebellious history of psychoanalysis; a disdain for bureaucracy, professional nit-picking, and jargon; a fear of labeling people by diseases; a sensitivity to the psychiatric encounter as a Buberian "I-Thou" relationship; a willingness to cite novelists and theologians; and a duty to the poor and powerless. Castigating himself as one of the erring members of the profession, Coles calls on psychiatrists "to affirm proudly the preciously individual in each human being" (*Fate*, 11). Although it is sometimes vague, the essay has a vigorous simplicity overall that Coles's later writing often lacks.

The second section, "The Work of Individuals," gathers articles about notable psychologists. The title also evokes Erikson's "life-history." There are early appreciations of Erikson and Anna Freud but also the Swiss therapist Bruno Bettelheim, the psychiatrist and social radical Franz Fanon, and the American ego psychologist Clara Thompson. Although Coles's portraits are often frankly admiring, there are exceptions. Among these is a reexamination of William James, which contrasts the enduring psychoanalytical influence of *The Varieties of Religious Experience* with James's own psychological problems (*Fate*, 154). In several essays Coles grapples with contemporary writers whose views he cannot wholeheartedly accept or who, in his view, have been embraced too quickly and uncritically. R. D. Laing falls into the first category; Jean Piaget into the second. In three pieces Coles develops the tension between the artist and the scientist, again couching their struggle within the large terms of a transcendent search. For example, "Faith as Doubt," on the psychoanalyst Alan Wheelis, rings changes on Erikson's concept of identity as a search to join the artistic, scientific, and existential aspects of mind: "[I]dentity is gained only through work, through an uneasy but dedicated search, through exercise of the passion that doubt generates and the artist (among others the analyst also) sometimes manages to bring under control. In a sense the writer and the doctor in Wheelis achieved a necessary alliance; they both have an uncertain time of it, and each has reason to live warily, in constant danger of failure" (105). Erikson achieved a more stable alliance, according to "The Artist as Psychoanalyst," a 1964 review of Erikson's *Insight and Responsibility*. Likewise, a description of Franz Fanon, in "What Colonialism Does," allies the scientist and artist. His treatise *The Wretched of the Earth* succeeds because "The crushed people are brought to life as only the novelist or clinician can do it, by detailed descriptions of their private lives, their fears and terrors" (102).

"The Achievement of Anna Freud" is an extended and important essay about this profound influence on Coles's thought and method. Originally published in 1966 in *The Massachusetts Review*, "Achievement" reached Anna Freud herself and so began her longtime professional association with Coles (*Anna Freud*, xxii). "Achievement" is a straightfor-

ward, skilled profile that explicates Anna Freud's major ideas in lay language. Taking up her works chronologically, it promotes her importance
as a thinker in her own right, while placing her ideas in the context of
her father's thought and the main strands of psychoanalytic history. It
sketches the main events of her life and her major contributions to psychoanalysis. Most important from Coles's standpoint is her emphasis on
the ego and her pioneering use of direct observation of children. Her
contribution to the field generally was *The Ego and the Mechanisms of
Defense*, although Coles is more interested in the imagery of defense
mechanisms than in their actual workings (*Fate*, 111). For Coles, direct
observation profoundly changed the possibilities of psychoanalytic study
(117). Anna Freud's skepticism about psychoanalysis as a means of raising children—a series of fads, really—also strikes a chord with Coles
(118–19). He would return to her summary of these fads again and
again.[5]

The articles of the third section, "Creativity, Leadership, and 'Psychohistory,' " all have books at their center, mostly fiction and history.
The books variously elicit Coles's delight, censure, and intricate intellectual analysis. A main theme of the section is the improper application of
psychoanalysis to the lives of artists, statesmen, and other noted figures.
Originated by Freud himself and called "psychohistory," this genre was
in vogue throughout the 1960s and 1970s after Erikson had renewed
and enlarged it, or rather a parallel genre called "life history." Coles,
however, uses the term *psychohistory* pejoratively to mean a reduction of
lives to psychopathology. That is, people's complexities are reduced to
infantile desires and unresolved neuroses. This section reveals a human-
ist and clinician engaged in a tough intellectual battle over the soul of
psychoanalysis. Coles wants psychoanalysis, history, and literature to
inform each other, in the manner that Erikson had outlined, but the
proliferation of crudely argued psychobiographies undermines the very
projects Erikson engages in. The articles on psychohistory, "A Bullitt to
Wilson," "Van Gogh: The Fever of Genius," and the long, learned essay
"On Psychohistory" are difficult reading for those not well versed in psychology and historiography; however, they show a range of tone and
approach rare in Coles's other writing, including some invective as well
as close scholarly argument. To oppose psychohistory, which paints lives
black with repressed desires, does not mean embracing a sunny vision of
human life. The third section closes with essays on the dark visions in
the fiction of August Strindberg and Cormac McCarthy. To Coles their
work suggests that "insight is often not redemptive," not even psycho-

analytic insight (*Fate*, 213). Against the internecine battles of psychoanalysis, the contemporary means to insight, Coles places an older religious tradition of scrutiny. The latter is just as scathing and nihilistic as its modern scientific cousin.

The final section, "Theory: Lectures on Child Development," contains two essays based on Coles's field studies. "The Inner and Outer World" is a 1971 lecture published first as a chapter in *The Infant at Risk* (*Fate*, 225; ed. Bergsma 1973). Describing the experience of a black child of Mississippi, the essay is typical of Coles's research in *Children of Crisis*. The thesis is that the boy's dreams cannot be reduced to symbols of infantile desires (*Fate*, 238). In "Children and Political Authority," the subject is children in different cultures, but the theme is again the subtle relations between children's psychological development and their understanding of their particular historical and political situation. The final section of this collection illustrates that Coles uses "theory" to describe comparatively modest generalizations from his observations. Earlier in *The Mind's Fate*, Coles defines theory as a "particular truth" (125). Theory is "something tentatively held, a vision that for the moment works, that for a while makes things clearer, lends them a certain order" (125). This definition would remain important to Coles; he would eventually add story as an integral part of theory.

Anna Freud: The Dream of Psychoanalysis

To most readers, Anna Freud is simply the daughter of Sigmund Freud. She is nonetheless a major contributor to psychoanalytic theory and research. She and Coles shared an informal professional association and mutual regard for over a quarter century, sparked by the younger researcher's profile of the older. A decade after the death of the renowned psychoanalyst in October, 1982, Coles published *Anna Freud: The Dream of Psychoanalysis* (1992), on the second of his two towering psychoanalytic mentors. Miss Freud's famed modesty was in part to blame for the delay (*Anna Freud*, xxiii–xxv). Because of their differences of opinion on many issues, amply illustrated in the biography, there may have been reluctance on Coles's part as well. *Anna Freud: The Dream of Psychoanalysis* shows the evolution of a writer over 20 years since the publication of *Erik H. Erikson*. Nevertheless, the stance toward psychoanalysis remains essentially the same.

Directed to a nontechnical audience, *Anna Freud: The Dream of Psychoanalysis* is part biography, part memoir, and part appreciation. A volume

in the Radcliffe Biography Series of extraordinary women, it illustrates
Anna Freud's "quality of mind" in writing, lecture, and conversation
(*Anna Freud*, 24). She is portrayed as a strong but humble person who
had a healthy doubt about psychoanalysis and her own contributions to
that field. Unlike *Erik H. Erikson*, which was the first extended biography of Erikson, *Anna Freud* followed several other biographies of Freud's
daughter (211). It is less ambitious than *Erik H. Erikson* and much
shorter, only 178 pages of body text. However, it also reprints "The
Achievement of Anna Freud" and includes several letters from Miss
Freud to Coles. After a brief overview of her life, "A Life with Children,"
the book is arranged by topics that stress Anna Freud's humanitarian
qualities: "Teacher," "Theorist," "Healer," "Leader," "Idealist," "Writer."
Although it draws on learned and primary sources, *Anna Freud* gives its
subject accessibility rather than comprehensive treatment, as reviewers
have noted.[6] Altogether, *Anna Freud* has been called "the foremost text
available" on the psychoanalyst.[7]

Erik H. Erikson* explicated its subject's major writing. *Anna Freud* shifts
the burden from published texts to oral history. In tone and organization,
Anna Freud is most like *Dorothy Day*, also written for the Radcliffe Biography Series. Like his 1987 study of Day, an American Catholic writer
and activist, major portions of *Anna Freud* excerpt Coles's conversations
with his subject. These took place mostly in the early 1970s, presumably
"in the Yale dormitories during her annual visits to the United States."[8]
The talks are organized as discussions on particular topics about which
Coles sought guidance from Miss Freud. Like *Dorothy Day*, *Anna Freud* is
a lesson in making conversation with a formidably intelligent woman
who knows the wiles of interviewers. And it also conveys the desultory
interplay of two friends and colleagues, one old, one much younger.

"A Life with Children" lightly touches on major aspects of Anna
Freud's life. Surrounded by young psychiatrists and psychoanalysts,
women as well as men, eager analysands (people undergoing psychoanalysis) as well as analysts, Anna Freud grew up in the ferment of a
major intellectual movement. As in *Erik H. Erikson*, the closeness of the
Vienna circle plays a part in the grace, energy, and integrity of the girl's
experiences. The sixth and last child of her famous father, Anna become
Sigmund Freud's "secretary, nurse, confidante, colleague" (*Anna Freud*,
4). She also undertook analysis with her father. Although Coles suggests
that this "unorthodox" procedure probably affected her entire life, especially her emotional relations, he approaches Miss Freud's personal life
with great delicacy and even what he calls lack of "nerve" (9). All her life

she had close friendships with women, especially the psychoanalyst Dorothy Burlingham, but besides her father, none with men (10). Like Erik Erikson, who became her student and analysand, Anna Freud became an analyst without university or medical education. But that was less a deterrent to becoming an analyst than was her unconventional analysis, which would be unheard of today (117).

"A Life with Children" also sketches Anna Freud's adult life, her personality, and her devotion to children's development, which Coles thinks was partly a consequence of her early experiences as a teacher. As in *Erik H. Erikson*, Coles deftly portrays the mixture of European intellectual ferment, Nazi aggression, wartime altruism, and maturing thought that formed Anna Freud. The sketch captures her reluctance to talk about herself. At times she is suddenly and inexplicably silent, as when she relates her decision to go to England in 1938, taking her terminally ill father with her (18). Coles informs us that she refrains from speaking of her fears or her own heroism in this flight to safety. She would spend the rest of her life in England, sheltering displaced children, establishing a clinic, and training new psychoanalysts.

Anna Freud stresses the energizing but unwarranted optimism of the psychoanalytic movement's early years. Its adherents thought that psychoanalysis would not only liberate them through insight but also enable them to emancipate others by strengthening families and schools. Anna Freud's wry but warm view of that idealism is a major theme of the volume: " 'Our dream was the dream of psychoanalysis— all it had to offer: not only individuals, but schools and universities and hospitals and the courts and the "reform schools" that worked with "delinquents," and social service agencies' " (*Anna Freud*, 152). Insight was itself considered freeing, a stance that Coles has criticized in *Fate*. The younger Freud, the Freud who analyzed his own daughter, is painted as a social dreamer. The biography's stance is historical: not to criticize the movement but to rekindle its early spirit for a new generation of readers.

Like Erikson, Anna Freud was interested in normal children as well as troubled ones. Her much repeated phrase "the best interests of the child" conveyed scientific detachment but also compassion (*Anna Freud*, 23). "Teacher" interweaves the philosophy of teaching with the philosophy of analysis. This chapter elaborates the ideas in Miss Freud's 1928 publication, *Psychoanalysis for Teachers and Parents*, with August Aichhorn, an analyst with whom she worked at an after-school program for poor children in Vienna, called the "Hort" (32). In particular, she rejects the idea that delinquent children are victims, prophets, saviors, or patients (49). Uncritical at best, this chapter is a simple plea to use Anna Freud's works in the classroom, as Coles has argued for using literature in *The Call of Stories*. However, Coles demonstrates that he knows teachers well, mindful of what they will and will not tolerate as advice for doing their jobs (45).

Anna Freud was a significant psychoanalytic theorist. Nonetheless, the chapter entitled "Theorist" approaches her thought not as a given but as a problem, from a decidedly antitheoretical standpoint. Whereas the chapter briefly reviews Miss Freud's major theoretical publications, *The Ego and the Mechanisms of Defense* and *Normality and Pathology in Childhood*, it is cast in the form of an ongoing conversation between Miss Freud and Coles. They discuss not only Miss Freud's work but also Coles's fieldwork in New Orleans and elsewhere. Coles has always maintained that theory is overrated and even dangerous compared to direct observation. In the course of the essay, the two have friendly disagreements. These are conveyed more by the flow of conversation and narratorial asides than by the exposition of ideas. Thus "Theorist" has some of the dramatic narrative tension that Coles used to good effect in *Day*. Gradually, and without seeming to leave the presence of the two conversationalists over their coffee and cake, the discussion becomes an explication of Miss Freud's major ideas in *The Ego and the Mechanisms of Defense*. The discussion casts Anna Freud as a heretic committing apostasy against her father (*Anna Freud*, 67). Coles comes to terms with Anna Freud's theorizing by claiming her as a rebel, artist, writer, and seeker on a journey: "Anna Freud was a theorist, as a poet can be; she sought through metaphor, simile, a semblance of control over life's astonishing, limitless variation. She used theory as a quiet resting place rather than a final destination" (78). Her respect for the individual life never allowed theory to triumph.

"Healer" concerns the ethics of analysis as well as the selecting and training of new analysts, a major activity in Miss Freud's life. In this context healing does not mean curing but having a strong capacity to empathize and thus help others—and ultimately oneself (*Anna Freud*, 82–84). That empathy is called "a leap toward another person," linking the psychoanalytic encounter to the existentialism of Marcel (83). Although there is a spiritual dimension to the discussion, Miss Freud avoids characterizing her own inspiration as religious faith. Drawing on accounts by Grete Bibring and Peter Heller, who was analyzed by Anna Freud, the essay portrays Miss Freud as an analyst: warm but austere, didactic but flexible. However, "Healer" also suggests discord and even rivalry between the main speakers. Although most of *Anna Freud* is deferential to its subject, in this essay Coles seems to test Miss Freud's understanding and moral commitment, especially regarding poverty and racism, his special field (90–96, 101–2). The scene is complex, the tone shifting several times. With her answers, the older analyst maintains the younger's respect—although not without fumbling a bit, revealing her lack of experience to this truculent, somewhat accusing person. For her part, Anna Freud delicately implies that his moral anguish may have roots that he has not examined (102).

Coles, always suspicious of power, rarely concerns himself with the workings of organizations or movements. Nonetheless, "Leader" touches on Anna Freud's role in the psychoanalytic profession, inheriting her father's mantle. Freud himself is acknowledged not only as a thinker but also as "in a sense, a political, an organizational, genius" (*Anna Freud*, 111). According to *Anna Freud*, his daughter preserved the heritage of the movement her father founded (124) and, more importantly, envisioned the future of psychoanalysis, especially in the training of new analysts. A major part of Anna Freud's leadership was her "bitter rivalry" with analyst Melanie Klein over matters of theory (Hegeman 16). In describing these disputes, which Miss Freud would not discuss with Coles, the chapter suggests that leadership is essentially agonistic (*Anna Freud*, 123). For example, Coles notes how much military imagery appears in Freud's and others' descriptions of their circle (108). Whereas Coles had once endorsed Freud's description of himself as a "conquistador," that is, as a bold, solitary discoverer, 20 years later Coles dwells on the word's military connotations (*Irony*, 1). Likewise, Anna Freud's disputes with the psychoanalyst Melanie Klein are couched in terms of war: "struggles," "in the trenches," "hard-fought contest," "tough protagonists," "give little or no quarter," "fought," and "political warfare" (*Anna Freud*, 121–25). Leadership is also territorial. The two analysts "divided up . . . important parts of the psychoanalytic terrain" (122). Above all, for Coles, the best leadership is by example, and he returns to her devotion to children as her finest legacy.

"Idealist" turns to Anna Freud's view of altruism, or selfless behavior, which she began studying in children during World War II. Two of Coles's books, *The Moral Life* and *Simone Weil*, are heavily influenced by Miss Freud's ideas on altruism. Miss Freud concludes that in many instances humans do act like real-life Cyranos de Bergerac, surrendering " 'our own instinctual impulses in favor of other people' " (139). However, she qualifies her answer, questioning " 'whether there is such a thing as a genuinely altruistic relation to one's fellow men' " (140). The chapter also returns to the desultory interplay of the two conversationalists. When Coles tries to characterize Miss Freud as an idealist, she demurs (141). On the subject of Simone Weil, Miss Freud becomes enlivened, vexed by the French social philosopher and mystic's capacity for self-criticism and self-dramatization. Her response is interesting in part because, in his 1987 biography of Weil, Coles uses not only Anna Freud's psychoanalytic ideas but also her words and presence to help elucidate the philosopher. The similarities between Anna Freud and Weil make their differences all the more profound. Both women were European, daughters of Jewish physicians, and of the same generation. Both sought to help others, perhaps at the expense of their own emotional lives. But Anna Freud eschews Weil's excesses of self-display, opting for "some kind of 'normality' of idealism," like the humble, dedicated work of the social workers, nurses, and teachers whom she has known (*Anna Freud*, 145–47). Coles would like to rescue Weil, but it is clear the two speakers must politely agree to disagree.

The concluding essay, "Writer," explores an aspect of Anna Freud dear to Coles's own heart. As a scientist, she "used language like a window, through which any reader might see the world being evoked, characterized" (*Anna Freud*, 157). Clarity in presenting difficult ideas distinguishes her prose. Yet the essay strives to give her the status of artist as well as scientist. Coles discovers that she loved the poetry of Rilke and aspired to study literature. In psychoanalysis she found " 'a road to the same kind of broad and deep understanding of human nature that writers possess' " (169). Coles judges her fine writing as a powerful part of her influence in psychoanalysis, enabling her to reach readers beyond professional analysts and thus influence her fellow specialists: "She had her father's gift for going public, as it were—with plain but strong and lucid prose that could command the interest of a broad range of educated readers, and stay with them" (169). Considerable time is spent on Anna Freud's rhetoric of argument, with its use of simile, stories, and even punctuation (175–76). Ultimately, her writing is faithful to human lives in the way that "good stories" are (*Anna Freud*, 178).

In *Anna Freud* Coles is often present as narrator. He watches, giving his silent reactions and guessing at hers. At times he is the bumbling character whose ineptness is a foil to make his subject shine more brightly. For example, at one point Anna Freud follows up his too-quick remark about the meaning of children's art, an exchange that makes her measured intelligence stand out (52–53). Elsewhere, she gently needles him about Simone Weil; he rankles, then blushes, and they laugh (145). The conversations give an intimacy to *Anna Freud* that colors the portrait of the distinguished analyst yet does not dispel the formality between mentor and mentored. The narrator's presence may also be "a reminder that Dr. Coles' thoughtful, sympathetic books are largely a sprawling, unedited autobiography" (Gean 1765). *Anna Freud* is both a skilled appreciation of the child analyst and a delicate comment on the challenges of biography and oral history. That comment comes in the form of the exchanges between narrator and various speakers in the book. For example, Dr. Grete Bibring chides Coles for his impertinence in raising the issue of Anna Freud's analysis by her father (*Anna Freud*, 11–12). Dr. Bibring's sharp words reveal her own discomfort, and Coles describes the moment they share in trying to resolve their mutual worries about Miss Freud's emotional life. This insight into the nature of biographical research, casually exploring the social and professional relations from which "facts" emerge, is sometimes more interesting and informative than the biographical narrative itself. The goal of mutuality sought between biographer and subject, as between analyst and analysand, is achieved through the form of *Anna Freud*.

Conclusion

In these works on psychiatry and psychoanalysis, Coles reflects on psychiatry's relationship to ordinary life, to history, and to literature. In psychoanalysis Coles originally sought both science and moral philosophy as well as an artistic elegance or purity of language. This was an ideal that the field could not meet—but that he has not abandoned. His books on psychoanalytic subjects aim to explicate for wider audiences the best that the discipline can offer, in his terms, and on occasion to fight battles for what he has regarded as the soul of psychoanalysis. His best weapon would turn out to be not the theories of Freud, Anna Freud, or even Erikson, but the unique application of their ideas in his fieldwork.

Chapter Three

"The 'Ground-Being' of Everyday Life": *Children of Crisis*

In the third chapter of *Children of Crisis: A Study in Courage and Fear* (1967), Robert Coles describes the drawings and words of Ruby Bridges, thus easing into the printed account of a six-year-old New Orleans schoolgirl who was the first black student to enroll in her elementary school in 1961. Listening to and shaping the words of particular children and adults has become an occupation of three decades. Their lives personify large, often hazy or distant historical events and social conditions: racism, integration, poverty, peonage, slow genocide, migration from the land to the cities, the rise of urban ghettos, the tide of illegal aliens, discrimination, disenfranchisement, political turmoil, and all the uneven ways that power and privilege come, or do not come, to the citizens of a nation.

Coles has labored to unpack those abstractions. The landmark statement of that labor is the five-volume series, *Children of Crisis*, spanning 18 years of research and writing from 1959 to 1977. The series is central to Robert Coles's body of work and his development as a writer and thinker. From the initial volume, *Children of Crisis: A Study in Courage and Fear* (1967), through the paired volumes *Migrants, Sharecroppers, Mountaineers* and *The South Goes North* (1971) to *Eskimos, Chicanos, Indians* (1977) and finally *Privileged Ones* (1977), Coles refined his methods of observation, his style and narrative stance, and not least, his purposes for writing. In 2,800 pages, *Children of Crisis* addresses many issues: the intricate ways in which individuals relate to a society and that society relates to them; the shortcomings of science, especially the social sciences and psychiatry, in understanding individuals in their daily lives; the limits of language and of one writer's viewpoint, given the particular social and historical situation in which he or she works; the many ways one can, or should, or might possibly be allowed to live a meaningful life in this, the latter part of the twentieth century in a rich, powerful, troubled, and hopeful nation. Simply put, the "method" of Coles's research is the repeated encounters by which he comes to know the people of whom he writes. It has its roots in his psychiatric training and wide reading in psychology, history, sociology, and literature. As Bruce A. Ronda has observed, there is a priority to his concerns: "For Coles, the pervasive issue is class, and then parental influence" (Ronda 1989, 137–38). As the series progresses, Coles extends the scientific method to encompass a literary technique and a philosophy—an ethics to be sure, but also an epistemology, or way of knowing. As a labor of travel, listening, and writing, this series of works is "an effort in human actuality," in James Agee's phrase, or an attempt to touch "the 'ground-being' of everyday life," in Paul Tillich's.[1] A number of Coles's later works employ the same approach, especially the three-volume series sometimes known as *The Lives of Children.* Still others draw on the research and insights of *Children of Crisis.*

The first three volumes in the series, *Children of Crisis: A Study in Courage and Fear*, *Migrants, Sharecroppers, Mountaineers*, and *The South Goes North*, share a common subject and area of research—the lives of poor children in the eastern United States, with a strong focus on children in the South or recently arrived from the South in Northern cities. The second and third volumes are paired, one on rural and one on urban children. These three works show Coles developing as a writer, forming strategies, a style, and thematic strands that have endured throughout his work. The fourth and fifth volumes, *Eskimos, Chicanos, Indians* and *Privileged Ones*, shift the emphasis geographically, economically, and culturally. They also amplify Coles's narrative strategies and deepen his exploration of the psyche, morality, and spiritual values.

Children of Crisis: A Study in Courage and Fear

Coles's first book, *Children of Crisis: A Study in Courage and Fear* (1967), documents the effects of racism on young children who were enrolling in the first integrated schools in New Orleans, Atlanta, and other Southern cities during the late 1950s and early 1960s. He set out to study the psychological stress of desegregation, which he postulated was as serious as the stress brought on by crippling disease, such as polio, a subject that he had previously examined. As he says repeatedly, Coles heard and saw more than he had bargained for and more than his hypothesis about stress could hope to describe. The title *Children of Crisis* was inspired by a 1940 American Council on Education (ACE) study of poor black people in New Orleans, *Children of Bondage* (*Courage*, 390). The title, which would become the name by which the series was

known, claims this first volume as a successor to the ACE study, showing progress from bondage to freedom by way of crisis. In this first volume the title comes to apply to all the people described, children and
adults, for or against integration. Hereafter the first volume will be
referred to as *Courage and Fear*, with the title *Children of Crisis* reserved
for the series.

Method

Coles's method, which he describes at the beginning of each volume,
combines techniques from psychoanalysis, child psychiatry, and anthropology. He speaks with and observes children and their families—not in
an office or clinical setting but in their homes and classrooms. To vali-
date this method he cites the research of Erik Erikson and Anna Freud,
among others. Often he asks young children to draw or paint scenes or
people from their lives, a technique from psychoanalysis. With older
children and adults he mainly talks and persuades them to talk. He visits some people weekly or even daily, over a period of months and then
makes less frequent visits to a few children so that they come to know
him over several years. For example, during part of this study Coles conducted interviews with high school students and younger children, aged
5 to 11, whom he saw weekly or more often. He spoke with adults—
teachers, parents, grandparents—periodically but less often (*Courage,*
41). Later the compiled notes and transcripts of taped interviews and
conversations are edited into narratives, so that the effect is of children,
their parents, friends, relatives, and others who know them speaking
from the page, as if in conversation with Coles. Each volume of *Children
of Crisis* contains color plates of selected drawings. *Courage and Fear* contains 13 drawings, and Coles intersperses analysis of these with the conversations and his commentary. Taking his cue from anthropologists,
who do not deny that they are newcomers and participant-observers in
the community culture, Coles is careful to respect those who agree to
meet and talk with him. He is also present as a person, a character if you
will, in the narrative. Indeed, early on his presence becomes a major
theme.

Structure

Courage and Fear is loosely organized as a scientific report. Part 1 contains two chapters justifying the study's method and purpose. With

Atlanta, New Orleans, and their rural environs as focal points, "The South" gives a Northerner's perspective on the complex interactions of locale, social interaction, and race. This opening description of setting would become a consistent feature of each volume of *Children of Crisis*, one of the few times that Coles regularly elaborates physical detail. "Observation and Participation" develops his method of study. Part 2, "The Children of Crisis," is equivalent to a scientific report's results section, presented in six chapters that contain about 20 narratives or case histories. Part 3, "Courage and Fear," offers four chapters of generalizations.

Narratives

The power of *Courage and Fear* arises from the narratives that make up Part 2. Maxine Greene calls the portraits "as alive with vital human characters as a novel," yet with the added impact of national crisis, a fact that she believes elevates the book above works like Oscar Lewis's *Children of Sanchez* and *La Vida*, which also use taped material.[2] The narratives move outward in concentric circles from the children, who are at ground zero of these historical events. After the children come their relatives who walk them into school every day, facing crowds or police guards or both, then their teachers, then activists, then interested bystanders during the crisis, and ultimately members of the mob itself. Some of the sections are clearly modeled on case histories, rotely describing family circumstances, infancy, appetite, toilet training, disposition, childhood traumas, and other features of psychological interest. Yet the sections frequently break free of this format.

Ruby's narrative, entitled "When I Draw the Lord He'll Be a Real Big Man," is the first "case" after a lengthy justification for the use of drawings in child psychiatry and social psychological observation (*Courage*, 45). But as soon as Ruby's drawings are described, the story of racism emerges, dramatic and numbing. Six years old and the only black child in her class, Ruby faces mobs every day at the school's door. However, for months she attends a virtually empty school, since most parents of white children kept them home rather than send them to school with Ruby. What Coles sees in her drawings is even more arresting than the mobs. For a long while Ruby does not use brown or black except for the ground; then it must be covered thickly with green grass: "She drew white people larger and more lifelike. Negroes were smaller, their bodies less intact" (47). Her drawings make other telling distinctions between

blacks and whites. Ruby comments about the mobs, her life, and their
work together as Coles meets with her and they draw, talk, have a Coke.
He concludes that her drawings, even those she had done before she
knew him, were "confounded and troubled at the representation of
racial differences" (50): "It was as if Ruby started drawing all people as
white, then turned some of them into Negroes by depriving them of a
limb or coloring a small section of their skin (she preferred the shoulder
or the stomach) brown" (50). Two years later Coles asked her why she
deliberated about how much brown she used. She replied: "When I
draw a white girl, I know she'll be okay, but with the colored it's not so
okay. So I try to give the colored as even a chance as I can, even if that's
not the way it will end up being" (50). Only when Ruby portrays her
grandfather, an independent farmer who represents hope and strength,
do her drawings give coherence to an African American figure. Coles
watches Ruby grow up. Her strength, her persistence, and her vision of
a future for herself recall her grandmother who accompanies her
through the mobs. They inspire the researcher-narrator's awe.

Coles's emotions are also evident in his description of Jimmie, one of
only two or three of Ruby's white classmates during her first year. He
describes his first reaction to the boy as "unfair" (53). Jimmie, who is
also interviewed over several years, has a hard time drawing Ruby or
imagining anything about her life (54). Ruby's, Jimmie's, and other
children's drawings and talk reveal that they already have highly developed senses of their own expectations in life, some of which are con-
strained or empowered by skin color. They perceive differences between
people's looks, activities, and homes as based on race, and changes in
their own lives brought by a new school or new and different children in
school.

The experiences of the older children are no less powerful, although
there are no drawings to dramatize the impact of their stories. In John
Washington, Coles finds a person whose life not only fails to support the
assumptions of Coles's psychiatric training but also demonstrates a surprising resilience (119–22). To try to explain John Washington's character, Coles draws on Erikson's maxim of multiple influences (121). Similarly, long discussions with the young civil rights workers of the
Mississippi Summer Project cause the researcher to question conventional psychiatric wisdom (226).

In the outer ripples of integration are other voices. Without the
words of those who opposed integration, white and black, *Courage and
Fear* would lose its edge. They are heard in "The Teachers" as well as

"Lookers-on and the Last Ditch." The "lookers-on" are passive. Like one black store owner, they " 'want no part of all this' "; his white counterpart agrees (295). Nonetheless, their views, like those of the teachers, are complex. The "Last Ditch" is the story of a "passionate segregationist" called John (300). Finding and gaining the trust of anti-integrationist protesters was one of the most difficult tasks Coles faced (26–27). John's story is rendered as a case history to help explain a terrorist's mind to readers. He likes violence and has seen "Negroes assaulted and killed" (298). Abuse, illness, and belittlement filled his childhood; unemployment dogs his youth and adulthood (301). A survivor, John is intelligent, sane, and hard working. Thus "we must all know that the animal in us can be elaborately rationalized in a society until an act of murder is seen as self-defense and dynamited houses become evidence of moral courage" (315). To those who ascribe racism to psychiatric causes or regional temperament, Coles gives no comfort.

Although in the main thoughtfully organized and lucidly written, *Courage and Fear* already exhibits a tension between the genre of social scientific study and an older tradition of nonfiction for the general, educated reader. Thus the tone shifts at times, and the report organization seems not to take full advantage of the material. Some reviewers were unsure whether to treat the work as social science or as humanistic exploration.[3] In fact Coles makes the tension a source of reflection and self-conscious literary technique, as when, in the third part, he pushes his observations toward philosophy: "children who in a moment—call it existential, call it historical, call it psychological—took what they had from the past, in their minds, out of their homes, and made of *all* those possessions something else: a change in the world, and in themselves, too" (365). The volume ends with a quotation from James Agee, on the uniqueness and paradoxical strength of each " 'new and incommunicably tender life' " (*Courage*, 381).

The choice of a period of historical crisis for psychiatric study is singular, although Erikson's biographical studies of Luther and Gandhi clearly influenced *Courage and Fear*. The section on student civil rights workers, in particular, reflects on why the conjunction of the individual's psychology with the historical moment is important. Without the dramatic setting of desegregation, these students' various identity crises would have been "rather pedestrian" (225). The conjoining of private and public becomes, for Coles, the basis of ethical action: "What emerges as unusual, as extraordinary is the ethical context chosen for the struggles—and allowed, even encouraged, by history. What indeed activates a youth's ego, causes him to generate an idealism of deeds as well as of thought? The mind's relentless, ever-present past? History's arbitrary encouragement, granted almost indiscriminately? Or an almost exquisite—defying questions and questionnaires—blend of the two?" (225). *Courage and Fear* is Coles's first extended attempt to ponder this juncture of history, psychology, and ethics.

Ruby, her family and classmates, and the activists are the first of Coles's questers. Some are flung into their quests, some choose them deliberately. Few of those who entered into the events of desegregation, regardless of their roles, knew what awaited them. The people that Coles comes to admire in *Courage and Fear*—the young integrating students, their parents and grandparents, a few teachers and professionals, and the student civil rights workers—gained a sense of personal commitment and historical moment. Compared with the heroic deeds of children in World War II studied by Anna Freud, their virtue consists more in endurance than bravery (226). Yet it is extraordinary because it shows "an everyday willingness to go about one's business under vague, continual, and in a flash dangerous hostility" (226). Because there is a struggle to present all the complexities of desegregation above the valorizing of individual participants, the quest is not a strong theme in *Courage and Fear*. However, the motif is implicit in the lengthy treatment of certain speakers. Later, in Coles's constant reworking of these persons' words and lives, it becomes an indelible part of his work.

Migrants, Sharecroppers, Mountaineers

The second volume of *Children of Crisis* is an electric book. *Migrants, Sharecroppers, Mountaineers* (1971) carries on the same method as *Courage and Fear* but is substantially different in confidence, energy, tone, and literary approach. With its companion volume, *The South Goes North*, *Migrants, Sharecroppers, Mountaineers* earned a share of the 1973 Pulitzer Prize for general nonfiction. Incorporating the previously published study *Uprooted Children: The Early Life of Migrant Farm Workers*, *Migrants, Sharecroppers, Mountaineers* concerns children in the rural South, divided into the three groups of the title. *The South Goes North*, on the other hand, treats urban children of families who moved North for jobs. The change from the first volume is immediately apparent. In *Courage and Fear* Coles remains the wary researcher, surprised by the resilience of the children he interviews. In *Migrants, Sharecroppers, Mountaineers*, Coles is abashed, ashamed, outraged, and helpless. His subjects' stories provoke him to write but also to question the value of his—or any professional's —concern. In its literary goal to convey "Lives, as opposed to problems," *Migrants, Sharecroppers, Mountaineers*, more than any of Coles's other works to date, carries the influence of James Agee's *Let Us Now Praise Famous Men*.[4] In 1941 Agee and the photographer Walker Evans published their 1936 documentary of the hard, somber lives of rural Alabamans. Coles's allusions to their collaboration befit the subject of *Migrants, Sharecroppers, Mountaineers* as well as his stance toward rural Southerners. Reviewers such as Adele V. Silver have noted Agee's influence.[5]

There are other differences from the first volume. The people of *Courage and Fear* share a commonality of purpose that unifies the book. All speak and take action with regard to the public issues and events surrounding desegregation. Those portrayed in *Migrants, Sharecroppers, Mountaineers* do not see themselves as participating in any larger culture. According to Paul Starr, the people of *Migrants, Sharecroppers, Mountaineers* and its companion, *South,* have "none of the sense of triumph and moral purpose that the movement for integration lent the first book."[6] The three groups—migrant workers, sharecroppers and tenant farmers, and mountain dwellers—all live on the land, but they differ in their relations to the land they work and are not even likely to come into contact with each other over a lifetime. Moreover, in 1971 they were (and today many remain) virtually invisible to the American educated middle class. *Courage and Fear* puts flesh and bones on the cultural drama of the civil rights movement; as a citizen, every American reader can presumably bring some knowledge and experience to that drama. In *Migrants, Sharecroppers, Mountaineers* there is a sense of eerily quiet worlds where very real people with quite ordinary concerns live, utterly cut off from a shared national life. Paradoxically the most mobile, the migrant farm workers, are the most cut off. In an impassioned review recapitulating the oppressive history of Appalachia and the South, Henry Caudill calls migrant workers "One of those alien nations" that inhabit the United States.[7]

Method

Coles's decision to study rural children evolved from interviewing for *Courage and Fear* as well as from his work in rural medical clinics and his trip through the Appalachians in 1967. The migration from farm to city had affected virtually every poor family in the South. Thirty families became his subjects: 10 who worked as sharecroppers or tenant farmers, 10 migrant families, and 10 mountain families. In addition Coles interviewed a migrant camp crew leader and others whose work touched the lives of poor rural people (*Migrants*, 32–35, 431). Despite its scientific purpose, the method chapter of *Migrants, Sharecroppers, Mountaineers* is marked by a new tone of urgency and exhortation, revealed by lists and staccato phrasing: "It does help, too—by God it does—to listen to the sounds of those voices, the rhythms and cadences, the pauses, the hesitations that suddenly are overcome, the hurry that is shown, followed by a relaxed stretch" (36). Like Agee, Coles employs effusive rhetoric to convey his indignation at the abject poverty that he witnesses. Reviewer Adele V. Silver called the prose of *Migrants, Sharecroppers, Mountaineers* "sometimes embarrassingly lyrical" (Silver 53), whereas Marge Piercy sees "a Biblical wash in it."[8] Of all Coles's research on children, *Migrants, Sharecroppers, Mountaineers* takes the most radical political stance. In "The Method" there is the protester's willingness to sweep the hand across the table, to reform society at all costs, but that dissolves, as is customary with Coles, into affirming lists that return to the subjects, the people, and the land. Ever liberal, ever the physician, Coles does not advocate radical action.

The method chapter also explains decisions that affect the rest of *Children of Crisis*. Most important is the decision to put people's words into standard American English (*Migrants*, 39). (The first volume also used standard English, but without comment.) That is a moral choice, as Marge Piercy has noted, akin to other decisions that aim at representing speakers as people, not distant "others" who require help or pity (Piercy 20). The choice brings further moral questions, however, which include minority groups' claim to their own speech. Other decisions show awareness of the tension between the genres of scientific case study, documentary, journalism, and literary essay. Literature, psychology, and sociology are cited as influences (*Migrants*, 25). The names of people and places are disguised. Some speakers are composites, that is, composed of two or more actual people (37). Readers who try to find the names of speakers in the index will usually be disappointed.

Structure

The same technical report organization that governs *Courage and Fear* is superficially evident in *Migrants, Sharecroppers, Mountaineers*. Again a spatial metaphor amplifies the conventional pattern. This volume has four parts: "The Setting," encompassing chapters describing "The Land" and "The Method"; "The Children" and "The World," which compose the bulk of the volume, taking up the three separate groups; and "The Rural Life," three chapters of generalizations. Each group is characterized by a single anguished term: migrant children are "uprooted"; sharecroppers' children are "stranded"; and mountaineers' children are "hidden." Like *Courage and Fear, Migrants, Sharecroppers, Mountaineers* generally proceeds from younger to older and from less to more worldly and connected persons. The middle sections are also organized by means of a dynamic image that resonates through the volume. In *Courage and Fear*, the outward "ripples" of the narrative section end on a bitter note, the words of anti-integrationists. *Migrants, Sharecroppers, Mountaineers* has a simple yet sophisticated geographic movement of ascent and descent, from the coastal plains to the mountains and back down again. The migrant workers travel the Southern lowlands and plains of Florida, the Carolinas, and northward. Sharecroppers and tenant farmers live on the middle ground, some in the Mississippi Delta, some further inland in the eastern Piedmont and Alabama clay. Mountain people obviously inhabit the uplands and steep hollows of the Appalachians. Once in the mountains, the book remains there until the opening of the third section, "The World of the Hollows," then moves back down the slopes to the sharecroppers and finally, again, to the migrant workers. This artful organization simplifies the varied geography of the South and the scattered states that Coles visited (*Migrants*, 38). For Piercy *Migrants* is more unified than its companion, *The South Goes North* (Piercy 1). The many locales blend into a larger image that allies the people with the land.

The ascent and descent also serve to define the quality of these lives. The miserably fragmented lives of black migrants of the "eastern stream" of farm workers yield to the more stable but also disrupted lives of black and white sharecroppers. These in turn pass to the enduring, traditional but very poor and threatened lives of the white mountaineers. According to Coles, the mountaineers' lives have a fundamental "coherence" (*Migrants*, 271) born of being on one's own land generation after generation and being in stable families. As the tightly knit world of the hollow binds their lives, the mountaineers' statements and their connected, but varied, culture bind this volume. As the mountains form the spine of the Eastern United States, the mountains' inhabitants organize the center of the book by what the other rural dwellers' lives, apparently similar in their harshness, lack by comparison.

The first chapter of *Migrants, Sharecroppers, Mountaineers*, "The Land,"
traces the profound influence of the land on its people, calling to mind
good historical writing and reportage. In depth and skill it sets a standard that would be met in the remaining volumes of *Children of Crisis*.
Early on, it touches the paradox of migrant workers' moving "settle-
ments" and elaborates that mobility and their desire for invisibility into
a metaphor for all three groups:

> Some of the settlements, of course, move across the land—a caravan of
> trucks, a few buses, a single car or maybe two, all filled to the brim with
> migrants. Yet, when the vehicles are brought to a stop it is done beside
> bushes and under trees. The point is to be inconspicuous, to hide, to disap-
> pear from sight; and so a number of families disperse, become little knots
> of people here and there, anxious for the ground as a resting-place and anx-
> ious to blend into things, merge with them, and thereby hide away from
> the rest of us, from the world that gazetteers and atlases and census
> bureaus take note of, from the world of the police and the government, but
> also from the merely curious and even the openly concerned. (4–5)

Like the migrants, sharecroppers, tenant farmers, and mountain dwellers
recede from the gaze of middle-class Americans. The passage sharply
distinguishes the strengths and interests of its subjects from what professional "helpers" and nostalgia buffs want from them.

Although many of the stories throughout *Migrants, Sharecroppers,
Mountaineers* are dramatic, the metaphor of movement is especially well
developed in the sections on migrant farm workers. Locale, being settled,
and motionlessness are set against constant motion and being uprooted.
The third chapter, "Uprooted Children," begins with an anthropological
gambit, the conditions of a migrant child's birth. But it is more than case
study. The chapter opening contrasts the cramped space of the womb
with the (apparent) freedom of movement of the young migrant children. However, by the time they are 9 or 10, their sense of freedom in
motion has made a disquieting change. Late in the chapter Coles brings
in the children's drawings and their comments on them. Compared with
Courage and Fear, these drawings and voices resist all clinical interpretation, and their words are treated more as a mythology of migrant life.
Coles distinguishes migrants from all other children he has known. He
gives in finally and passionately to the urge to generalize:

> Unlike migrant children, other children like to draw pastoral landscapes,
> like to drench them in sun, fill them with flowers, render them anything

but black. Unlike migrant children, other children don't draw roads that are fenced in and blocked off or lead nowhere and everywhere and never end. Unlike migrant children, most children don't worry about birth certificates, or doors and more doors and always doors—that belong, even in a few years of experience, to half a hundred or more houses. So it would be different if the little girl just quoted could have a solid, permanent home. (115–16)

These people inspire an outpouring of rage and rhetoric in the same way that sharecroppers gave James Agee a language (*Privileged Ones*, 554).

Sharecroppers' and tenant farmers' children occupy a middle place between migrants and mountaineers. Described in the chapters "Stranded Children" and "The World of the Black Belt," these children have roots, as it were, but their families live in virtual servitude to landowners. Malnourished in a fertile land, their experiences both emotionally free and grotesquely limited, they live out paradoxes of the rural life. "Hidden Children" and "The World of the Hollows" take mountain children and their families from discussion of their birth to death and also from the continuation of a way of life to its decline and death. The comparative coherence that mountain children know is seen in their drawings. For example, seven-year-old Sally, who is desperately poor even by Appalachian standards, is, the narrator tells us, "trying to look beyond" to a perspective on her whole world (*Migrants*, 261–63). In a sense she stands at the pinnacle of the spiny geography of *Migrants, Sharecroppers, Mountaineers* and gazes outward—a lucid perspective not afforded the other children of this volume. By its allusions to mining, industry, and the pressure that many feel to leave their mountain homes, the end of "The World of the Hollows" also reaches out to the companion volume, *The South Goes North*.

Persona

Throughout *Migrants, Sharecroppers, Mountaineers* Coles is present as a character, a feature noted by reviewers. Marge Piercy remarks on the importance of Coles's singular and paradoxical presence to rural people (Piercy 20). Adele V. Silver also comments on the narrator's quizzical demeanor, too shy for his suit and tie (53). This diffident, shambling persona is apparent to an Appalachian man, who describes him as " 'always coming back and not seeming to know exactly what he wants to hear or know' " (*Migrants*, 39). In another vignette, Coles has dinner at the house of a Mississippi tenant family's "bossman" (488). In a brief, complex story of middle-class mores and racism, the simple graciousness of well-prepared food becomes an occasion for the narrator's silent embarrassment and moral reflection.

Theory

Part Four, "The Rural Life," gives three chapters of qualified generalizations, using composite speakers. In contrast to the somewhat scattershot conclusions of *Courage and Fear*, *Migrants, Sharecroppers, Mountaineers* draws together its three disparate rural groups with considerable power. "Rural Youth" renders the fleeting adolescence of poor rural Americans. At 15 and 20 years of age, they perceive themselves as weathered, if not old. Although time has virtually stood still in these lands, these haunting voices capture a sense of time gone fast and without regret. "Rural Upheaval" shifts to political analysis, turning to the social issues and programs that brought rural poverty to national awareness. That would seem a fitting end for the book. Instead, Coles turns to people's beliefs and especially to what sustains their lives—religion. From "The Method" on, *Migrants, Sharecroppers, Mountaineers* deals with religion both as a feature of people's lives and as a source of turmoil for Coles himself, part of his moral quandaries about his project. Early on, for example, Coles chastises himself for allowing religious complacency to interfere with his project of reform (109). At times he regards people's religion as simply one of several respites from the backbreaking work, maybe even an "opiate." The migrants' relief from work is described thus:

> The only answer to such a fate is sex, when it becomes possible, and drink, when it is available, and always the old familiar answers—travel, work, rest when that can be had, and occasionally during the year a moment in church, where forgiveness can be asked, where the promise of salvation can be heard, where some wild, screaming, frantic, angry, frightened, nervous half-mad cry for help can be put into words and songs and really given the body's expression: turns and twists and grimaces and arms raised and trunks bent and legs spread and pulled together and feet used to stamp and kick and move—always that, move. (112)

For migrant workers, religion is part of the ceaseless movement of their lives: " 'We have to catch our praying on the go,' " remarks one (611).

But at least in church, movement is easier. A mother says, " 'I do a lot of walking and my feet are always tired, but in church I can walk up and down, but not too far; and my feet feel better, you know. It's because God must be near' " (112). And so *Migrants, Sharecroppers, Mountaineers* concludes with "Rural Religion." This prominent place is a challenge and an answer to liberals, white and black, who themselves have no need for an emotional, sustaining, and public spirituality. However, Coles emphasizes the earthly failures of organized religion, not its transcendence (617).

The South Goes North

The dominant mood of *Migrants, Sharecroppers, Mountaineers* is quiet, almost sepulchral. Except for the relatively short section "Rural Upheaval," the time covered could be the 1930s or 1940s rather than the 1960s. By contrast, the feel of *The South Goes North* (1971) is tumultuous and eager. Groups that knew little of each other in the rural South are tumbled into Northern cities. In their diversity and their knowledge of what middle-class readers regard as the everyday world, these urban residents may seem more familiar than the rural voices. A substantial number, mainly men, fill their statements with names and ideas from the politics of the 1960s. Blacks debate the competing philosophies of civil rights' nonviolence and black power's endorsement of terrorism. Whites, formerly isolated in the mountains, now face the claims of betting parlors and advertisements for thousands of consumer goods. These are woven into the fabric of family and religion. Published the same year, *The South Goes North* and *Migrants, Sharecroppers, Mountaineers* document two aspects of poverty, but both stem from one larger historical event: the massive twentieth-century American migration off the land. *The South Goes North* makes constant reference to rural life, which remains "home" for many relocated families.

Method

No abstract knowledge of American social history sent Coles to these cities; rather, it was the ties with Chicago he heard rural Southerners speak of that led him to ghettos and working-class suburbs (*South*, 28). In 1964 Boston began busing students to counter *de facto* segregation, another impetus to the studies that became *The South Goes North* (*South*, 33), which details five years of visits to 20 families, plus Coles's year

spent riding a Boston school bus (33–34). Acceptance rather than outrage marks the method chapter of *The South Goes North*. The urban
problems that Coles raises are no less grave than the rural ones (and
both remain today), but his tone is dispassionate. He reserves his ire—
the shadowboxing with specialists—for a later section, "The Schools."
Likewise, he shifts his occasional outburst of self-justification to the endnotes. As in *Irony in the Mind's Life*, the notes carry on a sub-rosa battle
with contemporary social critics. In general, the notes of the *Children of
Crisis* series often amount to separate essays, crammed with titles from
many fields as well as judgments about the cited works. In addition, the
notes to *The South Goes North* are leisurely, personal, enthusiastic, and
confrontational. One bibliographical note runs three-and-a-half pages
and contains the blunt phrase "made me want to scream" (*South*, 657).
Such apparatus reminds readers that, regardless of his diffidence toward
professional "helpers," Coles takes his scholarship seriously and regards
Children of Crisis as a challenge to the dominant mode of quantitative
social research.

Setting

The South Goes North opens, again, with locale. Rather than stress the
trite novelties of electricity and other urban conveniences, Coles depicts
"The Streets" in relation to the newcomers' subtle knowledge of home
and the land. They have defined a world view, a language, a sense of
time, music, and spirit on the rhythms of another place. Until they
moved, the land (described in *Migrants, Sharecroppers, Mountaineers*) had
been endless and seamless except for an occasional dirt track or road. In
the city, people immediately face a new definition of space occupied and
"possessed": "The street is flat, has no hills and no stream nearby, has no
bank to sit on and lie down upon and use to 'collect' one's strength"
(*South*, 5–6). There is the built world of cities, not just houses and
apartments, but many flights of stairs (6). Then there is the need for
security, so that " 'the nothing we have is all locked up' " (7). Coles elicits from his speakers their first thoughts on encountering the city as well
as how quickly those memories fade and become incomprehensible.
Each newcomer first applies her personal cosmology, then adapts it, and
then some way or another moves into city life. The same negotiating
process applies to all the newcomers' values, from the nature of work to
religion to preparing food and caring for children. All the blessings are
ambivalent.

Structure

Like *Migrants, Sharecroppers, Mountaineers, The South Goes North* has four major parts but lacks the majestic literary structure of the second volume. The introductory section, "The Setting," yields to "The People," where we meet first "Blacks in the City," then "White Visitors" and "White Northerners," moving outward from the orbit of recently arrived blacks' daily lives. The last major segment of "The People"—"In the Places Where the Mountains Are Gone"—concerns white "immigrants" from the hills of Kentucky and West Virginia. The third section, "The Schools," focuses on desegregation in the Northeast, Midwest, Upper South, and Far West. Then, returning to the shape of *Migrants, Sharecroppers, Mountaineers,* "The Way It Is" orchestrates individual voices and stories to address urban social issues. Where *The South Goes North* differs most from the second volume is in Part 3, "The Schools," which incorporates a study published separately, *Teachers and the Children of Poverty.* This portion of the book is both a highly organized research report and a lyrical polemic on racism in schools in 13 U.S. cities. Within this part, slightly past the book's center, are the drawings so characteristic of Coles's work. As in *Courage and Fear,* they are mainly of school buildings, teachers, and the students' self-portraits. Ultimately, "The Schools" fails. It is not integrated into the remainder of the volume, its purpose as a report is undermined by its placement in the larger context of closely rendered, somewhat literary case study, and literarily it pales by comparison to other sections of the volume.

Narratives

Speakers in *The South Goes North* are well able to summarize their former ways of life, often comparing the new urban and the old rural life. Rarely do speakers in *Migrants, Sharecroppers, Mountaineers* articulate their situation so directly. Lengthy stories about their lives are not particularly relevant for migrants' daily living. For example, for one migrant worker, one's chronological age is fluid and one's past is impossible to track, a meaningless passage of different camps (*Migrants,* 542–43). However, like it or not, those in the cities have a new point of reference for the older life. Even to talk to their city-raised children, let alone keep rural memories alive, they must characterize that life. For example, a former sharecropper now in Harlem has to answer his children's questions about his youth. They know about clean water and nutrition, but he did not: " '[Y]our daddy lived on grits and the water in

that pond, back in Peach County, Georgia. He didn't die. He *lived* on it,
you hear!' " (*South*, 23). It also—obviously—works the other way. Those
now in the cities can also describe their present way of life. Their
thoughts about the two aspects of their lives and memories are affected
by the change itself. In a sense they have received an education. When
they visit family at "home" back in Kentucky or Mississippi, they bring
these comparisons, somewhat muted, with them. This fluency with
words differentiates the narratives of *The South Goes North* from those of
Migrants, Sharecroppers, Mountaineers.

Persona

The speakers' relative self-consciousness or their comparative willingness to talk about their lives in middle-class terms also changes their
relation with the narrator. In *Migrants, Sharecroppers, Mountaineers*,
Coles's jagged, self-conscious voice often echoes alone. People talk at
length, but only a few voices directly acknowledge his moral outrage at
the unlivable conditions. Even fewer debate him in political terms—
usually professionals and local activists. Not so in *The South Goes North*.
Even children understand the wider politics of urban life. For example,
James Lewis, a 14-year-old black "street kid," engages Coles in spite of
himself (Ronda 1989, 49). He acknowledges the young man's "highly
developed political sensibility" as well as "a sense of his own personal
history and of his people's history" (*South*, 70). There are also Billy, who
is 10, and Billy's bus driver, who weaves his admiration of the students
integrating the Boston schools with observations about Dr. Martin
Luther King. Even those who do not directly talk about current events,
like a man named Henry Rollins, often suffuse a knowledge of the wider
world with their personal sense of identity (163).

Themes

The new knowledge gained by those who come to the cities weighs
against their abiding sense of exile and loss, the main themes of *The
South Goes North*. Having made an arduous, sometimes ongoing journey,
they closely explore the place where they have landed in spiritual as well
as material terms. Coles stresses loss from the opening chapter on. One
boy calls junkies and drunks " 'the *real* lost people' " while his mother
reflects on her past (*South*, 13). The final chapter, "The Lord in Our

Cities," elevates the theme of loss, exile, and journey in spiritual terms. The words of several speakers, mainly two women from Chicago and Boston, weave a concluding image that both parallels the end of *Migrants, Sharecroppers, Mountaineers* and forms a lyrical coda to the two volumes. Once again Coles proceeds from a nominally scientific assumption, in this case, that newcomers to the city will describe their experience in "a familiar and congenial 'frame of reference' " (617). Instead of hills and earth and woods, this time the frame of reference is religion. People use religious imagery to speak of their everyday life. Mrs. Clara Allen's family has moved "across rivers and deserts" to get to Chicago (620). Mrs. Josephine Williams, a Georgian widowed by a white man's hand, came to Boston thinking that " 'up here it would be the "triumphal march"—like the one of Jesus into Jerusalem' " (637). However, the narrator does not merely report and analyze. Moved by images, he cannot help but see "the virtually apocalyptic quality in their descriptions of city life" (622). Mrs. Allen and Mrs. Williams tell how their faith has changed in imagery and substance. Above all, they now feel absent from God (623). They still have a qualified, pragmatic hope, but the city is dark, built by man, " 'not God's world' " (625). This is Mrs. Williams:

> 'Before, we were in the wilderness, and it was touch and go if we'd make it. When we decided to come up here, I had a dream that we'd find the Holy City, but it's not a holy city, this one, that's for sure, though we eat better here. I have nightmares, and in them it's always the same: we're falling way down, down, down, the whole family, and we're bad off and there's no welfare check. Then I wake up and I know what a fool I was to think we'd ever reach that Holy City until we're dead and gone from this city here. But meanwhile my kids have their food in them. That's something.' (*South*, 629)

Coles accepts her biblical terms for her predicament. The narrator finds that those who came to the cities are in exile and describe a religion of exile. They give an image of the Heavenly City for which this move to northern ghettos and slums is one more trial, not a simulacrum of what is to come. They have taken a literal journey, but they are not home yet.

"The Lord in Our Cities" is one of Coles's earliest explorations of spiritual quest. Its placement gives an artful closure to *The South Goes North*, changing our gaze to the end of time and history. Yet that art is also intended to convey the moral and philosophical substance that social science cannot. The pride of place afforded "The Lord in Our Cities" and its companion in *Migrants, Sharecroppers, Mountaineers*, "Rural Religion," implies how seriously Coles regarded faith as early as 1971. Here he acknowledges his need for discovering the purpose of life, "a sense of destination" and "the conviction that we are on a journey that matters, the sense that we have something ahead of us, a place waiting" (*South*, 617). He recognizes how familiar Biblical imagery is to him and how he yearns to shake the intellectual baggage that he thinks divides social scientists from the passionate faith of one like Mrs. Williams (650). But his words suggest doubt. He feels separate, too, but not from the Heavenly City as such. He cannot simply affirm his belief in that city but must echo the testament of one who can. To Mrs. Williams's description of truly humane, humble Christians, the narrator adds only one line, "I believe I want more than anything to say amen to those words" (651). Adele V. Silver was one of the earliest commentators to observe that Coles did not simply report on the religion of his speakers but in fact placed spiritual purpose at the center of his writing: "Through all his writing runs the need to bear witness, almost a religious witness, to individual witness, to individual dignity and mystery—and to his own struggle to become and remain aware of that mystery. At heart his is a religious struggle" (Silver 53). If that were not so, Silver argues, Coles would realize that his goal—to raise the social consciousness of his readers—was doomed, merely adding books to help them give lip service to the poor (Silver 53). In this way Silver answers critics like Marge Piercy, who has questioned that activism can be a result of Coles's writing. Ronda also points out the religious tenor of the final chapters of the second and third volumes of *Children of Crisis* (Ronda 1989, 146).

Although *The South Goes North* was named with *Migrants, Sharecroppers, Mountaineers* for the 1973 Pulitzer Prize, for the most part the third volume has suffered by comparison with its companion. According to Marge Piercy, *The South Goes North*'s "thinner" treatment of urban poverty is partly due to circumstances within the urban environment itself (Piercy 1). However, Henry Caudill, a Kentucky writer and lawyer, praises *The South Goes North* for its historically accurate treatment of the complementary problems of urban and rural poverty: "Until the sickness of the land is healed the agony of the cities can only deepen" (23). Likewise, Silver finds that the "apocalyptic edge" to the end of *The South Goes North* complements the movement of *Migrants, Sharecroppers, Mountaineers* because the third volume reveals that "There is no place left to move to" (Silver 55).

Eskimos, Chicanos, Indians

The next two studies bring an important shift in the direction of *Children of Crisis*. For the most part the fourth and fifth volumes, both published in 1977, are outgrowths of Coles's earlier research. *Eskimos, Chicanos, Indians* (1977) began as a natural westward extension of his work with eastern migrant workers and became a study of three groups marginalized in the culture of the American West (*Eskimos,* xi). Yet, although still true to the purpose and method of the earlier works, *Eskimos, Chicanos, Indians* and its companion volume, *Privileged Ones,* posed new problems, the former by a complex set of historical events, the latter by seeming to abandon the series's basic subject. After more than a decade of fieldwork, Coles found himself facing new challenges as a researcher and self-professed, although modest, agent of change.

Between the early 1960s and the early 1970s the country and its politics had shifted. Those seeking social justice had become more militant. Although the new political awareness was already evident in *The South Goes North,* nowhere was it more prominent than in the emerging Chicano movement. Dedication to social change was no longer enough. A number of people had begun to demand their own voice, not "interpreted" by someone else. The someone else was usually white and an outsider. Moreover, the Native Americans that Coles also began to work with had already been much scrutinized by anthropologists and government officials. As he moved westward to study native and Spanish-speaking children, Coles faced a combination of new political winds and old cultural differences. These affected the purpose, method, and above all the narrative technique of *Eskimos, Chicanos, Indians.*

The foreword and method chapters of *Eskimos, Chicanos, Indians* describe these changes in detail. Because of identity politics and Coles's new self-consciousness about being a white researcher, his purpose in *Eskimos, Chicanos, Indians* is more limited than it was in the first three volumes. In *Eskimos, Chicanos, Indians* Coles presents himself, perhaps reluctantly, as more content to be a child psychiatrist and not an activist: "I have tried to stay strictly within my own bounds as a clinician . . . and as a child psychiatrist" (*Eskimos,* xvi). The very foundation of his reporting must be qualified. Rather than a straightforward documentarian and agent of change, Coles describes himself as a "mediator of sorts" and a "translator" (55, 57). The emphasis shifts from the author as liberator to the resisting subjects. Against his so-called translation stands each life's "own history, its own authority, dignity, fragility, rock-bottom strength" (57). In a sense, *Eskimos, Chicanos, Indians* shows how Coles grew along with the citizens he studied. He sees that change will increasingly be in the hands of people who come from the communities they serve (55). His role as a researcher, a "participant-observer," also shifts. To get around the image of the anthropologist as a timeworn, somewhat humorous figure among certain Native Americans, Coles relied on being a doctor (44). Another solution was participating in everyday tasks, chiefly among Eskimo families. During blizzards in Alaska, Coles mentions shoveling snow, getting water, feeding the sled dogs, and tending to sick people (52).

The Pueblo and Hopi children presented Coles with a final problem. They were even less inclined to talk than the wary Delta blacks and tight-lipped Appalachian whites to whom he had become accustomed. He learned to adjust to the Native Americans' taciturnity in ways that affected his whole research procedure and his narrative style as well (*Eskimos,* 44). Vision—just waiting, watching, and looking—became important. Coles admits that the photographer Alex Harris "taught me a lot about how to look, see, and keep my mouth shut" (xvii). He also began to view the drawings that he invited children to do with a different eye: "It was almost as if the picture, the representation put down on paper, possessed its own authority, energy, and requirements" (46). This knowledge is put to use in the volume's narrative technique.

Method

The method of *Eskimos, Chicanos, Indians* remains similar to that of earlier volumes in the series. Again, the research required extensive travel in the Rio Grande Valley of Texas, New Mexico, and Alaska, as well as intermittent visits to Los Angeles, California's Imperial Valley, Denver, and Tucson (*Eskimos,* 40). Unlike previous volumes, which focus on children and adolescents from about the ages of 6 to 18 or so, *Eskimos, Chicanos, Indians* contains the experience of children only, up to the age of 13 (53). Older Chicano and Native American adolescents are treated more as adults, an insight that Coles brought from his studies of rural Southerners (53).

Narrator

For the first time in *Children of Crisis* there is a sustained third-person narrator, as a few reviewers—including Bruce A. Ronda—have pointed out (Ronda 1989, 50). The decision was deliberate; Coles wanted the children to "move toward the reader on their own" (*Eskimos,* 61). The narrator rarely intrudes directly and even then casts himself as a shadowy "someone." For example, here is Domingo, a 12-year-old Chicano boy: "He is not really interested in carrying on a conversation—or in being helped to get his views across through the intervention of someone older, better educated, and convinced of his ability to organize and give direction to language" (267). The personal outrage that Coles so admires in Agee—and emulated in the tone of *Migrants, Sharecroppers, Mountaineers*—would seem arrogance with these speakers. Much of *Eskimos, Chicanos, Indians* concerns whites' or Anglos' (the latter is used by Chicano speakers) self-absorption, which makes the white narrator uncomfortable with the "vertical pronoun" (60). Furthermore, third-person narration lends itself to the theme of the interaction of landscape with ways of thinking. Ronda finds that such a text is "an invitation, a space to enter, an opportunity to cocreate a new reality in the space between our assumptions and lives as readers and those of the people here described" (Ronda 1989, 53). Coles would later use this same technique in *Women of Crisis.*

Structure

The organization of *Eskimos, Chicanos, Indians* is simpler than that of other volumes of *Children of Crisis,* although it shares important features with them. After a foreword, there is a chapter on setting, entitled "Once and Still the Frontier," and another on method. Each ethnic group then receives a section. The chapters within each section contain narratives of one or at most two children and their families. The sections end with summary chapters, similarly titled: "Growing Up Eskimo," "Growing Up Chicano," and "Growing Up Indian." These compare the children with each other and with others that Coles has studied. The final section, "References," consists of four bibliographical essays, streamlining the lengthy endnotes of earlier volumes. The overall effect of this exceptionally clear structure is to isolate the three groups from each other. This is a flaw, according to Peter Prescott, who finds that *Eskimos, Chicanos, Indians* "lacks its siblings' unity of focus," indicating that Coles's material may be exhausted.[9] Paul Starr, although noting the three distinct cultures of the volume, finds commonality in that all three are swept up in historical change, struggling to survive "against the current pulling them under and into the white society" (Starr 32). The organization, even though tending to separate into three parts, also allows more subtlety of narrative, metaphor, and theme within the sections. Although there is no controlling metaphor for the whole work, traces of the intricate geographic orchestration of *Migrants, Sharecroppers, Mountaineers* can be found in the Western volume's opening chapter, "Once and Still the Frontier."

The major sections on each group are deceptively simple in their presentation. Each section focuses on five to eight children and their families—often extended families. A number of the children in a section are siblings or cousins, living out different lives in somewhat different circumstances. Village, farm, and reservation life is treated before city life. Very young children—toddlers and preschoolers—have a featured place that is unusual in the series. This is particularly true in the section on Chicanos. There is considerable emphasis on the actions and speech of mothers and other caregivers in the household: an older sister, a grandparent, a father, an uncle. This emphasis on extended families spills over into two companion volumes to *Eskimos, Chicanos, Indians: Old Ones of New Mexico* and *Last and First Eskimos*. At each section's end, a summary chapter reviews, compares, and offers modest generalizations.

Setting

The opening chapter, "Once and Still the Frontier," deftly outlines the history, politics, and cultures of the West. These processes differ significantly from the ones that brought poverty and injustice to African Americans. Chicanos, Eskimos, and Native Americans also responded differently to these pressures. Each group has maintained a distinctive consciousness, a separation from mainstream American culture, to survive. For Native Americans of the Southwest, that consciousness is historical. For Chicanos, the Spanish language as well as a history of owning land in the Southwest has been a bulwark. Alaskan Eskimos, or the Inuit, have been physically isolated.

The theme, like the other chapters on setting in *Children of Crisis,* is the relationship between America's geography and the ways of life characteristic to each part: "To a degree every region is, among other things, a state of mind" (*Eskimos,* 4). Contrary to the volume's title and overall structure, this chapter first takes up the history of Spanish-speaking Americans, then Native Americans, and finally Eskimos. This order presents a number of obvious geographic and more subtle cultural links between the groups. Once the complex cultural and national heritage of

Spanish-American farmers and landowners is established, migrant workers provide the constant thread for a wide-ranging traversal of the Southwest. (Despite the strategy of this chapter, the focus of the Chicanos section is not migrants but children settled in Southwestern villages and cities.) The reader sees through the eyes of Chicano migrant children who watch the landscape from car windows. The historical link between the Native American child and the Chicano child with her Mexican and European roots is achieved by this contemporary perspective. The one has dwelt there since before recorded history and is united in fact and in spirit with the land; the other is a relative newcomer, yet closer than most whites to the land and its mystery. Through the Chicano's perspective, the reader gradually enters Pueblo and Hopi spaces and (if the reader is of European Judeo-Christian background) shares the child's surprise at the landscape's spirit. The Chicano child likewise takes us to Native Alaskan children, who are also nominally Christian and yet whose way of life is vastly different from either of the previous two cultures (22).

Narratives

In tone and texture, the three major sections are subdued but evocative. The chapters within each section read more like stories than the case histories in earlier volumes of *Children of Crisis,* largely because of the third-person narration. Each section is introduced via a tableau of a child and an elder. In each case the two figures are absorbed in what might be called a "gaze." There is some talk, but it is either indirectly reported or amounts to a few terse words. The Eskimo section is introduced by a five-year-old Eskimo girl and her grandfather, who walk to the river to stand and look at the ice (*Eskimos,* 65). Wind buffets them. Glances and gestures pervade the narrative. Then they turn home again. In similar fashion, the section on Chicanos opens with a silent ritual between a child and a father, each standing still as "a mirror image" of the other (232). "Indians" introduces both Pueblo and Hopi children in this manner, in two chapters. The tableau of a Pueblo girl and her mother places them outdoors. As a small plane flies overhead, each responds to the changed sky with a marked symmetry (395). "Hopi Girl" also opens with a mother and daughter out-of-doors, watching the sky (468). The narrative unfolds into a complex evocation of becoming a Hopi, how children construct their worlds from these seemingly small moments, often repeated. In their attention to gesture and gaze, *Privileged Ones* and later works like *Political Life* and *Dorothy Day* clearly show the influence of *Eskimos, Chicanos, Indians.*

Although the narrative technique departs radically from scientific reportage, observation is artfully blended with children's talk and drawings. The narratives are embedded in close observation of children's actions and words. *Eskimos, Chicanos, Indians* is especially good at portraying children's words and actions as arising coherently from their families' and peers' influence. Some stories change characters, but through thematic links seem to extend over more than one chapter. The links are subtle and unfold slowly. An example from the "Chicanos" section illustrates the connections. Three chapters, "Carlos: A Boy's Clues," "Forbidden Play," and "A Barrio Game," describe several cousins who range from toddlers to teenagers. The older children teach the younger ones a set of intricate behaviors toward Anglos: Never forget anger and oppression, but express nothing outwardly (*Eskimos,* 333–38). The summary chapter, "Growing Up Chicano," implicitly relies on these interconnected stories. As the progression from little Carlos to Francesca and her brother Eduardo to the barrio boy Luis shows, Chicano children's violent fantasies submerge but are not lost, developing into a nascent political consciousness. The sections on Chicano children have much in common with the later study, *The Political Life of Children.*

Stylistically, *Eskimos, Chicanos, Indians* also opens a new dimension in Coles's writing: the sustained interaction of two people on their own. As with any writer who relies on interviews, Coles has to deal with monologue's lack of drama. In earlier volumes, and indeed in most of his writing after *Children of Crisis,* his own presence in the narrative has afforded some tension. However, the Western volume of *Children of Crisis* concentrates on the drama that others play out. Only *Women of Crisis* and *Women of Crisis II* rival *Eskimos, Chicanos, Indians* for narrative sophistication.

Themes

Because the narratives of *Eskimos, Chicanos, Indians* are the most artfully worked and the least bound by case history, they are among the most thematically rich of *Children of Crisis.* Again and again, Coles returns to these themes: gaze and gesture, along with dreams and art—especially the children's drawings—as primary means by which these children develop a sense of identity and learn the subtleties of their heritage. By contrast, language is more problematic in their lives. For Chicano children, whose first language is Spanish, the English required at school challenges their loyalty to family and community. Early on, the speaking of Spanish is imbued with passion, mysticism, and overtones of political struggle *(Eskimos,* 282). For Native American and Alaskan children, the issue is how and when to verbalize. For example, Pueblo and Hopi children are taught to watch carefully, but they may not listen or speak so readily as teachers may wish (515). Used to following and giving terse directions that help them survive, Eskimo children may avoid speaking sentences (193). Thus the schools' attitude toward language conflicts with their upbringing. A final theme—by now a distinctive feature of *Children of Crisis*—is the life of the spirit, including the profound Catholicism of Chicano families and the evocative, haunting forms of spirituality of Native Americans, especially the Hopi, whose world view Coles regards with awe.

Although the mainstay of *Eskimos, Chicanos, Indians* is still talk, wordless communication—gesture, gaze, dreams, and art—assumes a place of importance and offers a means to critique the middle-class American preoccupation with language. The summary "Growing Up" chapters also make use of gesture and gaze to skirt the traps of sociological labeling, especially by the children's teachers. In keeping with its focus on the visual, this volume gives more attention to dreams than does any other in *Children of Crisis*. Dreams are interpreted largely as the children and their parents interpret them, without psychoanalytic ideas. Native American children's dreams receive special emphasis and form a bridge to the volume's conclusion. An ultimate refuge beyond the touch or understanding of whites, dreams are "a means of talking to oneself, a means of hearing the messages of ancestors long dead, a shared way for, say a mother and child to speak to one another about the values of a particular tribe" (544). Likewise, the drawings in *Eskimos, Chicanos, Indians* carry even more weight than those in the other volumes. In addition to evoking children's expectations, fears, and ambivalence about their lives and the lives of those around them, the drawings portray entire worldviews.

Finally, *Eskimos, Chicanos, Indians* treats religion, a hallmark of the conclusion to each volume of *Children of Crisis,* with a new sense of mysticism as Coles grapples with Hispanic Catholicism and the beliefs of the Pueblo, the Hopi, and the Eskimo. Eskimo children frequently talk about death and the spirit; some have "an almost uncanny kind of self-scrutiny" that differs from a Christian or Western conception of spirit and nature (203). In contrast, the abiding Catholicism of Chicano families is both a constant, reassuring presence and a reminder of political oppression (377). Yet faith is "an instrument, really, of self-knowledge and self-respect" as well as of community (359). Foreshadowing *Harvard Diary* and *Flannery O'Connor's South,* "Growing Up Chicano" describes "the tension between a rural, mystical, emotional Catholic faith and an agnostic, urban, materialistic culture, occasionally wrapped in fundamentalist Protestantism but, in the clutch, committed to Mammon" (*Eskimos,* 376). The theme of the Chicano section remains the conflicts inherent in being a Christian in twentieth-century America. The discussion of mysticism reaches a crescendo in "Growing Up Indian," concluding the volume. From the time they can walk, Pueblo and Hopi children learn an essentially contemplative way of life based on a complex response to the natural world (533). Gesture and gaze coalesce into an intense spiritual attention foreign to Christians: "For a Hopi or Pueblo child, the *world* is God, as compared to the white man's interest in *words* as a means of reaching and understanding God" (548). Contemplation includes not only the land but also the vast scope of history. An extended discussion of time traces how Native Americans have mingled Western ideas about time with their own, but still regard whites' obsession with linear time as foreign. Always concerned with the age by which children reach an understanding of moral, political, and spiritual realities, Coles points out that by the age of six or seven, Native American children have grasped the concept "forever" through the stories told of relatives and their spirits (518).

With their different perspective on time, the Hopi also revise Coles's understanding of the journey of life. A Hopi mother refers to the continuum of time, especially " 'the future time, when all life joins the world and stays with the world—no more moving around' " (533). This sense of life as a journey differs from the restless, linear, paradise-driven quest of *The South Goes North* and others of Coles's works. Finally, this nonlinear, spiritually rich historical gaze is turned full onto the moral history of whites. *Eskimos, Chicanos, Indians* ends with an extended treatment of Hopis' sense of themselves and whites, framed as a colloquy in which the Hopis are at once witness and teacher, or alternatively on a journey together with whites through time. The themes of journey and loss of self recur in the story of whites' spiritual emptiness: "For the Hopis, especially, white people are ravenous because for some reason they have become lost and show no signs of finding their way home" (550). For Coles there is no greater tribute than to bring someone up short, that is, to position one's existential being as a moral witness to another. Pueblo and Hopi children learn that their destiny, as it were, is "to be a witness to the depredations and excesses of others—and, maybe, a source of help, one day" (551). This sense of self, conceived in a spiritual history of the world, brings to Coles's mind his beloved Kierkegaard. The conclusion of *Eskimos, Chicanos, Indians* wrestles with Kierkegaard's and Hopi children's conception of spiritual resignation, a state that Coles elsewhere has called "man's highest task and least common achievement" (*South,* 389). What he seeks—and what he believes the Hopi have—is a "calculated, unremitting, entirely assertive resignation" (*Eskimos,* 551). That is, they know that there is "no hope of changing many people, at least in this world, only the hope of converting some, teaching some by example, winning some over spiritually" (552). Time is essential to this view, vast spans of time—and an anti-intellectual and antiprogressive outlook. In this portrayal, Pueblo and Hopi combine spiritual resistance with a transcendent view of history and a sense of the ineffability of life.

Privileged Ones

The final volume of *Children of Crisis* has a somewhat surprising subject, the lives of upper-middle-class and wealthy American children. Published with *Eskimos, Chicanos, Indians, Privileged Ones* (1977) was inspired by white and black parents who for years insisted that " 'The rich folks are the ones who decide how the poor folks live' " (*Privileged,* x). Earlier volumes of *Children of Crisis* include the voices of wealthy adults who affect the lives of impoverished children. Coles had also been talking with their sons and daughters, and gradually he began to do so in earnest. This volume benefits from two decades of meetings with the original "children of crisis" in the South, West, and North. Thus the children reported on here have been observed periodically for several years, during which time most have grown and changed dramatically. For example, the boy called Gordon is 9 at the outset of "Withdrawal," 14 at its close (306, 317).

Privileged Ones serves as the finale to *Children of Crisis* and a prologue to Coles's next projects, teaching literature and studying children outside the United States. There are many allusions to the other volumes, especially *Migrants, Sharecroppers, Mountaineers,* and the final sections of this last volume take up new subjects that would occupy Coles for many years to come. The epigraph of *Privileged Ones* comes from the book of Revelation, describing the New Jerusalem and those chosen of God, who "shall reign for ever and ever."[10] In this life, of course, it appears that well-off children already know the bliss of the New Jerusalem; their parents reign, and someday they will, too. The subtlety with which children so placed learn of their privilege is the subject of this work. Such learning ironically takes its toll on the spirit. Christopher Lasch, noting the Biblical terms, sums up *Privileged Ones*'s ironic stance: "Before they can inherit the earth, the children of privilege have to become incurious."[11]

Method

Privileged Ones documents work with 85 children living in or around New Orleans, Atlanta, Boston, Hartford, New York, Cleveland, Chicago, Albuquerque, and Anchorage; Charleston and Huntington, West Virginia; San Antonio and Crystal City, Texas; as well as rural eastern Kentucky, central Florida, and Mississippi (*Privileged*, 51). As is standard in *Children of Crisis,* actual names and places are altered, and the narratives are selective, occasionally composites of more than one person. Some families owned mines, retail stores, factories, plantations, huge farms, or ranches; others made a living from oil, ranching, medicine, law, or insurance (50–51). Some children's fathers were corporate executives or bankers. In the mid-1970s family resources ranged from "forty or fifty thousand dollars a year" to many millions (7).

Structure

The volume follows roughly the same plan as the first four. It is divided into 10 parts, the last of which is a long bibliographical essay. Part 1, "Comfortable, Comfortable Places" explores the setting, the physical dimensions of being privileged. It is followed by "The Method," while the next three parts give case studies divided broadly into geographic regions. The South is treated separately; so are Northern cities and suburbs across the United States. In between are placed the Appalachians, the Southwest, and Alaska. The final third of the book contains generalizing essays, treating "Entitlement," "The Schools," "Ethical Struggles: Idealism and Pragmatism," and the conclusion, "What Profit Under the Sun?" There is no overarching thematic or metaphoric structure to *Privileged Ones*. Rather, certain juxtaposed narratives and chapters resonate thematically with each other.

Narrator

As in *Eskimos, Chicanos, Indians,* the narration of the case studies is third person, without Coles's intrusion. But late in the volume, first-person point of view returns in force. For several reasons, the effect of third-person narration is somewhat different from the same technique in the fourth volume. Words are plentiful in the young mouths of *Privileged Ones.* These affluent children not only speak and read constantly, they hear their parents talk with each other and over the phone with associates and friends. The children also write, with their numerous school compositions often displayed and saved. Language is the ocean they swim in. Thus third-person narration is not required simply to "get into their heads." Rather, it helps give Coles, as narrator, needed distance from people quite like himself (43). There are other effects as well. The point of view, plus the lengthy time that Coles knew these children before writing their stories, affords a fictionlike freedom of narration that contributes to the greater drama of certain case studies. (The narrative impact of long knowledge also shows up in *Women of Crisis.*) For example, in "Tamed Rebel," a boy's tangled skein of preoccupations and experiences is told as if the narrator were omnipresent, a treatment very similar to fiction.

Setting

The opening chapter, "Comfortable, Comfortable Places," keeps the high standard achieved by the other volumes' essays on setting. However, the chapter succeeds not by bringing middle-class readers into strange spaces but by distancing them from familiar sights. It shows how wealthy Americans construct physical distance, landscaping, and a carefully established "semirural" setting as barriers to the rest of the world (5). This landscape figures largely in children's drawings. The estates and yards are described as one would approach them from the outside. Whether Appalachian wooded estates, Southern homes, or houses in suburban developments of Northern cities, these spaces depict the myriad social and aesthetic choices that are so important to well-to-do Americans. Many of these preferences pertain to a carefully nuanced and orchestrated notion of leisure, from acquiring art or other valuable possessions to repairing to a beachhouse, to playing golf or tennis. From the house or compound the essay moves out to places children visit. Although the essay also treats the physical restrictions and cultural riches of city life, there is special focus on suburban or exurban places, such as the country day school and the village store (16–22). Travel is also a major element in these children's lives and, along with possessions, contributes to their sense of limitless choices and prospects (*Privileged,* 25). In his review of *Privileged Ones,* Gore Vidal singled out this chapter, calling it "a sharp look" at upper-class American life.[12]

Narratives of Accommodation

The 16 named protagonists of this volume—and the term *protagonists* describes their understanding that they are likely to be the center of an interesting drama—range from Veronica, a Delta girl who lectures her friends on being " 'the true aristocrat,' " to Raymond, the son of an Atlanta businessman, who did not know he was black until he was five years old (*Privileged*, 64, 336). They include a young Alaskan; a "problem child" who has an absent, ambitious executive father and an alcoholic mother; and a Chicana girl who becomes her father's confidante and potential business partner. They are all described with great attention to their struggles and dignity as well as the irony of their circumstances. At several points this section pairs sister and brother, friend and friend. In one essay, "New Mexico Twins," a sister and brother display their delicate, loving, but development-minded sense of the land near Albuquerque, a sensibility that contrasts with the Pueblos of *Eskimos*. These pairings often juxtapose one child's moral dilemmas against the other's for the reader to evaluate. These predicaments are usually resolved by gradually acceding to elders' subtle wishes to maintain the status quo. For example, Coles draws a pointed moral contrast between the "Young Observers," Helen and her younger brother Geoff, who live in Boston and take up photography. Whereas Helen is older and more cosmopolitan in her photographic interests, Geoff takes pictures of workmen, including some firemen (304). These win honors at school, but Geoff is more concerned that a black classmate's father cannot get a job at the fire station. Not to be outdone, Helen devises a plan to photograph black children in another neighborhood, yet in the end decides not to go through with it. Her failure of moral nerve is clear. Although there are indications that she (and indeed most of the girls described) may have been subject to restrictions that Geoff was not, Coles is not interested in sexism as an excuse for moral weakness. Another pairing is developed between the chapters "Young Patriot" and "A Boy's Journey from Liberalism to Social Darwinism," the latter concerning a minor theme of *Privileged Ones:* the failure of liberalism.

Themes and Theories

The narratives illustrate the need for children—as they grow older—to accommodate their beliefs, a theme registered in Christopher Lasch's review (124). Although accommodation is also evident in other volumes of *Children of Crisis,* notably the "Chicanos" section of *Eskimos,* the accom-

modation of affluent children seems particularly shameful and gratu-
itous. In *Privileged Ones* this process takes the form of a dead hand, as
one child after another learns to quit asking questions about troublesome issues of race, money, class, human dealings. The lesson is so pronounced in so many of the chapters that the cases amount to moral
exempla.

Privileged Ones also sounds a warning on the perils of intellectualism.
For example, the chapter entitled "Withdrawal" shows how worthy pursuits (in this young man's case, marine biology and art) and the common maxim to plan one's future are the means by which a young man
escapes the wrenching moral complications of his world. The subject of
the essay, Gordon, is an activist who argues at school for integration and
against American defense policy (*Privileged,* 311). But whereas his teachers and parents seem to encourage his noble plans, they also influence
his choices and finally curb his activism. Gordon retreats into science,
admiring "scientists who withdraw from the world's distractions" (318).
His plight is expressed by one of his drawings. On an anchored ship
stands a person, "a portrait of the artist as sailor, scientist, explorer, and
not least, man removed from others, privileged to have his own activity,
while they [on shore] cling to each other and do nothing, get nowhere"
(318). As well as anything else, this painting symbolizes Coles's skepticism toward conventional intellectual and artistic endeavor. The efforts
of well-meaning, powerful people are stymied by their faith in a work-
able plan—or its absence. Withdrawing into ambition and excellence of
individual achievement is a relief but also a moral abdication.

As in *Eskimos, Privileged Ones* uses its narratives as springboards for
several generalizing chapters. However, the last four essays of *Privileged
Ones* are not just assemblages of observations but rather a serious
attempt to theorize the psychosocial development of middle- and upper-
class American children, as psychologist-critics Lasch and Starr have
noted. Often studied individually, this group has been understudied as a
group because of their families' reluctance to be subjects and, even
more, because of the layers of influences and choices that tend to
overemphasize differences between them (*Privileged,* 362). Drawing
heavily on psychoanalytic concepts, these four essays contain some of
the most difficult passages in Coles's body of work but at the same time
some of the most fascinating ideas and stories. They reward the specialist and the diligent generalist with a variety of insights.

The first essay, "Entitlement," elaborates a concept that is one of
Coles's genuine contributions to social psychology: "I use the word 'enti-

tlement' to describe what, perhaps, all quite well-off American families transmit to their children—an important psychological common denominator, I believe: an emotional expression, really, of those familiar, class-bound prerogatives, money and power" (363). To develop a theoretical framework for entitlement, the essay wades into psychoanalytical concepts of narcissism, then moves back to the distinctive shores of families' lives (363–64, 367–68). Through repeated and yet constantly varied conversations and experiences, children learn how privileged they are (371). Extended examples of particular unnamed children fill the essay. All the examples are multitude, all point several ways. Entitlement means money but also a host of other prerogatives. For example, wealthy children learn to cultivate the self: "With none of the other American children I have worked with have I heard such a continuous and strong emphasis put on the 'self' " (380). That self includes their appearance, bodies, and clothes as well as their interests and preferences, formed into discrete and approved activities such as tennis, sailing, riding, reading, photography, caring for pets and possessions, and certain kinds of charity. They are steered away from doing nothing and solitary pursuits unless these meet certain criteria of activity and competence (379). They also learn pleasure in competence (398). Even troubles, such as the serious illness of a parent, are framed by a basic optimism (398). Such confidence also has doubts, chiefly the need to "do everything right" all the time, as one boy writes in a composition (405). Doubt is countered by platitudes like " 'If you really work for the rewards, you'll get them' " (405). Yet the essay stresses that these children are not allowed to fall short.

Wealthy children learn to regard themselves as essentially different from others, who are often considered weak, immoral, unruly, or subject to the discipline of the rich. They learn to feel politically and economically vulnerable—and thus protective of what they have. They learn to use the so-called work ethic to judge people morally. They learn to tolerate, if not condone, parents' use of power, often by giving directions to others who must obey. These lessons are often contradictory and fraught with anxieties. One example of this delicacy is in wealthy children's attitude toward teachers, described at length in the essay entitled "The Schools." This essay extends the theory of entitlement to education, exploring the special social position that teachers occupy in these children's lives: "not a servant, but not really an equal either" (415). Education is taken seriously but with reservations, too.

The last two essays concern moral and spiritual issues of privilege. "Ethical Struggles: Idealism and Pragmatism" is important because it prepares the way for the concerns of *The Moral Life of Children*. Somewhat ponderous and shakily argued, the chapter has an important theoretical task: to explain why children who develop such superb competencies in every other area do not often do so in crucial matters of conscience. The how of such failures is well documented in the narratives and case studies. The whys are murkier. The essay lays the groundwork for explorations of "moral notice" in *The Moral Life of Children* and provides a rationale for the teaching of literature to privileged students in *The Call of Stories*. The essay proceeds from conscience and a cluster of psychoanalytic concepts to examples from children (*Privileged*, 473, 481–83).

For all affluent parents, the problem of ethics, Coles suggests, is a singularly knotty one because it conflicts with the need to keep certain people—and certain moral issues—at a distance (462). Coles plumbs the idealism of moneyed children versus their pragmatic need to accommodate to elders. The examples are arranged to show a kind of moral progress, and their cumulative effect is cautionary. For example, a mine owner's daughter grieves for the miners killed in a series of explosions, behavior at first tolerated by her parents, then as weeks go by, found exasperating (471). Finally her father orders her to stop praying. The portrayal of this family conflict, with its ironies and the childish behavior of the adults, recalls Coles's reading of James Agee's novel, *A Death in the Family*, in his 1974 study *Irony in the Mind's Life*. The essay contains other highlights for the nonspecialist reader, like a wonderful list that shows how ideals are a subtle blend of morality and manners; another passage that unmasks the privileges inherent in "volunteerism"; and a refutation of the idea that any behavior is natural (*Privileged*, 492–94). Ultimately these children are portrayed as victims.

In addition to describing the problem, "Ethical Struggles" also suggests one kind of solution. Children learn by repeated, varied experiences and by talking. By disclosing these children's blindness to others' less fortunate lives, this essay points the way to Coles's teaching of moral literature, documentary, and (eventually) art history (500). A year after *Privileged Ones* was published, Coles began offering "A Literature of Social Reflection" to Harvard College freshmen (*Stories*, xvi). This seminar grew to an entire set of academic courses, some with fieldwork, to make sure that a certain number of extraordinarily privileged college students do listen to others not of their experience.

Apocalyptic images haunt the final chapter, "What Profit Under the Sun?" (*Privileged*, 495). In this essay the voices of migrant farm workers are offered as perhaps an inevitable counterweight to those of wealthy children. The poorest of the working poor, they are invoked to round the entire series as well as to conclude this volume. Although not as lofty as *Eskimos'* discussion of spiritual resignation, "What Profit Under the Sun?" plays on the question form and the economic motif of its title, taken from Ecclesiastes. There are constant overtones of business loss contrasted with spiritual loss. This sometimes vague, provocative, and occasionally lyrical essay has two purposes vis-à-vis privileged children: It continues to summarize their mundane beliefs and attitudes, and it also considers their spiritual longings, which develop somehow alongside their full worldly lives. Organized religion is not treated except to note its convergence with maxims of hard work, the pieties that children learn. The subject is children's existential moments. That privileged children have any such moments is, for Coles, a source of awe, given the crowded, wonderful, material lives they lead. A precursor of *The Spiritual Life of Children* (1992), this chapter concludes the *Children of Crisis* series by repeating the line of James Agee that closes the first volume (*Privileged*, 554; *Courage*, 381). The end of *Privileged Ones* is a plea to keep searching and questioning.

Enduring Issues in *Children of Crisis*

The five volumes of *Children of Crisis* make up a sweeping study of American children, what K. L. Woodward has called "a kind of interior landscape of the American family, circa the 1960s."[13] Paul Starr summarizes the principal theme: "At an early age, society becomes part of our *internal* environment: our dreams, fantasies, ideals, intentions, our conceptions of ourselves, our assumptions about what the world has to offer and what we can expect from it" (Starr 1). In the language of psychology, the series portrays "the psychodynamics of socialization, the mental processes through which social life re-creates itself in the form of personality" (Lasch 124). Harry M. Caudill calls *Children of Crisis* "the definitive work on America's poor and powerless in the twentieth century," worthy to stand with W. A. Cash's *The Mind of the South* and James Baird Weaver's *A Call to Action* (Caudill 21).

However, the series underwent major changes between 1967 and 1977, most noticeably in the shifting focus of the title. Surveying all five volumes, Starr points out that the crisis changes from the clear crisis of desegregation to more diffuse predicaments, the racism and social oppression that black and white, poor and rich, adult and child, internalize on a daily basis (Starr 1). The different volumes each give their own meaning to "children of crisis." *Eskimos* expanded the series to encompass other marginalized groups in the United States; to do justice to them Coles adapts his narrative style, among other things. *Privileged Ones* then places the previous volumes on the poor "into sharp relief," creating "a vast portrait of children in America at various intersections of contemporary history, culture and class relations" (Starr 1).

Contemporary reviews of *Children of Crisis* not only establish its importance but also raise a number of persistent issues. Writers have been moved by the series, yet often unable to fit it into established categories of social science, general nonfiction, or reportage, revealing the sometimes artificial distinctions between the conventions of literature and science that have come to characterize late-twentieth-century nonfiction. The issues raised by their commentary reveals a great deal about the criteria we use to judge writing as well as about the series itself. Reviewers have compared his method with that of writers like Oscar Lewis, who also tape-recorded poor people. Maxine Greene, however, distinguishes Coles's purpose from Lewis's, not merely to portray a slice of life for its own sake but also to show how individuals are affected by national events (Greene 67). Depending on whether they treat Coles's purpose as literary or scientific, critics attribute his method's simplicity to either a certain literary admiration of taped conversations or a social-scientific obsession with data. For example, Joseph Epstein regards *Children of Crisis* as largely a mass of underanalyzed data from taped interviews.[14] Throughout his essay Epstein wavers between grudging admiration and contempt as he attempts to find a yardstick to measure the first three volumes of *Children of Crisis*. One early commentator, however, contends that this artlessness is achieved by considerable refinement, and others have followed suit. Sociologist Edgar Friedenberg observes of *Courage and Fear:* "Coles's writing is so forthright and unobtrusive that the reader may not notice how much his work owes to its methodological sophistication."[15] He asserts that "it is a delight to see data handled with such canny simplicity" (Friedenberg 1967, 28). "Canny simplicity" indeed describes the seemingly effortless monologues and stories that fill *Children of Crisis*. In foreword after foreword, Coles attempts to answer critics like Joseph Epstein who would dismiss either his way of gathering stories or his procedures for editing them. Coles's reports of his methods make it eminently clear that the volumes are highly shaped. Whether that result is good or bad depends on the reader's own often quite subtle expectations of purpose and genre.

Regardless of whether *Children of Crisis*—assuming that it belongs to one single genre—falls into the realm of history, social science, or social commentary, critics generally agree that it lacks a central argument, conclusions, and recommendations.[16] This opinion expresses another virtually unresolvable dilemma: Should the legacy of *Children of Crisis* be its research or its artistry—or something of both, something not quite grasped?

The commentators who are least disturbed by the genre question of *Children of Crisis* have regarded it as moral literature and its purpose as didactic. Starr and Mary Ellman assert that psychology must ultimately fail to encompass Coles's subject. They both locate the problem in contemporary psychology's historical dependence on existing social organization, and Ellman recommends that ethics is a better field for Coles's work[17] (Starr 33; Ellman 92). Like Piercy, Eliot Fremont-Smith emphasizes the series's advocacy, regarding Coles as not only a doctor, scientist, and citizen but also "a publicist and propagandist."[18] Nor is novelist and historian Gore Vidal daunted by genre, calling these works variously "monologues," "stories," and "moral literature" (Vidal 12, 14). He judges Coles to be "essentially a moralist" (Vidal 14). Prescott indicates that Coles's search is for "the truth of the spirit" and that in melding social documentary with art, his purpose is didactic; without the art, no one would read the social treatise (Prescott 76). Expanding this approach to genre, Bruce A. Ronda turns to the moral and social criticism of two older traditions: the American Transcendentalists and writers of the Progressive reform movement at the turn of the twentieth century. Ronda places Coles "in the space between these two approaches, in the territory between the Romantic and the sociological visions" (Ronda 1989, 105). Stories are simply part of the moral and social critic's traditional repertoire, as exemplified by the writing of Ralph Waldo Emerson, Nathaniel Hawthorne, Henry James, Harriet Beecher Stowe, Jane Addams, and Stephen Crane (Ronda 1989, 54, 105). Ronda blurs the distinction between writers of fiction and nonfiction to bring *Children of Crisis* into focus. Because Coles himself, as observer and narrator, must learn the lessons of *Children of Crisis,* the result can be charming instead of wearily didactic. Vidal has noted what many other commentators have grappled with, that Coles's research is his own search, his own autobiography (Vidal 9). The "beguiling" ironies of Coles's persona allow the children to express his outrage at injustice (Vidal 9), a disarming posture.

The prose of *Children of Crisis* has received considerable praise for its lack of psychiatric jargon, but many commentators also find Coles's style repetitive. Vidal finds the prose flat and the characters indistinct (Vidal 10). Piercy, although she likes Coles's prose, also finds that "middle-classing" the speech overly smoothes the individual speakers' dialogue (Piercy 20), whereas Ellman notes "a certain blandness of diction" that she attributes to psychiatric shorthand (Ellman 92). Charges of vagueness and effusion are also typical. In Coles's prose both Vidal and Epstein see the pernicious influence of Agee's overblown style. Other commentators, such as Lasch and Silver, applaud that influence. In all respects, flaws included, *Children of Crisis* is a "prodigious achievement" (Starr 32). Its tensions—of persona, style, genre, method, and purpose—are reflected in Coles's subsequent writing.

Chapter Four
Children across Cultures

Before *Children of Crisis* was completed, a new study of children began to take shape. This second study was to be, like *Children of Crisis*, a set of loosely related efforts, the subjects of which lived thousands of miles from each other. It too would take years to complete. However, this series focused not on class or race as such but on children's capacity for wisdom. The series composes *The Moral Life of Children* (1986), *The Political Life of Children* (1986), and *The Spiritual Life of Children* (1990). The three volumes not only add new material but reexamine Coles's earlier work. Coles regards the series as the culmination of 30 years of research (*Spiritual Life*, [xi]). The project was ambitious. The method, observing children across cultures and nations, required immense travel, fluency in languages (Coles speaks good Spanish and passable French), and assistance in gaining access and interpreting (*Political Life*, 163). Before 1974 Coles had never been in another country. By 1990, when *Spiritual Life* was published, he had made dozens of visits on four continents, often accompanied by one or more of his three sons.

The project was ambitious, too, because it was unorthodox. The assumption that children did indeed think about, imagine, and take part in the moral, political, and spiritual aspects of their cultures is a logical extension of Coles's previous work on race and class. *Children of Crisis* had demonstrated that children interact intensely with their culture through daily contact with their families and peers. Race and class did not do full justice to their comments, which had dimensions that suggested philosophical treatment. However, that line of reasoning is not generally part of psychoanalytic thought. Indeed, it harks back to ideas about children's innocence and virtue as well as to pre-Freudian conceptions of children as miniature adults. To ground the study in psychoanalysis, the series looks to the work of Anna Freud, who is invoked many times in these volumes. From her study of child heroes in World War II as well as her general observations of children and her theories about the ego, Coles extrapolates that notions like morality, honor, character, idealism, and altruism figure in psychological development.

The genesis of the series can be seen in the fourth and fifth volumes of *Children of Crisis*. For *Eskimos, Chicanos, Indians* Coles observed American children from cultures markedly different from the mainstream. They, particularly Chicano children, had political views, as did children in *Privileged Ones*. Coles became interested in extending cross-cultural study of children but credits his final decision to his 1974 visit to South Africa (*Political Life*, 11, 15). *Privileged Ones* had other influences on the series: Its discussion of the "ego-ideal" was elaborated in *The Moral Life of Children,* and during his research with well-off youngsters Coles learned that nonreligious children contemplated moral and spiritual issues (*Privileged*, 481–88; *Spiritual Life*, 350).

Nine years separate the publication of the last two volumes of *Children of Crisis* and the first two in this series. Between 1977 and 1986, Coles completed many projects, including literary appreciations of Walker Percy and Flannery O'Connor, and collaborated with Jane Hallowell Coles on the two *Women of Crisis* volumes. During this period he refined his technique of presenting "voices." The narratives of the *Lives of Children* benefit from this overall refinement. The books are substantial but considerably shorter than the volumes of *Children of Crisis*. The stories of children tend to represent highlights rather than exhaustive or even necessarily typical descriptions (*Spiritual Life*, 342). Thus the burden of presenting a fully documented work of research weighs less heavily on the writing than it did in *Children of Crisis*. Yet the series is still firmly anchored in the methods of psychoanalysis, psychology, sociology, anthropology, and political science. It also has a self-consciousness, a sense of personal quest for truth.

The Moral Life of Children

Rather than being a single, unified work, *The Moral Life of Children* (1986) is a series of seven essays on several distinct projects. Nonetheless it contains the results of prolonged research and maintains several themes. The underlying thread of *Moral Life* is the search for positive psychoanalytic and psychological sources for children's moral sense. Some of the research is retrospective, whereas other studies were specifically conducted for this volume. Although the structure is loose compared to Coles's other studies of children, *Moral Life* still follows a familiar pattern. Life stories are related, usually within a theoretical or topic-based discussion of morality. Stories are often paired, usually an American child with a child from another country.

The opening essay, "Psychoanalysis and Moral Development," builds directly on the later chapters of *Privileged Ones*. It offers a psychological explanation of the human moral sense and critiques the tradition of research on moral development exemplified by Sigmund Freud, Jean Piaget, Lawrence Kohlberg, and Carol Gilligan. The theory, for which Coles does not claim originality, is a rereading of Freud's "ego ideal" (*Moral Life*, 32), which is a positive reformulation of conscience, opposed to the primarily punitive action of the traditional superego. Somewhat confusingly presented, the theory mixes ancient touchstones like mind, heart, and will with Freudian concepts (29, 31, 287). At times the essay leaps from one person's sudden insight or fortuitous action straight to the fate of a nation (36). On the other hand, Kohlberg and others are justly criticized for their rigidity in defining moral development. Ruby Bridges, the schoolgirl first described in *Courage and Fear*, is brought forth to show the flaws of Kohlberg's influential developmental scheme. According to Kohlberg, the essay states, Ruby would be rated merely " 'preconventional' or 'premoral' " rather than possessing true moral insight (27).

One of the liveliest essays in the volume, "Movies and Moral Energy," adds Coles's early personal fascination with film to his research on morality. It is a frank admission that "Entertainment is an expression of our nature" and an attempt to integrate interest in film, stories, and myths generally to children's moral development (*Moral Life*, 83). Coles grapples with defining a "moral sensibility . . . provoked by artistic expression," an idea that he would later refer to as "moral imagination" in *The Call of Stories* (65). Movies can be one "source of moral energy," although the means by which this happens is somewhat loosely argued (92). The essay gives animated examples of the way children involve movies in the discussion of their moral dilemmas, citing *A Raisin in the Sun*, *To Kill a Mockingbird*, John Wayne movies, *Star Wars*, and *Dirty Harry*.

The next essay, "Moral Purpose and Vulnerability," also brings art— in this case literature—to bear on research observation and theory. The essay extends "Psychoanalysis and Moral Development" and in some ways offers a more coherent explanation than the earlier chapter affords. The chapter argues that some people who endure harsh circumstances in life not only survive without psychiatric illness, they maintain a solid, reflective moral sense without self-pity. Again rejecting the superego as a major influence, Coles names moral purpose—the sum of "small, everyday dreams"—and the ego ideal as sources of energy to aid one's instincts to survive in a grim world (*Moral Life*, 123).

"Moral Purpose and Vulnerability" also pays homage to George Orwell's documentary *The Road to Wigan Pier*. From Coles's research come two main voices: Eduardo, a 10-year-old boy from Rio de Janeiro, and Marty, the teenaged daughter of a Belle Glade, Florida, migrant family. Their nuanced stories, accompanied by drawings, capture the humorous, compassionate "decency" that some children have constructed from their circumstances (103). Homely details, such as the ice cream and cookies in Marty's tale, figure ironically in the development of a moral life. A lyrical description of a rainy night seen from a *favela,* a Brazilian hillside slum, figures in Eduardo's spiritual beliefs (135). The two marginalized cultures, a crowded Brazilian favela and a rural American migrant camp, play off each other. Although there are sentimental moments, the overall effect is arresting: These young people come to life as thoughtful characters in plays whose endings are uncertain.

"On Character" contrasts in method with those vivid stories and raises troubling questions about morality. The essay describes research conducted in 1980 in three American high schools (*Moral Life*, 140). Coles asked groups of students and teachers to discuss the meaning of "character," a word he wants to revive. The results reveal an interesting interplay between class and assumptions about psychology, sociology, and morality. For the wealthy and middle-class students, individuality was a focus. Inner-city students were less concerned with individuality as such; rather, they saw their very existence threatened by alcohol, drugs, and apathy. The class differences are marked in other ways. Private boarding-school students saw character not as "a possession, but something one searches for: a quality of mind and heart one struggles for" (144). The middle-class suburban students valued the use of psychiatry and psychoanalysis to judge character, and Coles could not dissuade them (149). Inner-city youth and teachers spoke of character as commitment, as either inner discipline or the outward discipline of rules (150–51). They valued nineteenth-century industrial virtues like punctuality and agreed that character belongs to the active, even the bold (153). Yet their confident assertions are called "exaggerated, romantic" (155). Indeed, "On Character" raises troubling questions about morality as class socialization rather than adherence to absolutes. Coles admits being frustrated with the students and teachers at the lower- and middle-class schools. However, by questioning the latter's conceptions of character, this essay seems to side with the wealthy students. This lack of irony or self-consciousness on Coles's part is unusual.

What inspires and sustains a young person to live a life of self-sacrifice and devotion? Is such a life a sign of previous emotional conflicts or arrested development? Is there such a thing as pure altruism? The next essay, "Young Idealism," tentatively answers these questions by telling the contrasting stories of two extraordinary but modest lives. First is Jimmie, a self-mocking New Englander who has settled in southwestern Georgia as a community organizer, helping poor, rural, mainly black residents. The narrative follows Jimmie for almost 20 years (*Moral Life*, 172). Coles poses Jimmie's story to Anna Freud, and their discussions provide a theoretical elaboration of the narrative. The other story is of a teenaged hairdresser and prostitute in Copacabana, Brazil (174–84). Despite her grim, degraded life, she regularly gives her earnings to the church. The chapter attempts to define a new relationship between the individual ego and social action. As they would later in *Anna Freud*, Coles the narrator and Miss Freud clash over conceptions of idealism (173). Ultimately the discussion of idealism is not as interesting or as germane to the daily life of altruistic people as is the evocation of the eerily quiet meals Jimmie takes in Georgia or the many-faceted exploration of Brazilian religion and squalor. Here as elsewhere in *Moral Life*, the stories carry the load when theory falters.

Altruism is a most attractive psychological function. One of the least attractive—moral attribution—is lucidly explored in the sixth essay, "Social Class and the Moral Other." One of the classic ego defense mechanisms, moral attribution occurs when "Through others we try to settle things for ourselves" (*Moral Life*, 222). Moral attribution involves dividing the world into "us" and "them," a division that is both psychological and moral. The other so created disguises secret wishes that are bound up with perceptions of class and race (205). The examples, drawn widely from Coles's cross-cultural research as well as from literature, examine children's "creation of the moral Other" (207), showing how early in life children begin to struggle with "ethical dilemmas" (216). The essay balances the stand of the moralist and the stance of the psychologist or social observer. For example, a boy who saves a friend from drowning yet utters invective against blacks seems a contradiction for the moralist but is consistent when viewed psychologically. Another set of stories comes from children's responses to the assassination of President John F. Kennedy, which many youngsters "dovetailed morally" with racism (223). In this chapter and others, the connections between the imaginative and the moral mark a turning point in Coles's work that would later find full expression in *The Call of Stories.*

There are only four drawings in *The Moral Life of Children.* The last of these depicts nuclear holocaust as drawn by an Atlanta girl whose story is prominent in the seventh and final essay, "Children and the Nuclear Bomb." Her mesmerizing picture of "artistic and moral" pessimism makes the extraordinarily abstract issue of nuclear holocaust concrete for herself and her interviewer (262–67). Like "On Character," this chapter presents a single research study, an evolving project that took place between about 1979 and 1981, when Ronald Reagan's conservative policies engendered fears of nuclear war in some American citizens. This essay makes a clear point: Social class largely determines which American children worry about the use of nuclear weapons. Coles found that it was mainly well-off children of professionals and businesspeople who heard about, read about, and speculated on nuclear holocaust.

Children of working-class parents showed much less concern. They felt more jeopardized by the potential aggression of other nations, not by nuclear weapons as such. Poor children who had even considered the threat of nuclear war were likely to treat it as a symbol of more immediate and for them equally devastating threats in their own communities (277). Coles coined the term *"moral notice"* to describe this selective awareness (275). The moral development of children from poor or working-class families is not the less because it does not include a commitment to ridding the world of nuclear weapons. Nor are affluent children who have such a commitment more developed or "evolved." Rather, children respond to the immediacies of the threats they experience. If the nuclear danger cannot be experienced as immediately as another peril can, it is morally hollow (273). Thus poor children find nuclear war too distant a threat compared with hunger, making a living, staying alive today.

In *The Moral Life of Children,* moral energy and action are mainly confined to awareness of race and class. That is, moral life is enacted in public life. While children struggle with ethical dilemmas based on their experiences at home and school, in the street and playgrounds—including watching television and movies—it is the complex web that is emphasized, not any particular defining moment of moral awareness. Jimmie, for example, is examined not on his initial commitment but on his staying power. In a sense, *Moral Life* is a collection of loose ends tied up and new and urgent issues set forth. The moral influence of movies, books, and popular culture generally, if not strictly speaking new to

Coles's thinking, is here reenvisioned. The change would affect other works, chiefly *The Call of Stories*.

The Political Life of Children

The Moral Life of Children turns inward, recalling Coles's struggles with psychological theory in *Irony in the Mind's Life* and *Privileged Ones*. The companion volume, published simultaneously, turns outward to international crises and tragedies. *The Political Life of Children* (1986) recalls the American struggle for desegregation in *Courage and Fear* and the multicultural world first explored in *Eskimos, Chicanos, Indians*. This outwardness gives *Political Life* the vitality of being in the thick of public crises and the historical moment. The drama of young lives is played out on a stage worthy of notice. The open sores of political tumult in Northern Ireland, South Africa, Nicaragua, French Canada, and Poland give way to economic crisis in Brazil and the United States. Then the volume proceeds to the aftermath of national upheaval in Southeast Asia, in the form of refugees trying to make new lives in other countries. As a narrator, Coles has a researcher's calm—rather than a reporter's urgency—about his choices of subject. Still, there is no doubt that he is energized by being with children living under daily political, economic, and cultural stress. The thesis of *Political Life* is "A nation's politics becomes a child's everyday psychology" (310).

Method

Political Life adds to the relatively small body of research on children's development of political understanding (313). Once disdainful of politics, Coles began to regard political knowledge as psychologists view sexuality and aggression—powerful enough to be repressed (11). *Political Life* draws on psychoanalysis, social psychology, and political science in its observations and theorizing. Although Coles recognizes that "political" refers to power relations in general, in this study the term is applied almost exclusively to attitudes toward nationalism (71). After his first trip to South Africa in 1974, he returned to that country in 1975 and eventually traveled to Northern Ireland, England, Nicaragua, Canada, Poland, Cambodia, Thailand, and Brazil and made further studies in the United States as well. His sons assisted him; indeed he relied on many other people who, for political reasons, cannot be named either in the acknowledgments or the narratives (16). In all he visited

Northern Ireland and South Africa for more than a decade, and they receive the most detailed treatment.

Drawings

Moral and political experiences rely heavily on stereotypical symbols and phrases. In *Moral Life*, Coles sometimes takes issue with children's use of these customary representations of moral life, especially in the essay "On Character." In *Political Life* he accepts the highly conventional, even trite, nature of children's words and drawings on these subjects for what they are: their attempts to negotiate these familiar symbols into political beliefs of their own. The children were asked to draw icons of nationalism or partisanship—a flag, a president, a map. This volume has 30 illustrations, some of them responses to that request. The essays agilely work the spaces in between the symbols and clichés.

Structure

The opening essays, "Children and Political Authority" and "The Homeland: Psychoanalysis and the Political Thought of Children," review definitions, theory, and context for children's political lives, in particular elaborating the idea of "homeland." There follow six chapters that form the bulk of the volume. Each chapter explores a theme that influences children's understanding of nationalism, and each theme is exemplified by observations of children in one or two countries. The six chapters proceed from obvious sources of political differences—religion, ideology, language, and culture—to more subtle but equally important influences on children's political lives, like race, class, and exile. In *Political Life* the former, obvious sources tend to make children knowledgeable and outspoken about nationalism, whereas the latter, subtler ones can repress nationalism or make it irrelevant. The volume may also be described as moving toward and then away from the idea of homeland as a fiercely defended idea, with various forces introducing strains and irony. As the chapter titles, such as "Religion and Nationalism," show, dual allegiances are a major theme. A final chapter summarizes the themes and ties the volume to *Moral Life*. In all *Political Life* has a coherence that is lacking in its companion volume.

The two opening essays construct a basis for children's political life, the first employing concepts from social psychology and the second, psychoanalysis. The theories that Coles develops are grounded in many examples and narratives. The first essay, "Political Authority and the Young," discusses children's " 'political socialization' " (*Political Life*, 24). Based on Coles's 1974 Davie lecture at the University of Cape Town, the essay argues that children do reflect on political matters because it is absolutely in their interest to learn "exactly what it is that works for or against them in the world" (27). Coles's analogy for their day-to-day political socialization is the ancient Roman " 'spectacle of gladiatorial games,' " an allusion to Simone Weil's 1939 essay "The Great Beast," comparing Nazi Germany and imperial Rome (21). Weil argued that powerful nations maintain themselves not only through propaganda and constant war but also through a system of political beliefs sustained by ordinary, daily activity, that is, "spectacles" or constant object lessons about power that young people see around them. The theme of the spectacle of nationalism echoes throughout *Political Life*. The games described are less public than the Romans', but equally orchestrated. They include the whipping an American man gets from a sheriff " 'for saying he wanted to register to vote,' " a spectacle that is replayed years later in taunts that the same sheriff gives the man's son and grandchild (31). The essay also offers Hopi children's ironic but highly moral attitude toward political authority, an idea that is treated again in the final chapter.

"The Homeland: Psychoanalysis and the Political Thought of Children" is primarily a case study of one Belfast child, whose ardent patriotism is an intimate part of her homelife (*Political Life*, 59). This case study elaborates the idea of homeland, Coles's word for nationalism "as an instrument of the ego" (62). Homeland is how children encounter "A nation's name, its flag, its music, its currency, its slogans, its history, its political life" (61). Like home, it is both a place and a "source of nourishment," almost "parental" in the close, familial feeling it engenders (63, 60). Poverty is no barrier to national feeling; rather, nationalism may help children consider their own survival important and linked to the nation's. The homely, somewhat dreamy description of the girl's life captures the sense of warmth by which objects, songs, slogans, and events associated with Great Britain's nationalism become themselves warm, secure, and reassuring. Other children's patriotism is described during a discussion of nationalism and political superego or conscience (66). The essay concludes that for a state or political authority to continue, generations of its members must be able to see it as a homeland.

Narratives

The chapters on nationalism also begin with Northern Ireland. In "Religion and Nationalism: Northern Ireland," the longest chapter in the volume, both Catholic and Protestant children believe that their patriotism is "religiously sanctioned" (*Political Life*, 138). As in "The Homeland," symbols of nationalism are a source of tremendous energy and purpose. But here they also confuse, for in practice, the flag and the nation are never one—even less so the nation and the faith. Drawing on interviews over at least five years, this section is particularly rich in its portrayals of individual voices. The essay also details the knotty geographical, historical, and linguistic divisions that Belfast embraces. The homeland is exquisitely concrete: this street but not that one, this house, this section of town (88). The children teach Coles the intricate manifestations of the city's "double past" (82). Aggression, whether in play or in earnest, is encouraged by adults. In the children's drawings, regardless of the artist's gender, walls rise and armaments bristle. The main portion of the essay develops the moral outlook of six children, all girls, through their day-to-day experiences and the impact of a major political event, the 1981 hunger strike by Irish Republican Army members jailed in Maze Prison (94–139). Because of its effect on children, the strike is accorded the same respect that *Courage and Fear* gave the early civil rights movement. Faced with the hunger strikers' "dramatically unsettling, even eerie selflessness," both Catholic and Protestant groups felt that they were suddenly in a transcendent, Biblical time (105). Children blamed themselves for the strike's failure.

The remaining chapters on nationalism offer a welter of children's stories, sensitive analyses of their drawings and conversations, and generalizations about the complex interactions of a nation's life with children's self-concepts. "Ideology and Nationalism" describes Nicaraguan children under the Sandinista government, four years after the fall of Somoza. The essay emphasizes the coexistence of Church and Marxism, even if there is much tension between them. (*Harvard Diary* also has three essays on the history of U.S.-Nicaragua relations and the tensions between the Catholic Church and the government.) A sense of nationalism that is separate from the state is the subject of the fifth essay, "Language, Culture, and Nationalism: French Canada and Poland." Although in general *Political Life* seems to equate the terms *state* and *nation*, the distinction between the two is the subject of this chapter.

French Canadians and Poles are enthusiastically nationalist, as a source of identity, but treat state authority with disdain. In this regard, homeland and nation are closely allied. Both of these peoples carry their sense of nation through language. Young Poles also maintain their national identity by means of "stories, poems, legends, myths, and social memories" as well as through religious faith and a profound sense of alienation from what was, in 1986, a government under Soviet influence (*Political Life*, 160, 178).

In "Race and Nationalism: South Africa," the theme is pain. Like no other country, South Africa has embodied "the melancholy, the outrage" of moral people (180). In political terms, the country is complex. Each of the three main groups—blacks, "coloreds" (persons of mixed race), and whites (Afrikaners and English)—relates differently to nationalism and is taken up separately. Furthermore, the government's white nationalist policies under apartheid affected the research. The essay alludes to covert meetings and people whose names cannot be acknowledged. Indeed, Coles's meetings with a banned black South African under house arrest set the tone of the essay. The man, a Zulu who had often been tortured under the policies of apartheid, gives Coles advice about the complexity of South Africa's racism and its reception in the United States (183).

Following his advisor's lead, Coles first explores the political and racial attitudes of white children, both Afrikaner and English. Petrus, an Afrikaner boy, and Brian, of English ancestry, are bright and personable. But for them, as for all the white South African children Coles encountered, he reluctantly concludes that racial separatism and nationalism are inextricable (201). White Christian churches of the time did nothing to mitigate this profound sense of white separatism. Interpreting the drawings of children as keys to their self-understanding, Coles turns to the effect of being "colored," an official racial category during apartheid. These children demonstrate the intricate ways in which loss or confusion of identity is also reflected in confusions about national identity. Colored South African children's "confusion takes explicit form in the ways in which they color themselves colored, in the conflict of colors, actually, one sees in so many of their drawings" (205). This section recalls the moving self-portraits in *Children of Crisis*.

The section on black children of Soweto and the Crossroads settlement reveals further disturbing relations between personal and national identity. Continuing the theme of naming begun in the essay on Northern Ireland, Coles notes that Soweto, the South West Township, is "a place without any real name" (212). Black South African children rarely draw themselves alone. According to the essay, many features of their drawings imply that in 1986 black South Africans were still "stateless— weak, that is, in an ultimate manner" (220). By showing the huge differences in nationalist and personal identity that race has opened, this chapter evokes the strongest connections with the opening essay on Weil's Great Beast.

How being poor or rich affects one's nationalism is the subject of "Class and Nationalism: Brazil and the United States." The essay revisits a number of situations and insights from *The Moral Life of Children*, which prominently featured the children of Rio's favelas, and various portions of *Children of Crisis*, such as *Privileged Ones*, where patriotism was often a theme of wealthier children's identity (*Political Life*, 247). The essay is divided into three sections: two about Brazilian children and the third about Americans. The first section, which is highly constructed and literary in style, demonstrates how class all but prevents a favela boy from having a sense of his country. Images portray his geographical and political distance from nationalism. A police car winds its way up the steep hillside to the favela, which commands a view of the city below but places young Carlos a world away from it. Functionally illiterate like other favelado children, 11-year-old Carlos is ignorant of civics. He is unaware of the national anthem or flag (234). Carlos does understand the drug trade; his fascination with money and his knowledge of the police constitute his link with the nation's life. He calls the police " 'the rope of Brazil,' " a chillingly accurate image of cohesion through force (233). Here too is the shadow of the Great Beast. The remaining two sections of "Class and Nationalism" strongly recall *Privileged Ones*, telling thought-provoking stories of two Brazilian girls and several American children. The essay concludes that in general class serves as "the most significant lens" for magnifying or shrinking a child's nationalism (259).

The lyrical eighth chapter, "Exile and Nationalism: Children of Southeast Asia," is about memories of a homeland and accommodation to a new one. Ostensibly about Asian refugees' loss of a physical homeland, the essay becomes a commentary on the devastating psychological effects of losing one's parents—again winding together children's psychological perceptions of place and family. Coles focuses on Cambodian, Laotian, and Vietnamese children in American schools but also visited Thailand's refugee camps (*Political Life*, 275). However, their drawings depict an earlier life with soldiers, guns, bombs, and warplanes (264).

What other children have dreaded—disappearance of themselves, their country—has happened to these children. What gives a child strength and purpose in the new country is her parents, who must be present and up to the task of making a new life. A child without parents struggles.

"Exile and Nationalism" tells the stories of several troubled refugees. Lon, a Cambodian boy living in Boston, does poorly in school. He "saw both his parents die before his eyes at age five" (269). His story shows "how remarks about *country* come to be connected to memories about a tragedy, and further connected to the mind's effort to heal itself, to come to terms with an indescribably painful past" (272). Lon cannot recall his mother's face. The essay weaves a suggestive account of grief and anger through the images of Lon's Cambodian village, the Khmer murderers, and his mother's leaving of the children to meet what now he knows was certain death. A Buddhist, Lon also speaks of his country's gentleness and his own faith, which leaves its mark on his conception of America as his new life. With little analysis, the images are allowed to linger for the reader to interpret (278). Another survivor of the Khmer, Sarann, has "twin loyalties" to her new and her old homeland, shown best by her taped-together drawings of the two national flags (284).

"Political Morality: The Hard Dream of Survival" concludes with an appeal for "political morality," a phrase that ties the volume to *The Moral Life of Children*. Like its companion, this final essay concentrates on nuclear attack. A complex narrative focuses the larger issues. In South Africa, as part of a going-away party, Coles is given an enigmatic painting of a nuclear bomb. Inspired by a bad dream, the young Afrikaner painter Hendrick regards his work as a warning to " 'stop fighting' " (*Political Life*, 300). Coles decides that the act demonstrates a form of political morality, "a commanding ethics of survival" (302). He argues that children possess a political morality because they know that their countries' policies affect the conduct of their lives and even their personal survival. Only where there is "moral deterioration" born of "political desperation," as in Ulster, do children advocate rather than shun the use of nuclear bombs (304). Thus *The Political Life of Children* concludes with a dream or ideal, a theme in the essays on South Africa and Brazil (223). When a person is utterly estranged from his government, he dreams, the dream being "the last island of individuality, the dream as the one repository of secrets no torturer can extract, because the victim is no more privy to them than the bloodthirsty jailer" (181). Coles implies, too, that these dreams are the seeds of political morality, for Hendrick as well as for other children whose stories are told here.

The Spiritual Life of Children

As early as 1985, Coles decided to undertake a third study, on children's "religious and spiritual life" (*Spiritual Life*, xv). However, between *The Political Life of Children* and the final volume of this series, three other books on religious subjects intervened: *Simone Weil, Dorothy Day*, and *Harvard Diary*. As a set of essays on Coles's own faith, *Harvard Diary* in particular led the way for *The Spiritual Life of Children* (1990). Another important influence on the form of this volume is *The Call of Stories* (1989). *The Spiritual Life of Children* marks the end of Coles's formal research and has a strong sense of closure: "It is a project that, finally, helped me see children as seekers, as young pilgrims well aware that life is a finite journey and as anxious to make sense of it as those of us who are farther along in the time allotted us" (xvi). The study concerns children's own constructions of the spiritual (xviii), which is distinguished from the religious. The terms overlap, however, and Coles does not seek a precise definition (xvii). Indeed, the children represent mainly the world's great monotheistic faiths, although nonreligious children are included, and Hopi children's beliefs have a significant place. *The Spiritual Life of Children* apparently struck a chord with the public, becoming a 1991 bestseller on the *New York Times Book Review* list (Woodruff and Woodruff xxiii).

Method

The chapter on method is a relaxed summary, giving the reader new to Coles details about how he conducts research. The more than 500 children interviewed range from 6 to 13 years old; most are 8 to 12 (*Spiritual Life*, 36). They live in the Americas, Europe, the Middle East, and Africa; they are primarily Protestant, Catholic, Jewish, and Islamic. (Japanese Buddhist children were interviewed but not by Coles himself, so they were not included in the final version [xix].) Children in his hometown of Concord and the working-class city of Lawrence, Massachusetts, were a mainstay (37). Coles's sons and students materially assisted the research (xviii). As Kohlberg's stages of moral development were criticized in *Moral Life*, so rigid "faith development" schemes come under fire in *Spiritual Life*. To show the poverty of those efforts, Coles offers stories of a Hopi girl and a Sunday school class in Massachusetts.

Structure

The volume is organized using parallel essays, similar to the structure of *Political Life*. After a chapter on theory, "Psychoanalysis and Religion," and one on method, two chapters consider the face and the voice of God; three more then examine aspects of "young spirituality." The last of these, "Young Spirituality: Visionary Moments," has the dual theme of keen vision in the world and transcendent visions, and it embraces the 16 plates of children's drawings in the center of the book. The eighth chapter, "Representations," interprets the drawings. Otherwise, the chapter stands alone and can be likened to the "Interlude" portion of *The Call of Stories*. *The Spiritual Life of Children* is the only volume of Coles's research to treat the drawings as a structural unit in the text itself. Following "Representations" are three essays on children of major Western religions and one on children of secular upbringing. These chapters each have a main theme or image, such as "Islamic Surrender." "The Child as Pilgrim" concludes the volume. Resources for studying spirituality are also included, particularly in the notes to the first and second chapters. Although there is no grand metaphor, *Spiritual Life* is shapely, its chapters arranged to peak first at the midpoint, in the extraordinary drawings and the corresponding chapter "Representations," and once again at the concluding chapter on the child as pilgrim. This order emphasizes the theme of vision, on the one hand, and spiritual inquiry on the other.

Point of View

The narratives of *Spiritual Life* benefit from years of refining technique in volumes like *Eskimos* and *The Call of Stories*. Ample third-person narration is intermixed with some first-person comments, as Coles usually keeps himself in the scene conversing with his young speakers. Often as narrator he must confront his own discomfort, particularly toward young people of fundamentalist Christian or Islamic faith, whose narrow vision of the world is focused on believers (*Spiritual Life*, 55). Children also react to him, often ironically (42). His presence adds drama to what would otherwise be monologues and keeps the reader aware of the somewhat artificial research situation. Occasionally a third voice is added, such as that of his son Bob, and at rare times children speak to each other, like the speakers named Norman and Sylvia in "Secular Soul-Searching" (55, 215, 295).

Theory

In "Psychoanalysis and Religion," the opening essay, Coles develops a robust, accessible, theoretical framework for spirituality that employs neo-Freudian and even some Jungian concepts. By applying the ideas of "object relations" psychologists like D. W. Winnicott, the essay accounts for the nature of images in shaping thought, a breakthrough in Coles's theorizing about children's drawings.[1] In particular, "Psychoanalysis and Religion" adapts the work of the American psychoanalyst Ana-Maria Rizzuto, author of *The Birth of the Living God*. Rizzuto explains how symbolic representations are essential to any definition of the spiritual (*Spiritual Life*, 4–6). Previously, Coles had treated children's drawings as a "technique" to uncover Freudian "agencies" (4–6). Here drawings, as symbolic representations, are integrated into a theory of children's spiritual development. Putting Rizzuto's ideas into an existential context, "Psychoanalysis and Religion" also moves beyond the strictures of Søren Kierkegaard, the Danish philosopher who serves as a major early influence in Coles's views of psychoanalysis and theology. Kierkegaard rejected aesthetic inquiry, that is, art, as a means to spirituality.[2] In contrast, *Spiritual Life* considers children's imagined life as integral to their understanding of things spiritual. Yet "Psychoanalysis and Religion" is not simply theory. It tells personal stories and surveys scholarship on faith and spirituality, primarily from psychoanalysis, but also sociology, history, philosophy, and religious studies.

Vision is thus a major motif, and the chapters that expand the visual are especially interesting. In his study of politics, Coles asked children to draw the flag, and in his research on spirituality Coles often asked children to picture God. "The Face of God" takes these visual images as a starting point for discussions of the ways in which children conceive of the deity. With its visual theme, this chapter strikes a keynote for the entire volume. For some children, the face of God is abstract—triangular, or a rainbow, the sun, and the earth (*Spiritual Life*, 59, 63). Sometimes these conceptions can be traced to family discussions or images in the home, sometimes not. Dreams are another potent source of spiritual experience, including seeing God's face. For one Seventh-Day Adventist boy in Tennessee, God's eyes and smile (48–50) become part of a complex personal theology. Those children whose faith forbids them to picture God reveal not only their knowledge of that prohibition but also their struggles to comply and their unbidden visions (64, 66). Children also demonstrate a subtle awareness of social and artistic conventions for race (44). "The Face of God" is about the metaphoric, symbolic experience of God's physical presence, here a visual presence. Its visual texture is reminiscent of the Hopi chapters in *Eskimos, Chicanos, Indians*. Interestingly, none of the drawings reproduced in this volume are of the face of God, perhaps out of respect for Jewish and Islamic readers. In any case, the point of "The Face of God" is that the nature of the Supreme Being is personal, idiosyncratic, and speculative as well as culturally constructed.

"The Voice of God" especially considers children of Islam and Judaism, for whom hearing is the paramount sense for receiving the experience of God. The story of the first young speaker, Haroon, a Pakistani boy living in London, plays on sensations of foreignness—otherness—and the meaning of hearing as *understanding*. Although Haroon struggles with Coles's non-Muslim belief and repeatedly assures him that " 'I am sure you will understand,' " hearing is not always understanding (69). In a later chapter, the call to prayer brings on Islamic children a stillness that is related to their vision of the natural world (200). This chapter presents hearing as a more difficult, or less familiar, mode of spiritual perception than vision is. The last story of this essay, about Margarita, an uneducated, unreligious favela girl, recalls the arresting description of churchgoing in *Migrants, Sharecroppers, Mountaineers*.

The next essays consider three aspects of children's spiritual life: psychological, philosophical, and visionary. "Young Spirituality: Psychological Themes" views children's conceptions of God as expressions of their desires, fears, and ambitions. Drawing on observations that range over decades, the essay explores the following thesis: "Children try to understand not only what is happening to them but why; and in doing that, they call upon the religious life they have experienced, the spiritual values they have received, as well as other sources of potential explanation" (*Spiritual Life*, 100). The first part of the chapter traces how suffering, such as serious illness, can psychologically energize or "arouse" spiritual reflection (101). Later, the essay explains how children give God a human psychology, often "as a judge, a critic, or a benefactor" (114). Coles used works of art to inspire fourth-grade students to these reflections and analyzes their responses in terms of the psychoanalytical superego and ego ideal (120). Finally, religious dreams and Biblical stories can become sources of psychological support and psychic inspiration for some children, as illustrated by two complex stories, one of a young West Roxbury boy and his grandmother and the other of an East Tennessee girl of fundamentalist beliefs.

"Young Spirituality: Philosophical Reflections" briefly examines spirituality from the perspective of existential questions—humanity and nature, death, the purpose of life, and its mystery. The stories of two children dominate the chapter. Mary, the Tennessee girl of the previous chapter, has a nightmare that she relates to her family. The minister gives a pat moral explanation; the narrator Coles, an equally pat psychosexual interpretation. But the girl comes to regard the dream as a "gift" from Jesus and as a result of this interpretation, she becomes more serious and purposive (133). In the second story, Gil, the son of devout but broad-minded Jews, speculates about his people, whom he sees through a modern filter of space travel and astronomy. According to Coles, Gil is trying to make "his own 'system,' his own set of principles," "trying to assemble what he had learned in a narrative of his own, which he could offer to others" (146). For Coles, the story making and story interpreting that these children do is essential to the spiritual search, as demonstrated later in "The Child as Pilgrim" (334).

Moral scrutiny is primary in Coles's rendering of spirituality. Yet "Young Spirituality: Visionary Moments" deals with another aspect of spirituality: mysticism, or, as couched here, the possibility of vision through the unexpected "spiritual horizon" (148). The setting is New Mexico, where Coles observes a new generation of Hopi children and their "extraordinary spiritual life" (148). Their stories are paired with that of a Catholic girl, the daughter of a Boston policeman. Mystical vision fascinates Coles, but it is not an easy concept for him. Vision occurs "when a mix of psychological surrender and philosophical transcendence offers the nearest thing to Kierkegaard's 'leap of faith' I can expect to see" (148). With vision comes a loss of words. This essay is heavy with the theme of the inadequacy of language and the potential for silence. Fittingly, it embraces the 16 drawings and paintings by children at the center of *Spiritual Life* and in effect opens a space in the volume for visualizing.

Like "Interlude" in *The Call of Stories*, the chapter "Representations" offers a respite from the intellectual approaches of the first half of *Spiritual Life* and the faith-specific organization of the second half. After a short introduction that resumes the themes of silence and vision, the essay explicates each of the volume's drawings. Christian themes predominate, but several drawings are by Jewish, Muslim, and nonreligious children. All are highly personal compositions, and the children's stories and reflections are as arresting as the drawings themselves. As in "Psychoanalysis and Religion," there is a recognition that the phenomenon of these drawings is more than a research technique. In his excellent readings, Coles notices the ways that color is used to make otherwise abstract connections, the intensity of line and shading, the quality of light, and the subtle composition of drawings. A drawing's salient feature can be rendered in a phrase. For example, in a portrayal of the Crucifixion, flowers bow their heads: "the landscape as a pietà" (*Spiritual Life*, 190).

The selected drawings show a recurring interest in Christ's miracles and children's "desire for supernatural transformations," whether God's or the work of comic books and fantasies (191). The paintings and drawings themselves are full of energy and wonder, from a Swedish boy's abstract rendering of heaven and hell to a Tunisian boy's drawing of an abundant natural world, recalling other Muslim children's illustrations of "huge suns with large features, skies choked with stars arranged in such a way that the viewer thinks of the human form" (199). The chapter ends by describing a deceptively simple drawing (Plate 16, also incorporated into the jacket design). A brown girl kneels beside a bed covered in pink. Her arms are raised. The line depicting the bottom of the bed runs through her body, making her seem transparent or cut in half. Without explanation, the drawing may seem crude, conventional. The girl is the artist, Leola. She is paraplegic. The bed defines much of her life. Kneeling is difficult, and she holds herself up with her arms. She says, " 'Praying is when I walk like I used to walk—to meet Him!' " Coles eloquently interprets her drawing as the essence of prayer. Every feature speaks of "the austere aloneness of meeting God, the transport of prayer" (201). The drawing gathers the themes of *Spiritual Life*: suffering, scrutiny, silence, vision. It epitomizes how a child can construct the spiritual.

After "Representations," a quartet of essays summarizes how children answered this question: " 'How would you describe the heart of your religion, its central message for you and others?' " (202). For Christians, the answer is manifest in the word "salvation"; for Muslims, "surrender"; for Jews, "righteousness"; and for secular children, "soul searching." These chapters show children's spirituality as it has been shaped by the teachings of several great traditions. Like languages, religions are passed on from early childhood. These interwoven stories refresh the major symbols and events of faith, criticize aspects of religion, and demonstrate that children also learn how other faiths impinge on their own.

A main theme is Coles's search to approach and know others. The discussions often reveal Coles trying to articulate his own internal pilgrimage. The children give Coles a glimpse of the spiritual life through their dialogue with him. Dialogue is necessary for spiritual search, according to the French existentialist theologian and novelist Gabriel Marcel. For Marcel the spiritual search requires knowing another person who can help a searcher, whom Marcel calls *homo viator*, toward greater responsibility and consciousness of his existence (*Percy*, 171). In "Christian Salvation," Coles mentions another theologian, Karl Barth, who focuses on "*God's* search" (224). Ultimately, God is the Other. In the meantime, Coles sees children as the others who enable him to approach the mysteries of life.

The chapters also explore how otherness is differently inflected, depending on faith. For Sajid, a Muslim boy, other people distract him from his duties. Only God is to be surrendered to. The notion of Muslim "surrender" includes a twilight world where God draws near (243–44). In "Jewish Righteousness" otherness has a dual meaning. It refers to the unique position that Jews feel that they occupy in humanity as well as to the ideal of righteousness, that is, "the *mitzvah*, the good deed every Jew should strive to do today and tomorrow, a lifelong obligation" (253). These two aspects of otherness combine in one boy's statement: " 'To be a Jew is to side with all the people who are in trouble' " (252). "Jewish Righteousness" also expresses empathy with the rites of that faith in a way unequaled elsewhere in Coles's work. Finally, children of secular upbringing also feel apart, learning "doubtfulness" at home that may turn them toward moral and spiritual scrutiny (278, 300). Nature and art inspire several of these children's reflections, and indeed Coles himself is inclined to regard contemplation of a great painting as an act of devotion (300).

The final chapter, "The Child as Pilgrim," gathers preoccupations from Coles's entire career: psychiatry, teaching, activism, stories. It first recapitulates Coles's history in child psychiatry, criticizing the profession but not punishing anyone (a contrast to the self-flagellation of *Harvard Diary*). This summary concludes that spiritual life must be counted among the child's unique capacities (308). The essay then shifts to a lively vignette from Coles's Cambridge public school teaching, from which emerges a homely image of " 'a march through life,' " one child's metaphor for the journey (320). This child, named Ginny, wonders about her ultimate future and so joins the ranks of "a Piers Plowman or a John Bunyan, or any number of awakened voyagers" (324). But spiritual models like these touch us only insofar as they conceive of their lives as stories and then tell their stories: "This is what we do as we hear a sto-

ryteller speak: let our own imagination, our past experiences, our various passions and problems, help form images that accompany the words
we're hearing" (334). Others tell stories that call us to ourselves. We re-
ciprocate by telling stories of our own. In this way Coles combines existential theology with psychology, literature, visual art, and, finally, with
his listening to children. Mary Gordon has called *Spiritual Life* "the natural third panel of a triptych," suggesting that the narratives partake of
the tradition of great religious art.[3]

The Lives of Children as a Series

The Lives of Children is both a continuation of *Children of Crisis* and a new
direction. Published simultaneously, *Moral Life* and *Political Life* were
usually reviewed together as complementary, with *Political Life* receiving
the bulk of the attention as offering more new insight. One reviewer,
Donald H. Heinrich, has commented on the series as a whole, aligning
it with *Children of Crisis* in its method and compassion.[4] Chester E. Finn
also views *The Lives of Children* as a continuation of the earlier series.[5]
Finn concludes, "If he did not invent this genre—part sociology, part
biography (and autobiography), part essay, part clinical file—Robert
Coles is surely its foremost contemporary practitioner" (Finn 63). Heinrich considers the "haziness" that blurs the children's and Coles's own
views as a skill, not a hazard, because Coles's research is not doctrinaire
(173). He is "exquisitely, sometimes painfully self-conscious about his
own words and behavior during these conversations, striving to elimi-
nate static and distortion" from the situation (Finn 63). Compared with
Children of Crisis, this series reads rather more simply. In the narratives, if
not always in the theoretical portions, the style is quite direct and the
structures, transparent. These three volumes seem less inclined than
Children of Crisis to appropriate the lives of others for Coles's ends, but in
turn they have somewhat less energy. They rework Coles's entire corpus
of data, and some loss is understandable. *The Spiritual Life of Children*,
culturally perhaps less daring than *Moral Life* or *Political Life*, is the most
confident work of the three, taking the next step theoretically and bene-
fiting from the structure and technique of *The Call of Stories*.

Chapter Five
Adults in the Margin

Over the years observation of children has been coupled with interest in adults. Ego psychologists like Anna Freud have stressed the mind's life beyond infancy and early childhood. Erik Erikson called attention to adolescence and adulthood, to "life history," as no psychoanalytic researcher before him had ever done. Coles's own research concerns mainly school-age children and teenagers who can articulate their lives. As he met with some of them over years, even decades, they grew up. Furthermore, he talked with their parents, grandparents, aunts, and uncles. These interviews with adults bring him closer to Studs Terkel, a writer with whom Coles is sometimes paired, as well as George Orwell.

In the early 1970s, Coles's first efforts to portray adult lives were combined with photographs. The purpose of these works is more documentary than scientific, and the text is comparatively short. (The documentary impulse is treated in more detail in chapter 6.) Nonetheless, these early photographic volumes do establish a pattern. As with children, Coles has sought out adults in the margin, people whose views and lives have not been a staple in academic surveys or in the media. Coles has listened to and written about blue-collar white Americans as well as Hispanic and Alaskan Inuit elders. But not until *Women of Crisis*, which he coauthored with Jane Hallowell Coles, did he give adult lives extended treatment on their own terms. This chapter treats five works, *The Middle Americans: Proud and Uncertain* (1971), *Farewell to the South* (1972), *The Old Ones of New Mexico* (1973), *The Last and First Eskimos* (1978), *Women of Crisis* (1978), and *Women of Crisis II* (1980).

The Middle Americans: Proud and Uncertain

In the late 1960s, a large group of Americans came to be known, in political terms, as "the silent majority." (The term was used by Richard M. Nixon in his 1968 presidential campaign.) They were white, employed, patriotic, and uninterested in or opposed to activism and identity politics. In his conversations with families of children affected by desegregation, particularly around Boston and other Northern cities,

Robert Coles has encountered many such people. He calls them "middle
Americans" because in many ways they feel caught in the middle of soci-
etal forces. They figure in a 1966 essay, "The White Northerner," which
was elaborated into *The Middle Americans: Proud and Uncertain* (1971).
Accompanied by several dozen photographs by Jon Erikson, the son of
Erik Erikson, *The Middle Americans* portrays a few men and women
through their conversations, whereas the photographs, taken over a
year, show a "broader and more comprehensive" picture of American
lives.[1] Those interviewed pursue trades, have a small business, teach
school, or keep house and raise children. The eight chapters, which aver-
age only 8 to 10 pages each, alternate with sections of photographs. As
is typical of Coles's collaborations with photographers, the text does not
comment on the photographs but provides a parallel experience; the
photos do not picture the speakers but rather people like them. The
preface defines middle Americans as they tend to define themselves, by
negatives: "[T]hey decide who they are *not*, perhaps do so rather defi-
antly and persistently: they are not black, not red, not brown, not
unemployed, not eligible for or desirous of welfare, not intellectuals, not
hippies, not members of a drug scene, a youth cult, a 'counterculture,'
not in general against our military position in the world, not rich, not
professional men, not 'big businessmen,' not individuals exceptionally
well-born, well-to-do, well-educated" (v). Their families are headed by
men (vi). The stated purpose of *The Middle Americans* is to show "how
such people come to psychological terms with the particular set of social
and economic circumstances that characterize their everyday existence"
(vii). In other terms, *The Middle Americans* aims to present values, "what
they *really* believe"—often narrowed to political values (143). The opening chapter, which presents the views of three people, establishes a common denominator of mixed feelings among ordinary white Americans.
It sounds a familiar litany. The speakers feel that the country is declin-
ing morally, economically, and politically, yet they decry those, especially
professionals and experts, who see only bad. They are convinced that
some Americans of color are decent people yet give vent to cascades of
racism. They mistrust politicians. They are patriotic. They may wish
their children to go to college but cannot abide the student protests and
liberal professors. Above all, they feel unappreciated (13).

   The Middle Americans gives an interesting, enduring portrait typical of
many white Americans. But despite the preface's claim of diverse,
unique voices and despite the upbeat photographs that include white

Americans' family and patriotic celebrations, the text's portrait is static and quite glum. Stories are rare. In chapter 2, for example, the speaker is proud of his Polish heritage, but no history or stories support his pride. Likewise, in the final essay, the speaker and her family, like many Americans, have crossed the country to make another life. However, this story is not probed—just the woman's present economic and political values (*Middle Americans*, 143). Other chapters are more successful. The police sergeant of the third chapter renders his life well, against the grain of the antiwar movement's stereotypes of the "pigs" (52). In the ups and downs of his monologue, some truths—as well as his own biases—come out. He is eloquent about the useless "consultant" from the university coming to tell people—here, the police—how to do their jobs (55). The fifth chapter evokes lives with some complexity and without either pity or valorizing. One woman points barbs at student protesters and liberal sympathizers but also criticizes the companies that pollute the river near her home. Like other speakers, she cannot explain these problems: "To her they have all suddenly appeared in recent years, out of nowhere it seems" (105). The sixth essay is a saga of what might have been. A couple whose oldest son was killed in Vietnam ruminate over decisions made before his birth that might have spared him being drafted. Vietnam, government policy, and the antiwar movement are seen from parents' eyes. For a while the narrative breaks free of the rote political whining that characterizes most of the essays but is still flawed by Coles's endless mulling over psychological contradictions (*Middle Americans*, 130).

In tone *The Middle Americans* uneasily walks a line between critique and apology. Ultimately a slight work, it is too skewed to the purpose of refuting (or confirming) political and media buzzwords to offer a fresh look at these Americans. Because of the focus on psychological aspects of political beliefs, the volume's narratives are not fleshed out. Yet *The Middle Americans* does tell stories with a self-conscious art. Although it assumes that it is men who participate in the national culture, its steady examination of two women's lives (chapters 5 and 8) previews the focus of *Women of Crisis*. In addition, *The Middle Americans* connects directly to the project that became *Privileged Ones*. In this work Coles ponders the differences in what he calls " 'tone' or 'edge' " between lower- and upper-middle-class Americans' economic expectations, differences that later would give rise to the social psychological idea of "entitlement" (*Middle Americans*, 173).

Farewell to the South

As he turned seriously to research in the North and then the West, Coles gathered 30 essays published between 1963 and 1971 as a "postlude" to *Courage and Fear* (*Farewell*, 14). The result, *Farewell to the South* (1972), is a set of often urgently worded reports from a region and a culture marginalized in American society. They originally appeared in a variety of liberal magazines as well as scholarly journals. The collection does not focus on adults, yet it complements Coles's other volumes that do.

The essays are divided into three sections, "The Region," "Children and Youth," and "Changes." The first section is the most varied, reaching across the Deep South from Texas to South Carolina and touching on documentary film and literature as well as politics. Politics does dominate these articles, from the ringing call to national action in "Who's Blocking Desegregation?" to expositions of local politicians and the effects of their governing on the poor in Georgia, South Carolina, and Texas. James Baldwin's polemical autobiography, *The Fire Next Time*, is reviewed, and the mood of the South is conveyed through reviews of stark, foreboding novels by Shirley Ann Grau ("Mood and Revelation in the South"), Alice Walker ("To Try Men's Souls"), and Cormac McCarthy ("The Empty Road"). Living and working conditions for black citizens are also portrayed in reviews of the documentaries *Black Natchez* and *Strike City* ("Natchez, Lovely Natchez" and "Mississippi Frontier").

The second section has three subjects: the children who were desegregating Southern schools in the early 1960s; the diseases of rural Southern children; and young civil rights activists. For example, "Children in Mississippi" presents the full report to the Southern Regional Council that Coles and five other physicians made following their observations of rural health during 1967. However, the heart of this section is the seven pieces on civil rights workers. Arranged in chronological order, the essays offer a personal history as well as a commentary on "The Movement" as Coles knew it. Many could be called brief reports filed from the trenches of the civil rights movement and from what would later be called the "war on poverty." The analogy with war is more than coincidental; it was "in many senses, a real war" (*Farewell*, 255). The reports of the Mississippi Summer Project of 1964, including references to the murders of James Cheney, Michael Schwerner, and Andrew Goodman— as well as Coles's presence in the students' training and his gradual involvement in the movement—stand as important personal documentary accounts.

The third section, "Changes," focuses on the changes in individuals between 1960 and 1971 as a way to comment on developments in the South and the civil rights movement during that period. "The Weather of the Years" takes up four young voices as they mature, including an unnamed New Orleans girl (apparently Ruby Bridges). Other essays follow a black civil rights worker, whose altruism is portrayed in a way that prefigures sections of *The Moral Life of Children*; a white student agitator; and a Klansman. This section is a carefully rounded postscript to *Courage and Fear* and has that work's power of voice.

These essays have an immediacy that recalls Orwell's *The Road to Wigan Pier* and *Down and Out in Paris and London*. Of all of Coles's writing, *Farewell to the South* is most like journalism. With its simple declarative sentences, it lacks the lyrical, rolling phrases of *Migrants* (1971) and many other volumes. Similarly, there are few genuflections to the giants—Freud, Erikson, and Anna Freud—and none to lesser psychological cataloguers. Rather, like the great Southern historian C. Vann Woodward, Coles has already "found enormous resources in the rich body of Southern fiction," as Jonathan Yardley has noted.[2] Moreover, Coles links these writers of fiction with moral philosophers: "I have learned that one does not have to be a political or social or philosophical 'romantic' to comprehend and appreciate the kind of truth that binds a Faulkner to a Tolstoy, an Agee to a Bernanos, a Simon [sic] Weil to an Orwell" (*Farewell*, 276). These couplings would bear more and more fruit as he went on.

Farewell to the South is neither as polemical as some contemporaneous writing nor as neutral as the psychiatric point of view might have dictated. The tone is of a man caught in the swirl of events, in the lives and goals of the people he is with, unsure what his training has to do with his being there except as a passport. He is an impassioned advocate, but he does not use the politicized language of the partisan. *Farewell to the South* often reads like the dispatches of a war correspondent; he is with the troops but not really of them. Like Orwell, Coles works as well as watches. He is in a position to be of some service. With the civil rights workers, especially, his uncertain role brings no illusions.

The Old Ones of New Mexico

Coles's next sustained look at adult Americans was much more artful than *Middle Americans*. *The Old Ones of New Mexico* (1973) marks his first collaboration with photographer Alex Harris, a fruitful byproduct of his research for *Eskimos, Chicanos, Indians,* which would be published four years later. The two circumstances, working with Harris and trying to communicate with the very taciturn residents of the Southwest, also marked a new development in Coles's literary style, which became more visual. *The Old Ones of New Mexico* demonstrates this new style in a study of Hispanic elders living in the American Southwest. The subjects were mainly the grandparents of children whom Coles was interviewing for the fourth volume of *Children of Crisis.* The grandparents, Coles perceived, were vitally important to the children's development: In a later work he claims that these elders "had a kind of moral custody of their grandchildren."[3]

"Old ones," a translation from Spanish, identifies the subjects not only by their age—most claim to be near 80 or more—but also by their families' long presence in New Mexico. The title also acknowledges language as an important part of their cultural integrity and dignity. Coles encouraged people to speak Spanish with him, so that *Old Ones* in effect translates their words.[4] The "old ones" have wisdom bought of long survival. By implication the general respect and status accorded older Hispanics in their rural communities contrasts with the age bias in society at large (xxxiii). Alex Harris accompanied Coles on his visits, but the two men worked independently (*Old Ones,* xv). Those speaking and those photographed are not the same people (xv). The result is 40 black-and-white plates depicting a variety of *ancianos* against their sunlit houses and the desert landscape. Their dignity is everywhere evident.

The text, which follows the photographs, is divided into five chapters: "Two Languages, One Soul"; "Una Anciana"; "La Necesidad"; "The Age of a Reputation"; and "The Old Church, the Spanish Church, the American Church." As in *Middle Americans,* each chapter focuses on one or two speakers. However, third-person narration is frequently added to describe activities during the long silences of these laconic people. The conversations, Coles notes, are constructed from exchanges that took place over months (*Old Ones,* 10). In 1977 Coles told listeners that in *Old Ones* he was trying to render the silence that is "part of their being."[5] The result is a set of highly worked narratives that reflect the stateliness and dignity of the photographs. For example, in "Two Languages, One Soul," a grandmother recounts her recent collapse outdoors in the fierce sun. Her thoughts about her own death, captured by a series of subtle mood shifts—faith, stoicism, humor, and regret—are one of the arresting moments of the book. Slowly, the essay turns to language and questions about education, bilingual or otherwise. "Una Anciana" also exemplifies the new narrative technique. Dolores Garcia's wordless actions around the house and farmyard are described by a "visitor" (*Old Ones*, 26): "She turns to lunch. She stirs the soup. She warms up the bread. She reaches for the eggs. She sets a simple, careful table, a large spoon and a knife for herself, her husband, and their guest" (29). Into this story are embedded Dolores's words, which are full of evocative metaphors. She describes the coming of morning in terms of her husband's homely actions: "[L]ike Domingo's knife with chickens, the night is cut up; it becomes a shadow of what it was" (20). The narrative method consciously represents the quality of these lives.

In a method usually associated with New Journalism, Coles sometimes attributes emotions to the residents at large. For example, the sound of an airplane prompts not anger but "the pain, confusion, and sorrow one world feels for another" (66). The main speaker in this essay is a priest, who, by his gestures, may be the same priest alluded to in the first chapter. The essays are tied together by such gestures and allusions. The priest feels allegiance to two churches, one Spanish and traditional, one American and young. His words of humorous resignation end the book.

The Last and First Eskimos

The poetic essay and photographic collection entitled *The Last and First Eskimos* (1978) reunited Alex Harris with Coles. The volume parallels *The Old Ones of New Mexico* in documenting the lives of adults whose children appear in the Western volume of *Children of Crisis*. Like *The Old Ones*, the text of *The Last and First Eskimos* is divided into chapters, in this case four essays. However, the 1978 volume claims a distinctive purpose: to document "a decisive moment of Eskimo social history" witnessed across generations (*Last*, 10). The title, from an elderly woman's phrase, signifies the transition from an old to a new way of life during the 1970s, as gas-powered snowmobiles, oil drilling, and government intervened even in remote villages. Old and young alike were aware of the change (*Last*, 11–12). Thus *The Last and First Eskimos* focuses on adults but includes all generations.

The four essays are grouped into two complementary pairs that define major characteristics of Eskimo time and space. "The Madness of Dark" contrasts its winter and age with the summer and youth of "Light's Coming." This pair touches on the experience of insanity, a subject that Coles rarely takes up. In the second pair, "Distances" complements "Closeness." As in "Two Languages, One Soul" of *Old Ones*, "The Madness of Dark" is an old woman's tale of illness and near death. As the sun plays a part in the New Mexican woman's thoughts on leaving life, the sea, the snow, and the cold preoccupy the Eskimo woman's waking and sleeping, figuring large in her pondering of death's mysteries. Her way of describing emotions not only eludes Western psychology but is incomprehensible even to her children. Is she insane? Coles poses the question but does not answer. The brief summer brings its own hints of madness, as the young hunter-father of "Light's Coming" attests. The intense, almost unrelenting light brings him "agitation," a sense of being drunk and dizzy (119). "The sun can be a whip," he observes (120). The mythology of summer, its conflicted importance to his and other Eskimos' psyches, preoccupies him as much as the sea does the old woman.

"Distances" has an unusual theme, the need to find a distant visual horizon to orient oneself. That orientation is emotional as well as kinesthetic; it enables the speaker, a young woman, to stabilize and "come to" herself as a vulnerable but knowing human being. Her psychic life is "a matter of balancing horizons—that of the water, that of the land, that of the air" (*Last*, 131). Ample description of landscape and the speaker's unusual perspective make "Distances" more than cultural documentary. The final essay, "Closeness," reports the "drawing-in" of activity as summer wanes as well as the need for children to learn to stay close to their elders to survive (137). Closeness is built up by many small details, such as fish nets, clothing, and other necessities being drawn up to the house. A mother, the essay's focus, describes closeness and distance not only in terms of her watching her children but also as part of the urge to go to the "lower forty-eight" to become educated. Like her children, she is pulled to consider these advantages of distance and yet worries she will lose sight of her home base. Through stories, she shrewdly assesses the cultural threats to her village. Thus the closeness enforced by winter winds metaphorically through the whole Eskimo way of viewing life.

The Last and First Eskimos lyrically explores the concrete basis of abstractions like "territoriality, accessibility, jeopardy, vulnerability" (138). Although remaining artistic and impressionistic, it unfolds important social concepts from the material circumstances in which people live. The volume is both an artistic work and a study of anthropological psychology. Like *Old Ones*, the text is complemented by Alex Harris's photographs, which depict the cramped interiors of cabins and tents as well as open spaces. Taken over five years, the pictures show new commodities as well as traditional gear and activities; also included are two engaging "narrative" sequences, a mother with her child and a man who gestures and talks as if telling a story. The volume closes with another section of photographs, snapshots taken by Eskimos themselves.

Women of Crisis: Lives of Struggle and Hope

In the same year as *The Last and First Eskimos*, Robert and Jane Hallowell Coles published the first of two book-length collaborations on the lives of women. *Women of Crisis: Lives of Struggle and Hope* (1978) was a personal and intellectual watershed. Robert Coles has many times expressed his adherence to the values of the early civil rights movement and his ambivalence toward the identity politics that splintered the broader movement. But identity politics, including the women's, Chicano, and Native American movements, profoundly affected his research, as seen in the fourth volume of *Children of Crisis, Eskimos, Chicanos, Indians*, published in 1977. *Women of Crisis* is unusual because it reexamines the lives of women whom Coles had interviewed mainly as children's caregivers—or as children themselves. People close to the Coleses, like Ruby Bridges, the unlikely six-year-old heroine of *Courage and Fear*, now grown, and several Radcliffe College students whom Robert had taught, urged him to do the volume.[6] Not incidentally, *Women of Crisis* also recognizes Jane Hallowell Coles's part in her husband's research and writing. Above all, *Women of Crisis* is a serious attempt to grant poor women their own voices and, in Lillian Smith's words, " 'the right to live their own lives' " (*Women*, 273). Their example may inspire others. As a volume in the Radcliffe Biography Series of the "lives of extraordinary American women," *Women of Crisis* has the lofty educational purpose of all biography, which is, in the words of the series editor, Matina S. Horner, to provide "lifelong models" ([v]).

The Coleses reread years' worth of their previous research and then reinterviewed certain women. The advantages of this long perspective are clear. Most of the speakers are seen over years, even decades. Several mature from children to adults. The women in these essays are diverse and competent but ordinary, their lives unremarked by the larger society. Thus the epigraph from George Eliot's *Middlemarch* compares the majority of women to unsung saints or ugly ducklings who never discovered that they were swans. The book has an introduction and six

parts. Five of the latter are extended studies of particular women from
Florida to Alaska. The sixth part, "References," is a bibliographical
essay, broad in scope and aimed at a general or even student audience.
Women of Crisis's organization naturally mirrors the overall drift of the
five-volume *Children of Crisis*, whence come its subjects.

"Living on the Road," the first essay, focuses on a woman here called
Ruth James. She is from a migrant worker family in Belle Glade,
Florida. The Coleses had interviewed her a number of times between
1964 and 1976, when she turned 35 (*Women*, 13, 69). Ruth James's
story is a saga worthy of George Eliot. Never seeing more than fields
and the nearby road, Ruth lives, dreams, and plays out the drama of a
woman trying to find a modicum of freedom in what is not only a man's
world but a particularly brutal world. With only a tiny range of experience by the standards of most Americans, Ruth's life twists and turns
with all the suspense of a novel. What happens to Ruth is full of irony
and fierce integrity yet also the peculiar accommodations that people
make with their circumstances. The hushed prison of the fields typical of
Migrants, Sharecroppers, Mountaineers here gives way to a sexually charged
cauldron of greed, retribution, and favoritism. This world has only a
handful of roles for adult women and men to play—perhaps only two
for women: mother or whore, or both. What Ruth James chooses goes
far beyond those roles and stereotypes.

The next three chapters sustain the suspense of the first, with characters haunted by dreams and inexplicable journeys of the soul. In the second essay, "Mountain Dreams," Hannah Morgan now lives in Dayton
but was born and raised in Harlan County, Kentucky. Her story gathers
elements of *Migrants, Sharecroppers, Mountaineers* and *The South Goes
North*. It is a story of a firm mountain faith, one's sense of entitlement to
a hard but good life wrested from the land now being shaken by city
life. It is also a story of relationships between women: sister and sister,
mother and daughter, friend and friend. Hannah and her daughter take
refuge in long walks and talks. Supplemented with expository passages
of great finesse, Hannah's dialogue portrays her as a woman of gesture
as much as words.

The second narrative gives way to the third, "Sometimes, *Una Chicana*," which focuses on a young Mexican woman's moral dilemmas in
the city of San Antonio. Like Ruth James, much of Theresa's life
revolves around her complex negotiations with men who seek to use her
and with her family, who give her mixed messages. Her story is a chilling tale of initiative, vulnerability, and confusion complicated by her

Spanish Catholic heritage of female silence. The fourth essay, "Eskimo Women Spirits," is the quirky tale of Lorna. Its contrast of Eskimo ways with those of the "lower forty-eight" has much in common with Robert Coles's *Eskimos, Chicanos, Indians* and *The Last and First Eskimos*. However, its dramatic tale of an odd romantic alliance in a tiny Arctic village is also reminiscent of contemporary Northern works like the film *The Map of the Human Heart*. Like her grandfather, Lorna spurns both rigid gender roles and the notion of private property as un-Eskimo. She also feels the presence of women who once lived in the village and is deeply affected by a Fairbanks prostitute who fleetingly befriends her. As Lorna's deeply private experiences slowly become political, she becomes a kind of leader in the village. The transformation is beautifully told, a blueprint for those who study organizations and leadership, whether earthly or spiritual.

"Class and Sex," the fifth essay, at first seems a letdown. In the vein of *Children of Crisis*, "Class and Sex" attempts to generalize the experiences of poor women. Like the summarizing essay of *Children of Crisis*, the early portion of this chapter suffers from obliqueness and rather stereotyped examples. It draws heavily on the research for *Privileged Ones*, especially the idea of entitlement. Eventually the essay focuses on the experiences of Helen, a white maid from Somerville, Massachusetts, who offers telling comparisons with the wealthy woman she works for. Helen and her employer are both limited by their gender, despite their differences in upbringing and attitudes (*Women*, 249, 258). Over time Helen also applies to her own world some of the feminist vocabulary and critical awareness she hears about (250, 253). "Class and Sex" assumes that class is a more important variable in women's lives than gender is. Thus changing the roles of some well-off women may simply mask problems in the existing class system. Contrary to what is so often said about poor women—that "they are their own worst enemies"—all of these women struggle, dream, and learn (270). Like Helen, they are aware of themselves and other women in that struggle.

Silence, solitude, and the profundity of women's relationships are themes throughout *Women*. In the main narratives, women's silence is shown as a powerful threat to certain men, like Ruth James's crew leader and Theresa's boss, Peter. The men sense that silence is resistance. Women are also shown alone and adrift, without consistent support from the obvious sources of family, church, or school. "Mountain Dreams" best demonstrates the power of women's relationships inside and outside the family, although these ties seem constantly threatened and happenstance. The women of this book are also charmed. They walk alone through the streets of rough migrant encampments, out beyond the Dayton city limits, through red light districts in San Antonio and Fairbanks, and somehow some spirit protects them. Possessed of a crazy willfulness, they restlessly walk and dream. Pilgrims all, they seek larger meanings. In their narrow circumstances they open themselves to experience. They see good in evil. They walk through fire unscathed. Their menfolk may try to educate them about " 'the facts of life,' " but these women have arrived at a truth beyond the facts (*Women,* 216). The narratives trace psychic arcs across barren land- and cityscapes, leaving sociology for literature.

Women of Crisis II: Lives of Work and Dreams

A second volume on women soon followed. *Women of Crisis II: Lives of Work and Dreams* was published in 1980, also part of the Radcliffe Biography Series. The sequel expands the collaboration of Robert and Jane Hallowell Coles. The five essays in the volume add the experiences of middle-class women to the first volume's portraits of poor women. Robert Coles wrote the introduction and two of the essays, Jane Hallowell the other three essays.[7] Interestingly, there is no concluding essay or attempt at generalizing. The portraits stand on their own. The introduction serves well to preface both volumes on women. It not only explains the method of "cross-cultural, naturalistic observation" but also strongly articulates feminist perspectives (*Women II,* 2). The theme of dreams and daydreams is noted, a feature that is also prominent in the earlier work.

Four of the essays deal with white women, whereas the fifth is about a Pueblo woman who runs a crafts business with her husband. Although these women are better off than their counterparts in the first volume, they too struggle. They reached maturity in the '50s or very early '60s, so they span eras of traditional and new roles for women. All work: The volume describes a manager, a bank teller, a civil rights activist, a photographer and potter, and a nurse. There is a new focus on women in management. As did the first volume, *Women of Crisis II* traces the shape of women's lives. These lives are planned—worked out by the girls' constant dreams, ambitions, and assessment of their circumstances. They are also touched by fate.

One important thread is mentors. Mentors are people to whom the young women look for guidance and inspiration, especially in giving meaning to life through work. The mentors are all outside the subjects'

families, although each speaker recognizes the influence, usually positive, of her upbringing. (The Coleses are careful to note the extraordinary and good influence that parents have on children's values, anticipating *The Moral Life of Children*.) In the first essay, "Bossing,"
advertising manager Laura Willis recalls being shattered by her older
sister's hospitalization and death. Laura found a friend in a medical student, Joan, who modeled female initiative for Laura, helping the
younger woman to see past her parents' and high-school counselors'
limited notions of women's futures. Her elders treat her interest in Joan
as a "crush," with veiled overtones of lesbianism, but looking back,
Laura scoffs at these innuendoes (*Women II*, 22).

In the second essay, Maisie, of "Managing," has an entirely different
sort of guide-figure. After discovering that her father is having an affair,
she confronts his lover, named Kathy McNulty. Their brief encounter
leads Maisie "to construct a mythic story: the sad, abused woman who
will never escape her fate as a mistress to one two-timer after another"
(79). Her memory of Kathy serves as a moral tale, guiding Maisie away
from certain decisions but also allowing her to envision some sort of
future for herself. Maria, of "Climbing the Mesa," is a fiercely proud
Pueblo. Ironically, she finds mentors in two young Anglo photographers
who climb her favorite mesa with her. They enable her to turn aimless
desires into a passionate craft. In the last essay, "Dreaming," Eileen's
experience parallels Laura's in the first essay. Eileen too has an older sister who is hospitalized, and by turning to a friend whose mother is a
nurse, Eileen decides to pursue that profession, an unheard-of luxury for
her poor family. Eileen persists in her goal, taking menial jobs in the
hospital and eventually succeeding in becoming a registered nurse.

"Fighting," the middle essay, is also a story of mentors, but it stands
out from the other narratives. The speaker is given no name. She is
allowed to speak entirely in her own voice, with little editing, and her
section is prefaced with an introduction that further sets this chapter
apart (*Women II*, 108). She tells the story of being a female activist in the
early, awful, glorious days of the civil rights movement. Several people
influence her life: her college roommate, the daughter of Italian immigrants; a black woman who introduces her to the movement in Atlanta;
and especially Paul, a fellow activist in the Student Non-violent Coordinating Committee (SNCC). From Paul she learned how to critique the
movement, including its bias against women (142). Her experiences
recall the volume's dedication to two older activists, one a Southerner,
Lillian Smith, and one a Northerner, Dorothy Day, both of whom the

Coleses knew and admired (13, 108). These women also knew that the stories of female civil rights activists had been submerged.

Sexuality is also somewhat more openly discussed in this volume than is usual in Coles's work. That is particularly true of the last essay, "Dreaming," in which Eileen describes the hard decisions she has had to make about birth control. Her decision to use birth control becomes her "journey." These women, raised in the '40s and '50s, do not easily discuss sexuality, but they show how girls' and women's daily lives are fraught with decisions related to sex.

The theme of dreams continues from the first volume of *Women of Crisis*. In both volumes, these include not just nighttime dreams and career goals but sudden, out-of-character events and journeys that take on the mythic quality of dreams. As in *Women I*, each journey has an impact that lets the sojourner integrate her vague desires and experiences. On a whim Laura flies to London and bids on a painting. Maisie tracks down her father's lover on a city street. The speaker of "Fighting" takes a fateful drive down a Mississippi highway. Never having set foot off the reservation, Maria, unbeknownst to her family, boards a bus to Albuquerque. The subjects all return to their mundane lives and responsibilities—but changed. These women are like the character Binx Bolling of Walker Percy's *The Moviegoer*, a favorite novel of Robert Coles. In a sudden journey comes the existential moment that transforms a life.

The stories of *Women of Crisis II* are less stark and less surprising than those of the first volume, perhaps because these women are somewhat more prosperous. But without the apparatus of *Women I*, the narratives shine by themselves. *Women I* and *Women II* are a literary as well as a sociological achievement. Each portrait combines a sociological "demographic" into a work of feminist and literary moment. These collaborations with Jane Coles are the most fully realized narratives found in Robert Coles's work. All the choices are literary: the focus on "odd" girls who felt solitary and different; the span of years; the twists and turns of lives that nonetheless have a coherence to them; the free rein given to the dreams and journeys with their existential meanings; the preference shown to literary criteria over a sociological and psychological thesis; the ample discussion of relationships, friends, family, lovers, and spouses that children cannot give. It is not too much to call these biographical sketches novellas.

Conclusion

Coles's works exploring adult lives both summarize and break free of the research project he set himself in *Children of Crisis* and *The Lives of Chil-*

dren series. Many of his adults inhabit a dual world. On the one hand they are bound by the necessities of caring for children, grandchildren, and husbands as well as toiling incessantly at jobs. At work their minds rove while their hands make the required motions and their voices, the required sounds. These people reflect capably on their lives. Devoted as they are, their words can be banal and repetitive. On the other hand they have quixotic dreams. They walk ordinary streets and roads, yet invest them with nightmares, memories, spirits. Some may even be said to be mad. These Americans—like the women of *The Last and First Eskimos* and *Women of Crisis*—share more with the characters of Walker Percy, Louise Erdrich, and other fiction writers than they do with the creatures of popular sociology and psychology.

Even as these works partake of fiction, they raise questions about nonfiction genres. With adults the question of authentic voice arises even more urgently than it does with children. To what extent are these oral histories? To what extent do the speakers share in the authorship? To what extent are their voices muted or appropriated by the Coleses? These works may perhaps best be viewed as products of an era, as one aspect of the struggle for mainstream recognition of marginalized voices. The worth of these volumes is unquestioned, but perhaps today the speakers would be able to write their own stories.

Chapter Six

"No Ideas but in Things": Writing about Photography and Children's Drawings

When *Children of Crisis* was published in 1967, Coles was already lending his assistance to projects on hunger, poverty, and school desegregation.[1] Several of these activities resulted in books that combined documentary photographs with his accompanying text. By including photography, the books draw on the American documentary tradition of *Let Us Now Praise Famous Men*, a portrait of Depression life in rural Alabama. *Let Us Now Praise Famous Men*, full of realistic but lyrical photographs and even more lyrical prose, was the result of a brief, celebrated collaboration between the fiction writer and film critic James Agee and the photographer Walker Evans. With the projects sponsored by the Farm Security Administration, in which professional photographers like Evans and Dorothea Lange traveled the United States and took pictures that were published in national magazines like *Life*, *Let Us Now Praise Famous Men* helped to establish a prestigious as well as popular American tradition of social documentary. According to William Stott, "Social documentary encourages social improvement" through public awareness of "conditions neither permanent nor necessary," such as racial discrimination.[2] The form, especially documentary books that combined photographs and text, flourished in the 1930s, but Agee and Evans's work transcended its time (Stott 25).

Originally published in 1941, *Let Us Now Praise Famous Men* became a touchstone for Coles as it was for many in the 1960s who sought to document the plight of poor and undernourished Americans. It is never far from his writing about photography. Like Agee, Coles found in documentary photography a source complementary to nonfiction: Let people see as well as read so that they will better understand and be moved to do something about poverty and racism. Of Agee and Evans, "those two extraordinary social observers," Coles has remarked: "They went. They saw. They were moved. They tried to tell others. They showed their intense moral anguish, their struggle to know and comprehend the world" (*Irony*, 57). What documentary photography shares with imaginative literature is the passion to record experience in all its complexity. That endeavor is moral as well as intellectual. Moreover, Coles agrees with Agee's views that text and photographs should be "coequal, mutually independent, and fully collaborative," each form standing on its own depicting different aspects of the same reality (Agee and Evans xv).

Coles's research has made the interpretation of children's art into a unique and subtle method, so one might expect his interpretive bent to carry over to photography. That is not the case. Much of his writing that accompanies photographs does not treat specific photographs at all. Rather, it offers a verbal parallel to the visual experience. Coles usually refrains from analyzing photographs as aesthetic objects, in keeping with his view that the "emotional impulse of the print" makes photography a superb medium to move viewers to moral awareness and action.[3] For most of his career Coles has kept his two major visual interests—children's drawings and documentary photography—separate. However, in 1992, the publication of *Their Eyes Meeting the World*, exclusively devoted to children's art, suggests that the two interests have moved under the common umbrella of the visual rather than remain in the separate fields of documentary and psychiatry.

This chapter gives a brief history of Robert Coles's collaborations that combine photography and writing. Four of these partnerships are treated at length in chapter 5 of this volume. Then several essays on photography and children's art are discussed to amplify the place of the visual in Coles's thinking.

A History of Working with Photographers

To maintain the children's anonymity, photographs are not included in Robert Coles's major investigative series *Children of Crisis* and *The Lives of Children*, although snapshots, usually taken by Jane Hallowell Coles, have always been an informal part of his research (*Photography*, 141–42). Photography entered Coles's published work through his social activism. Between 1967 and 1970 he contributed to at least four projects that included photographs, even though he did not undertake direct collaboration with the photographers: *Still Hungry in America* (1969), *Wages of Neglect* (1969), *The Image Is You* (1969), and *Teachers and the Children of Poverty* (1970). These works vary in purpose and the degree of Coles's contribution, but all concern poor children and share the purpose of showing affluent Americans the conditions of these children's lives. Where these books include material from his research, Coles is careful to note that the speakers in the text and the subjects of the photographs are not the same. *The Buses Roll* (1974)—a later collection commemorating 10 years of the city of Berkeley's desegregation—is similar to these works, although its purpose is to celebrate as well as to raise social awareness. Beyond their common purpose, these works vary in Coles's tone toward documentary photography and toward his audience. Two of them will demonstrate the contrasts.

Still Hungry in America documents the conditions that Coles saw when he accompanied Senator Robert Kennedy through the Appalachians. This handsome, well-produced book thoroughly integrates the text contributed by Coles with the photographic sequence, although he and photographer Al Clayton did not travel together. The photographs are disturbing but by no means a collection of atrocities. The essay, impassioned but restrained, actively complements the photographs. It draws on Coles's medical observations plus his conversations with various informants, mainly parents speaking about their infants and children. The stories are mostly short and dramatic, such as one that a woman tells of delivering a baby that soon dies. Beginning with pregnancy, the text describes the unseen aspects of hunger and malnutrition as well as the hopes and fears that children bring to their parents' lives.

Still Hungry in America also comments on photography and writing, invoking *Let Us Now Praise Famous Men* because this is after all the landscape that Agee and Evans walked (*Hungry*, 106). In the tradition of Agee and George Orwell, Coles sees photography as essential "to capture the actual look and feel of privation" (4). Photography has an advantage over writing and even film because narration can come between the reader (or viewer) and the experience. A photograph, being "static," can have "visible coherence and impact" through its greater ability to interrupt and confront the viewer (6). *Still Hungry in America* shows Coles speculating and theorizing about photography's impact, perhaps more idealistically than he would later but in much the same vein. The book has the "terse eloquence" of Coles's prose joined to "Al Clayton's stark photographs," according to Gerald Walker.[4]

In the same year, 1969, an unpretentious, small-format book with the arresting title *The Image Is You* appeared with a 53-page essay by Coles. The project was simple: Give ghetto kids Polaroid cameras—donated by the company—to take pictures of their world, then publish the results. The photographers were preteens and teenagers at a community center in Roxbury, a neighborhood of Boston. The contrast between the photographs and the text is striking. The pictures, which take up the first part of the book, are accessible and even lighthearted snapshots of children, adults, and the stark but sunny neighborhoods they inhabit. On the other hand, the essay that follows is somber, uneven, and at times difficult. With its oblique references to Italian film and Agee's film criticism, the first part of the essay seems addressed to an intellectual audience. Rather than displaying the uncritical faith in documentary professed in *Still Hungry in America*, this essay warns that photography's emotional impact is simplistic, sentimentalizing the poor.[5]

The second, more accessible part of the essay is the edited words of Roxbury children and those adults near them, presumably relatives and community persons. The essay also reaffirms a core belief in language (*Image*, 101). What photography can best do is what words can do: "inspire admiration and surprise and awe and doubt and suspicion and skepticism" (57). Both must show human complexity and challenge easy assumptions. Steven Weiland has argued that this essay is "about photography itself," including the "dialectic typical of collaborative style."[6] Weiland argues that Coles understands the nature of documentary photography and the writer's roles in collaborating with photographers: "[A]t its best collaborative documentary can internalize its own potential paradoxes and contradictions. And by highlighting them for readers it can assume a response true to the complexity of its material" (Weiland 141). Yet in the conclusion, these matter-of-fact, complicated children are romanticized by being placed in a cosmic allegory, as Agee might do: "I believe that these children—using cameras—have told us (and themselves) something; even as I believe that I am being told something when I hear people talking—to me, at me, at times almost through me, as though I were not there and they were roaring and moaning and shouting in the presence of History itself, in the presence of their Fate, their Destiny; as though Something Larger were being addressed, beseeched, and I fear cursed also" (*Image*, 101). One influence that Coles took from Agee was a taste for bombast, and this kind of rhetoric would be found again in 1971, in *Migrants, Sharecroppers, Mountaineers*. Here the writer and perhaps the photographer, too, recede into oblivion, simply a passive conduit of a transcendent reality.

Around 1970 Coles began to join more deliberately with photographers, especially Alex Harris, on projects of his own choosing. Several of these works—primarily studies of adults —might be called "collaborative documentary" in the tradition of *Let Us Now Praise Famous Men* and Dorothea Lange and Paul Taylor's *An American Exodus* (Weiland 135). With Jon Erikson, son of his mentor Erik Erikson, Coles produced two volumes, *The Middle Americans* (1971) and *A Spectacle Unto the World* (1973). Writer and photographer worked independently (*Spectacle*, xii–xiii). In *The Middle Americans* this autonomy is evident in the contrast between the text's narrow focus on a few residents near Boston and the photographs' "broader and more comprehensive" picture of white Americans' lives (*Middle Americans*, vii). There is also a contrast between the pessimism of the text, heavy with speakers' worries about money, desegregation, and politics, and the photographs' conventional optimism of picnics, parades, and family life. Weiland, in agreement with other commentators, has called the photographs "lacking in intensity and psychological interest," while the text lacks the courage of its claims (Weiland 140). *A Spectacle Unto the World* celebrates 40 years of publication for *The Catholic Worker* newspaper, which Dorothy Day cofounded in 1933 with Peter Maurin (*Spectacle*, ix–x). As in *The Middle Americans*, Erikson's photographs have a strong narrative arrangement. The text complements the photographs of the mission's daily life, providing history and larger context, one of the functions that words fulfill in this documentary tradition (Weiland 135). Rather than trying to mimic photographic effects, *A Spectacle*'s text fills in what photography misses.

Teaming with Alex Harris marked a new type of alliance, which coincided with the research for *Eskimos, Chicanos, Indians*. Coles realized that Pueblo, Hopi, and Inuit children challenged his previous methods of rendering mental experience. He sought a more visual style, and Harris was instrumental in this effort (*Photography*, 151). Still working largely independently of each other but united by a vision, they produced two books that approach the lyrical, otherworldly quality of *Let Us Now Praise Famous Men*. These are *The Old Ones of New Mexico* (1973) and *The Last and First Eskimos* (1978). To approximate the impact of photography, Coles turned to omniscient narration and visual description of people's actions, making the text of *The Old Ones* distinct from Coles's earlier writing. That text is discussed in more detail in chapter 5 of this volume.

Since 1974, Coles has turned some of his efforts to the history and the future of documentary photography. He contributed essays to retrospective collections, including *The Darkness and the Light* (1974), on Doris Ulmann, *Dorothea Lange* (1982), and *In the Street*, a collection of children's drawings photographed by Helen Levitt (1987). His biographical reflection on James Agee, opening the collection of memoirs and photographs entitled *Agee: A Life Remembered*, is in a vein similar to his contributions to photographic retrospectives. In the mid-1970s Coles began serving as a contributing editor to *Aperture*, a photographic journal whose scope is documentary as well as aesthetic and the publisher of his studies of Ulmann and Lange. Coles also cofounded the Center for Documentary Studies at Duke University, which furthers cross-disciplinary uses of oral history, reportage, and photography. Photography is also a part of his everyday life. On the walls of his Concord house are prints by Walker Evans, Alex Harris, and Doris Ulmann (*Photography*, 142).

Major Statements about Documentary

Three of these later essays offer insight into his views on photography. Two are on single photographers, Doris Ulmann and Dorothea Lange. The third is an essay compiled from an interview and remarks that Coles made at a 1975 symposium at Wellesley College. During his early research in the South, Coles was influenced by the work of Doris Ulmann, whose photographs were "a 'methodological aid' " to him (*Photography*, 145). Eventually he contributed a long essay to a major compilation of Ulmann's work, entitled *The Darkness and the Light* (1974). Born in New York, Doris Ulmann was a professional portrait photographer who turned to rural subjects especially during the 1920s and 1930s. She traveled extensively in the South at a time when few photographers, and fewer women, ventured there. The book's photographs are taken from her 1933 collection *Roll, Jordan, Roll*, a collaboration with South Carolina writer Julia Peterkin that depicts the lives of Gullah men and women, a group of black Americans whose culture had remained intact for over a century. In *The Darkness and the Light* the photographs appear without Peterkin's racist text, which Coles labels at best "condescending" and at worst "offensive."[7] Often in soft focus, the photographs show very poor, plain people who possess the integrity of a close-knit community and an other-worldly spirituality.

Coles's 30-page essay, entitled "A New Heaven and a New Earth," is an edgy, sophisticated foray intended to complicate the viewer's experience of Ulmann's seemingly transparent photographs. The intricate opening sentence immediately asks readers to ponder the meaning of life, not in the artist's terms but rather in the scientist's and the theologian's search for those meanings. Its beginning is ornate: "Life's thickness, its more than occasional impenetrability, its complexity that only seems to yield to various formulations . . ." (*Darkness*, 81). By implication, Doris Ulmann is a scientist and a pilgrim as well as a photographer. The essay then juxtaposes the 1930s photos with the words of 1960s and 1970s black rural Southerners, offering a kind of parallel verbal experience (92). One of these speakers acts as a sort of contemporary Ulmann, in Coles's terms, who "depicts" and "realizes" her mother as a camera would (86). This speaker is also like the "echoing voices" of *Flannery O'Connor's South*. Too, the essay draws back the camera's focus to provide context. Ulmann pictures a society that is apparently self-sufficient, culturally, economically, and spiritually. Its powerful, dynamic wholeness is only one part of a complex truth. The photographs leave out racism, which the essay's speakers try to describe as they saw their parents, who knew the 1930s well, experience it.

In its judgment of Ulmann, "A New Heaven and a New Earth" takes no interest in photographic technique, composition, or schools of image making. Although Ulmann belonged to the Pictorialist Society, which emphasized technique, Coles maintains that her achievement was primarily the result of a philosophical process of selection rather than artistry (*Darkness*, 95). Disturbed by the "ethereal" quality of the photographs and the impression that the people portrayed are "incredibly highbred and wellborn," he nevertheless brushes these flaws away by asserting their ability to make viewers ponder the paradoxes of life's complexity (96). Ulmann's work is called "reflective" and thus moral: "[S]he meditates on people to whom she is drawn; she is reached by those people, has touched them, and so can come forward with much of them, which, it can be said, has become hers to know and present to others" (96). In *The Darkness and the Light* Coles treats documentary photography as a moral force but also an experience that the viewer can misinterpret. Steven Weiland finds this retrospective to be in the collaborative tradition, indeed "more truly collaborative" than Coles's other work with photographers in his attention to the "fit between pictures and prose, the tone or point of view of each, and the social intentions of the whole" (Weiland 141). Weiland praises Coles's avoidance of "explanation" and his choice of "a loosely organized soundtrack, or vocal documentary" to accompany the photographs (142).

The most illuminating exposition of Coles's ideas about photography comes from remarks he made in 1975, at a monthlong symposium on photography held at Wellesley College. The remarks were edited into a first-person essay included in a collection of symposium proceedings entitled *Photography within the Humanities*. (Because of the essay's format, it does not necessarily represent his most considered views.) Coles was the final speaker at an event that featured a distinguished set of photographers, filmmakers, and critics. The interview takes up several themes: the tension between writers and photographers, the nature of good and bad documentary photography, the role of criticism, and Coles's own visual education and his reliance on the visual in his writing. Early on, the essay presents a radical view that pits writers against photographers. In this culture, words have power and represent tradition; they can even be instruments of persecution. Those who rely on words, like writers and especially social scientists and psychiatrists, are subject to a "malignant wordiness" (*Photography*, 142). The silence of photography may even be interpreted as resistance (141). However, the verbal and the visual are not foes. Rather, words and wordsmiths need help from another way of seeing.

In a similar vein, the essay faults photographic critics whose judgments determine whose work is shown to a public (140). The main subject for photography is people, seen through an artist's unique moral vision (150). Thus Coles admires the work of Eugene Smith (also a member of the symposium) but not that of Diane Arbus, even though their subjects, handicapped persons and so-called "freaks," may seem similar. Smith's photographs have a "humanity, to use that cliché, in all its wickedness and grandeur" whereas Arbus's are "a caricature" (147). Admirable photographers seek the higher nature of their subjects (149). As in *The Darkness and the Light*, Coles is impatient with photographic composition or technique. Getting involved and knowing one's subjects is the important issue. Thus he lauds the apparent artlessness of a documentary photographer like Alex Harris, who lives with people before he takes pictures (*Photography*, 142). Clearly, like Walker Evans, Coles deplores sentimental, polemical documentary photography that manipulates its subjects and dupes its viewers to make a point (Stott 222–23).

The later portion of the essay discusses learning to see, covering not only Alex Harris's tutelage in photography but also a unique discussion of Coles's visual memory during his research. These passages on the development of culturally colored "vision" offer subtle insights into Coles's thinking as he finished *Eskimos, Chicanos, Indians*, which was a watershed in his style and his aesthetic. Coles rehearses the history of photography's influence on his writing up through his turning-point collaboration with Alex Harris in the Southwest. To render the Native Americans' silence that "is part of their being," he looked to Harris's visual images and his activities as a photographer as a parallel that inspired the writer's experimental techniques (*Photography*, 151). Then Coles turns from photographs to his experiences of his memories as highly composed and emotionally charged still lifes. It is clear, as he contrasts two remembered images of a migrant family in Belle Glade, Florida, that he applies a visual artist's judgment in reconstructing these memories.

One image is the family, desperately poor, standing before a cabin; the other, inside the cabin, recalls the mother of the same family watering a plant with one hand and laying the other hand on her daughter's shoulder. The former image is appalling; the latter, poignant. The contrast of the two images—the family in two aspects—creates the necessary complexity of their existence for him: "Now there was a softness to that moment that came across in her body, and the light was there, and the plant was there to get the sun. It was so different from those same people standing in front of that cabin looking like the end of America" (147). The memory is emotional and also visual; the sunlight and the woman's pose form a beautiful scene. He argues that the writer and the photographer must respond to both images, "different moments in the same lives" (147).

This passage offers a rare glimpse of Coles's own visual imagination at work and the way it informs his moral sense. The essay concludes that photographs are no more real than words, simply that "photography is another way of being" (152). Similarly, in his introduction to a 1975 *Aperture* collection of documentary photographs by Mark Goodman, Helen Levitt, and Milton Rogovin, Coles emphasizes that he does not want "to make one kind of human response a competitor of another kind."[8] In its wide-ranging consideration of photography and aesthetics, these remarks make *Photography within the Humanities* an important document, especially for its connection of photography with Coles's own visual experiences and his writing.

For readers who know little about documentary photography, as well as for readers steeped in that tradition, Coles's next collaboration, *Dorothea Lange* (1982), is an excellent discussion of the genre and his view of it. The 35-page essay that opens the volume is one of Coles's most accomplished treatments of a major artist as well as his most comprehensive essay on a photographer. Dorothea Lange is best known for a 1936 photograph taken for the Farm Security Administration. The picture, usually titled *Migrant Mother*, continues to be reprinted as one of the most telling documentary images ever made. It was only one of hundreds of photographs that Lange made in the Southwestern and Southern United States during the Depression.

The essay proceeds conventionally, giving a biography of Lange and then an assessment of Lange's major achievement. It also offers a concise defense of the particular documentary tradition of photography and writing that Coles sees in his own work as well as Lange's. The discussion draws on archival material and interviews, including one with Paul Taylor, an economist and the husband of Dorothea Lange. Finally the essay grapples with the critique of photography that emerged in the 1970s, responding in particular to Susan Sontag's treatise *On Photography* (*Lange*, 36). Profusely illustrated with pictures of Lange, her family, and other subjects, the essay precedes 126 pages of her photographs and brief excerpts from her writing. The biographical sketch squarely confronts Lange's weaknesses as well as her strengths. A survivor of childhood polio, and never free of debilitating illnesses, Lange had "a nervous, irritable temperament" (*Lange*, 41). Lonely herself, she cultivated being unobtrusive and empathetic to the wary people she photographed. The sketch details many complementary aspects of Lange: her journey from studio photographer to documentarian, her weakness in the darkroom coupled with her excellent written descriptions of her photographs, her need for artistic independence balanced with the ability to collaborate, and her failures as well as her successes. Lange's two marriages and her family life are treated with a candor rare in Coles's other biographies.

The essay also contains Coles's signature touches. These include a letter from Lillian Smith, author of *Strange Fruit* and other works on segregation, and statements from sharecroppers and others to whom Coles has talked in his research (*Lange*, 27, 29). These additions fill in aspects of Lange's fieldwork but also downplay Lange as an icon. If ordinary people, people such as she photographed, can discuss the purposes and effects of documentary, then her work is not solely the possession of critics and scholars. They make clear the "connection [that good artists have] to the individuals who are their subjects" (8).

The essay portrays Dorothea Lange as an artist whose motives and methods Coles appreciated as his own. Lange was at the height of her art in the two decades from 1930 to the mid-1950s, a time of extraordinary confluence of photography, literature, and social science. She combined the observational powers of the scientist and the artist, "the intuitive sense necessary for accurate social observation" as well as "the personal vision and developed gifts of the artist" (*Lange*, 8). For Coles the key to Lange's achievement comes from a quotation from Francis Bacon that hung in her studio: "The contemplation of things as they are, without substitution or imposture, without error or confusion, is in itself a nobler thing than a whole harvest of invention" (*Lange*, 15). It was important that Lange had no "*preconceived photographic aesthetic.*"[9] Coles praises her methods as objective and scientific: "First came the image, then the research that interlocked the intricate features of the history she was recording. Obviously this is the closest anyone can approach to objectivity" (*Lange*, 31). Here, reality may be mediated, but through careful observation an artist/scientist can come close to knowing it.

Lange was a pilgrim, too, in that she had "a kind of hobo spirit, a companionable feeling for the down and out" that led to art with "moral passion" (8). Through her ability to awaken viewers' connections to the subjects, her photographs "acquire a measure of universality" and "transcendent power" (8). Pilgrimage is also taking risks. The union of art and science is dangerous because it attempts social and political change, as shown by the criticism that Lange and her husband Paul Taylor endured for going outside their fields (25–26). Finally, Lange's work did help prompt social and political action from national leaders (25). *Dorothea Lange* is both a sensitive exposition of Lange's vision and an important statement by Coles on the nature and purpose of documentary.

Children's Art as Art

Coles began asking children to draw while he was a psychiatric resident, a practice that his supervisor did not approve.[10] In a lengthy 1976 interview, he explained how art helps him establish relationships with children and how art can be used in child psychiatry (McNiff 117). It is clear that at this time he regarded drawing mainly as a "natural" alternative to talk in a therapy session (119). However, asserting that psychoanalytically the visual precedes words, he stresses the role of the visual in his own life, connecting his interests in art, art history, and documentary photography, even saying "I like to draw" while discounting his abilities as an artist (McNiff 118–19, 123). He also values children's drawings as "the actual landscape" of their minds, suggesting that the artwork is not merely a means to a clinical end (117). Eventually, in *The Spiritual Life of Children*, he would bring children's art as art to the forefront of his psychological thinking.

With Coles's views on photography honed by American social documentary, in all its complex relations to its subject and its emphasis on "actuality," it is not surprising that photography did not form a continuum with his work with children's drawings. But there have been crossing points. In 1987 Coles appended a very brief essay to a retrospective collection by Helen Levitt. Levitt, who had once collaborated with James Agee, captured urban children's frank, aggressive street writings and pictures in wry photographs decades before the current explosion of graffiti. Coles has praised some of Levitt's photographs as "lively, joyful, dramatic," with an "appropriate and tactful" use of color ("Looking," 7). This collection, entitled *In the Street: Chalk Drawings and Messages, New York City, 1938–1948* (1987), indirectly links Coles's writing about documentary photography and children's art. The essay, entitled "Robert Coles: Children as Visionaries," resonates with themes in two later volumes: *The Spiritual Life of Children* (1990) and especially *Their Eyes Meeting the World: The Drawings and Paintings of Children* (1992), his first work to focus exclusively on art. Children's art is not about "innocence" nor is it strictly a mirror of their upbringing and culture.[11] Rather art is one way that children negotiate with others and construct their individual experiences in terms of the culture. No explicit statements connect photography and art, but children's individuality expressed in drawings shares something with the artist's purpose and originality (*Street*, 6). The brief essay prepares for a fuller statement about children's art in *Their Eyes Meeting the World* (1992), a retrospective of children's drawings and paintings from Coles's research.

Some selections in *Their Eyes Meeting the World* are from the *Children of Crisis* and *Lives of Children* series; others have never been published. Published for the Center for Documentary Studies at Duke University, the collection has in part a documentary purpose. What is more, it capitalizes on the success of *The Spiritual Life of Children*, taking the folksy tone that sometimes characterizes Coles's writing about children.[12] But more than that, *Their Eyes Meeting the World* recognizes visual expression as not simply a means to describe children's psyches but also as worthy in itself. Like *In the Street*, the volume portrays young artists as well able to represent their own worlds. The title refers to William Carlos Williams's statement: "Look at them, looking, their eyes meeting the world" (*Eyes*, 1). After a 57-page essay entitled "Young Visionaries," illustrated with 14 drawings, the book contains a series of some three dozen color plates with Coles's facing page descriptions. Much more detailed than the captions in the *Children of Crisis* and *Life* series, the statements are thumb-

nail sketches of the young artists and the circumstances that inform—
literally, that the children have used to form—the pictures they have
drawn.

With its clear divisions and relatively short sections, the commentary
has a spare, "framed" quality—unusual in Coles's work—that complements the visual focus of the volume. The opening essay, "Young Visionaries," employs his more typical method, in which one story dissolves
seamlessly into the next. The essay, long but readable, blends personal
history with detailed readings of 14 drawings and paintings by children
with whom Coles worked. Theories about children's art making are
notable by their absence. Rather, through his own history as a doctor,
researcher, and teacher, Coles describes the wellsprings of art in children's lives, including their views of the process and the finished products. Some children, for example, destroyed their drawings rather than
give them to him.

The essay and commentary on the drawings display Coles's visual
sophistication. He prefers work that has "a mix of the aesthetic, cogni-
tive, and emotional" and early on is struck by a child artist who "knew
how to use symbols, make a subtle presentation, draw upon imagery
that would provoke others to thought" (*Eyes*, 5–6). At one point a boy's
politically tinged drawing calls forth references to poster art (49). At
another, abstract expressionism is suggested. Throughout, Coles plays
on the various senses of "look," "see," "vision," and "visionary." The
plates begin with children's depiction of self and move outward to their
contemplation of interior, exterior, and cultural landscapes largely
beyond the self. However, the series has a rhythm rather than a strong
narrative. The selections are diverse in culture and subject, and the commentary qualifies the Western notion of "self" in interpreting the children's statements. The selections dwell on inner conflicts, moral ambi-
guities (especially the everyday workings of racism), and renderings of
the spiritual. The last seem especially powerful, for they show children
expressing their own versions of what for all humans is a metaphoric,
symbolic world. How a moment of youthful awareness becomes knotted
with strands of enduring culture—religious, political, economic, racial,
artistic—is what Coles conveys and "reads" so well.

Although usually reluctant to analyze photographs, Coles willingly
interprets artwork and literature. The commentary of *Their Eyes* invokes
two post-Romantic traditions: the psychoanalytic interpretation of
dreams (mental "pictures") and the interpretation of painting as a fine
art. The commentary freely brings in the Western art critic's analytical

tools—the organization of space on a page, for example. The commentary reminds us that Coles's astute psychological observations in *Children of Crisis* and *Inner Lives of Children* rely heavily on his skilled "readings" of the visual, his ability to treat children's works with the same subtlety and seriousness that art historians give masterpieces. These readings are always placed in context. The conditions under which the drawings have been made are described, down to the artist's gestures, Coles's own promptings, and the swirl of family, school, political, religious, and cultural events that inform the child-artist's vision. *Their Eyes* allows the visual to emerge from Coles's research on children and to take its place with his other commanding medium: photography.

In all, Coles's works on photography and children's art display how important the visual imagination has been to his own purposes as a writer. They play a significant part in his aesthetic, including his understanding of literature.

Chapter Seven

"A More Intricate, a More Subtle Kind of, Psychology": Writing about Literature

At Harvard, Coles majored in English and history, writing his thesis on William Carlos Williams's long poem *Paterson* and later becoming acquainted with the doctor-poet, whom he regarded as a mentor. Personal acquaintance with living authors is one hallmark of Coles's literary writing. Another is his focus on characters' unseen futures and the half-spoken dilemmas that form, resolve, and re-form over the years of a life. Finally, Coles believes that the artist lives with, not above, other people. That is, Coles's interest in literature is intensely personal, moral, and spiritual. The writers who have engaged his interest the longest tend to have rural ties and often portray themselves as intelligent but anti-intellectual (*O'Connor*, 123). His first two book-length works on literature demonstrate these concerns: *Irony in the Mind's Life: Essays on Novels by James Agee, Elizabeth Bowen, and George Eliot* (1974) and *William Carlos Williams: The Knack of Survival in America* (1975). But they are even clearer in the later works, *Walker Percy, An American Search* (1978) and *Flannery O'Connor's South* (1980). *Walker Percy*, especially, influenced Coles's view of his work with children, as well as his aesthetic and philosophy. *A Festering Sweetness* (1978) and *Rumors of Separate Worlds* (1989) show him experimenting with poetry, while the anthologies *That Red Wheelbarrow* (1988) and *Times of Surrender* (1988) intimate a new confidence. Yet it was *The Call of Stories: Teaching and the Moral Imagination* (1989) that made literature a means of harmonizing Coles's projects, truly becoming what Dr. Elizabeth Zetzel had once suggested to him that fiction was: "a more intricate, a more subtle kind of, psychology" (*Irony*, 5). Eventually he has come to regard himself as a " 'novelist manqué,' " a writer without " 'the novelist's gifts' " but with " 'that set of mind.' "[1]

These works feature Victorian fiction, American (especially Southern) writers of the mid-twentieth century, and social, economic, and moral issues. Nonetheless, Coles's publications on literature range across genres and nationalities. He has created a volume of poems, *A Festering Sweetness* (1978), from the taped interviews of children and working people, and published another volume of his own poems, *A Rumor of Separate Worlds* (1989). He has edited *The Doctor Stories* of William Carlos Williams (1984), which serves as a text in a course for medical students. With Ross Spears and Jude Cassidy, he has collaborated on *Agee: His Life Remembered* (1985). A prolific reviewer and essayist, Coles has gathered an anthology of his literary essays, *That Red Wheelbarrow* (1988), and devoted sections to literature in the anthologies *The Mind's Fate* (1975) and *Times of Surrender* (1988).[2]

Writing about literature becomes part of Coles's project of developing an integrated philosophy to describe his passions and writing. In literary analysis he shapes his approach to his research and other writing and comments at length on his own work. At first he explicated works by authors whom he admires, using straightforward techniques of literary criticism. (Many of these were originally given as lectures at universities.) As in *Erik H. Erikson* and other works on intellectual subjects, the prose in these first studies is more elaborate than in his works of social observation. Yet even in the earliest studies, the literary criticism is animated by Coles's own experiences with people and deepened by his positions on psychology, philosophy, and religion. Over time, the prose simplifies, here and there approaching the conversational tones of the *Children of Crisis* and *Lives of Children* series. By the time of *The Call of Stories,* literary, social, and moral commentary had been integrated into a unique form.

Irony in the Mind's Life

Coles's first book-length study of literature contends with serious ideas in Western culture. As its complex title suggests, *Irony in the Mind's Life: Essays on Novels by James Agee, Elizabeth Bowen, and George Eliot* (1974) steps off an ambitious plot of intellectual ground: the intersection of literature, philosophy, religion, and psychology as a discourse about human nature. Originally delivered as the 1973 Page-Barbour Lectures at the University of Virginia, the four essays that compose the book offer moral and cultural critique as well as literary analysis. With so much at stake, the first essay and parts of the other three are densely written, full of allusions to the range of Western thought.

After a philosophical excursion into "Human Nature in Christian and Secular Thought," *Irony in the Mind's Life* explores an unusual group of three novels, *A Death in the Family*, *The Death of the Heart*, and *Middle-march*. Only the last is considered a major novel by a major writer. Clearly, historical period, national origin, and the literary canon are not Coles's main concerns. Rather, *Irony* advances an argument that may even be considered a psychosocial and literary manifesto. According to *Irony*, human nature is essentially unchanging and fundamentally contradictory, a mixture of Christian good and evil as well as psychoanalytical drives tempered by culture. The novels are chosen to illustrate the irony of human nature at various points: *Death in the Family* represents childhood; *The Death of the Heart*, adolescence; and *Middlemarch*, maturity. *Irony* indicates a debt to the ideas of Erik Erikson, but his stages of the life cycle are subordinate to more broadly Freudian and also Christian concepts. The first essay, "Human Nature in Christian and Secular Thought," opens with a distinction made by theologian Paul Tillich between "the pastoral and the prophetic modes of existence" (*Irony*, 5). The pastoral mode concentrates on a life of service whereas the prophetic mode encourages us to be bold, curious, and intellectual (5). Both modes are necessary to a full life, but they conflict with each other.

Irony also purports to offer broad cultural criticism by taking aim at the utopian thinking fashionable in the late 1960s and the 1970s. Through a series of footnotes and somewhat oblique references in the text, *Irony* targets "a whole range of political theorists, educational philosophers, [and] sociologists" (*Irony*, 98). The main subject of criticism is Charles Reich, whose *Greening of America* appeared in 1970. Reich and other writers capitalized on the student and youth movements of the era, interpreting them as major cultural phenomena. These "meliorists," who believe that human nature can be perfected or improved, argued that young people had a new approach to enlightened life that others must not only heed, but follow (*Irony*, 137). As the chapters develop, this critique of utopian thought emerges literally as a subtext, presented most candidly in a series of biting footnotes.

For Coles, the problem with these popular books is that they oversimplify human nature, promising a kind of redemption on earth to those who accept the observations of social science as a guiding philosophy of life. Twentieth-century parents are especially vulnerable to so-called expert advice (15). "Meliorist" books not only romanticize youth but reduce human experience to a few categories (137). For this reason Reich's book in particular draws Coles's ire. Against these contemporary utopians, "Human Nature" places philosophers such as Saint Augustine, Blaise Pascal, Søren Kierkegaard, Thomas Hobbes, and John Locke, as well as more recent thinkers like Sigmund Freud and Jean Piaget. The title, *Irony in the Mind's Life*, alludes to Kierkegaard. Coles finds this irony in all worthwhile literature and philosophical writing, including the Bible (8). This ambitious overview of good and evil in Western thought is the basis for the three chapters on "Childhood," "Youth," and "Maturity."

Despite the philosophical ponderings, fiction is the centerpiece of *Irony*. The epigraph, from George Eliot's prelude to *Middlemarch*, warns against foolish prophesying: "Every limit is a beginning as well as an ending. Who can quit young lives after being long in company with them, and not desire to know what befell them in their after-years? For the fragment of a life, however typical, is not the sample of an even web: promises may not be kept, and an ardent outset may be followed by declension; latent powers may find their long-waited opportunity; a past error may urge a grand retrieval" (*Irony*, xii). This passage serves as a literary parallel to the "life history" concepts of Erik Erikson. It warns psychoanalysts who overemphasize the early stages of life and social observers in general, including Coles himself, to beware facile generalization about an individual's promise, pain, or inner resources. The passage, cited often in *Irony* and Coles's later writing, summarizes his view of the human condition.

Like "Human Nature in Christian and Secular Thought," the three essays on the novels proceed by ambiguity and irony. They find tentative answers to humanity's future in sensitive portrayals of individual pasts. The sustained close readings show Coles's skill as an interpreter of literature. He is careful to shape the "ironies and paradoxes" (*Irony*, 9) that characters find themselves facing. That is, his own readings attempt to be as detailed, nuanced, and unsentimental as the novels themselves. The readings are broadened with explanations from psychoanalysts like Anna Freud and historians like Philippe Ariès, as well as the thinkers praised in "Human Nature." In addition, the second chapter offers a miniature appreciation of the documentary *Let Us Now Praise Famous Men*, developing connections between fiction, documentary nonfiction, and social commentary (57). James Agee and Walker Evans are social observers who were deeply philosophical but not led to make improbable theories (59). The philosopher Immanuel Kant and Jean-Jacques Rousseau would have admired them (57). A main theme of the second and third chapters is the ambivalent nature of childhood and innocence. Coles's reading of Agee's *A Death in the Family* focuses on the adults as well as six-year-old Rufus, the main character. For Coles, innocence is a term meaningful only to those who are beyond it. As demonstrated in the third essay, "Youth," innocents can harm others by the seeming willfulness of their innocence. To transcend innocence is to show a capacity for feeling what others feel and to enter into life as a participant. That is the nucleus of Coles's reading of Bowen's novel *Death of the Heart*. The novel's heroine Portia has a troubled adolescence, but it is no less difficult than the lingering ghosts of youth that haunt her adult relatives and friends. We may treat youth and childhood with nostalgia, but it is a mixed memory.

The fourth chapter takes up adulthood, which psychoanalysis typically regards as an afterthought to childhood traumas. Against this view, Coles places his reading of the nineteenth-century British novel *Middlemarch*, with its vast social landscape of "grown-up, serious, intelligent people" (*Irony*, 203–04). The essay concentrates on the moral and religious struggle of the banker Bulstrode, but it also treats other characters, including a harshly moral reading of the idealistic Dorothea Brooke and a sensitive discussion of the working-class Mary Garth. Adults, not children, suffer the most spiritually from the narrow psychoanalytic focus on infancy and childhood. The essay concludes hopefully, with the idea that adult life is indeed "a quest" (204). In *Irony*, Coles begins to explore in earnest the tension between story and theory, a central issue in his own documentary writing as well as his approach toward literature. In "Human Nature" Coles wrestles with ideas that, in *The Call of Stories,* he would express with more assurance, clarity, and grace.

William Carlos Williams

In three books published from 1975 to 1980, Coles turns exclusively to American and regional literature. *William Carlos Williams: The Knack of Survival in America* (1975) arose from the Mason Gross lectures Coles had given at Rutgers University in 1974, but the book is simply his lengthiest treatment of a writer to whom he returns again and again. Coles frankly admires Williams, who insisted on being both a serious writer and a doctor to the working-class people of Paterson, New Jersey. Representing a lonely holdout to Coles, Williams is set against the expatriate tradition of his early twentieth-century contemporaries and against the fashion of ennui and cosmic boredom that is typified by poets such as T. S. Eliot (*Williams*, 9). The "knack of survival" of the book's subtitle refers both to the ability of Williams's characters to survive working-class life in the United States and to the art that Williams himself so successfully practiced, as writer and as doctor, away from the nourishment of celebrity. Writers and critics, literary as well as social, must pay attention to people whom it is easy to ignore (xiii). *William Carlos Williams* deepens the connections among imaginative literature, nonfiction, and social criticism set forth in *Irony in the Mind's Life*.

Like Williams, Coles thinks that writers have abandoned to the social scientists the serious mission of documenting the conditions of life for the powerless and poor (*Williams*, 21). The study looks to literature— and particularly its language—as purifying and remedying the ills of theory, at least up to a point. *Williams* shows what Coles values and tries to emulate in his own work and writing: the language, subjects, method, structure, and goals carried from fiction into those very social sciences. The book also casts light on Coles's understanding of genre, poetry, and fiction, and the relations between fiction and autobiography. Like *Irony in the Mind's Life*, *William Carlos Williams* joins literary appreciation with considerations of the nature and purpose of literature.

After an introduction, *William Carlos Williams* is divided into three essays that discuss Williams's long poem *Paterson*, the collection of short stories *Life Along the Passaic River*, and the three novels *White Mule*, *In the Money*, and *The Build-Up*, collectively known as the Stecher trilogy. It is the frustrated and ambivalent social critic Dr. Williams that Coles discusses, not the intimate lyricist represented in anthologies of modern poetry. To a greater degree than Coles's other book-length criticism, *William Carlos Williams* treats an author with his contemporaries. As a poet, Williams is compared with Eliot and Ezra Pound; as a writer of immigrant and political fiction, he is compared with John Dos Passos and other writers of the 1930s and 1940s.

Williams also displays Coles's talent for close reading, as in the explications of the short stories "A Face of Stone" and "Jean Beicke" as well as *The White Mule* and the "Night" chapter of *In the Money*. The readings focus on a doctor's difficulties in coming to terms with his patients as people rather than as ignorant, acquisitive immigrants or grimacing infants. The interpretations also demonstrate how the psychological terrors of children and their parents play out in a family's economic dilemmas. Coles is sensitive to language, especially the ellipses and allusions that play between the lines of Williams's terse, realistic dialogue. That sensitivity to Williams's clear writing also shows in the direct style of the entire book, a contrast to *Irony in the Mind's Life*. What Coles finds most characteristic of Williams is the older writer's "unrelenting insistence on balance" in his social view of humanity, and the "possibility of love,"

that is, the overcoming of selfhood (9, 10). That balance means a willingness to look outside oneself toward others and to look for a long
time. The Stecher trilogy stays with characters over many pages and
many years (138). Williams enacts " 'the truth of the detail,' " one of the
values that his character Joe Stecher professes (152).

Williams also discusses techniques that presumably apply to research
writing as well as to literature. According to Coles, the technique of
pure stream of consciousness is highly artificial, like its psychoanalytic
counterpart, the patient's discourse (97). Coles prefers Williams's more
interactive technique, presenting a character's reveries in response to
others' speech or to events: "We don't carry on with ourselves extended
monologues. . . . We are constantly engaged in *conversations*" (97;
emphasis Coles's). The implications for Coles's own work and writing
are clear. He too spends long periods of time away from the seats of
intellectual power, carrying on his work: the observing of poor people.
His writing about children, although often cast into monologues, has a
larger context of conversation.

Above all, Coles finds Williams's fiction instructive and at least as
critical of the professionals as of the patients. In his next two books on
literature, Coles will continue that focus on the moral world of the professional. In discussing *White Mule*, Coles characterizes Williams as having "a sharp eye for that intersection of the private and the public which
determines the moral character of human beings; how they combine
their obligations to the demands of the world with their sense of what
they want for themselves and those they call their own" (101). Bruce A.
Ronda has used that characterization to describe Coles himself.[3] In other
words, the intersection of public and private is itself one's moral life.

Walker Percy, An American Search

Several years after Coles discovered the poetry and fiction of Dr.
Williams, he began to read another physician's work. Introduced to
Walker Percy's early philosophical articles by the theologian Paul Tillich,
Coles can legitimately claim to have followed the rise of the Louisiana
writer's career. His interest culminated in *Walker Percy, An American
Search* (1978), which followed his giving of the 1976 Trumbull Lectures
at Yale University and a lengthy profile for *The New Yorker*, for which
Coles interviewed Percy. There are some obvious similarities between
them. Percy, like Coles, attended medical school at Columbia University.
Both undertook psychoanalysis. Rather than an end in itself, medical

training became just one aspect of an intellectual and moral exploration of the world. Literature, philosophy, and theology—however different in specifics—were a part of childhood and youth. When each began to write, he had one foot in the conventions of academic articles and one in the broader intellectual traditions of literature and social observation. Both are very American, yet neither has hesitated to draw on a European intellectual tradition. Most of all, like Coles's friend William Carlos Williams, Walker Percy had set himself off to one side of the cultural mainstream. Thus he offered an intriguing stance for a psychiatrist who found himself immersed in that stream, yet bucking the current. There were obvious differences as well. Whereas Coles was a New England psychiatrist active in clinical practice and research, increasingly turned toward the lives of poor Americans, Percy was a reclusive Louisiana writer whose tuberculosis had cut short a medical career. Percy was Catholic; Coles, a nonchurchgoer of Episcopalian and secular Jewish heritage.

In *Walker Percy* Coles strengthens his views on literature, psychoanalysis, social criticism, and moral philosophy. He also employs a major new strategy, bringing stories from his fieldwork to bear on literature. He was already engaged in the cross-cultural research that would become *The Lives of Children*, and those experiences figure large in *Walker Percy*. The organization of *Walker Percy, An American Search* strongly suggests that of *Erik H. Erikson*, reflecting Percy's importance as a thinker on a par with the psychoanalyst and researcher. Although this book is slim (250 pages) compared with *Erik H. Erikson*, both volumes draw on the tradition of intellectual biography. The first chapter is entitled "Philosophical Roots," preceding two chapters that discuss Percy's essays and novels. The second and third chapters trace Percy's maturation from philosophical essays to fiction. With Martin Luschei's important early discussion of Percy's existentialism, *The Sovereign Wayfarer: Walker Percy's Diagnosis of the Malaise* (1972), scholarship on Percy was underway but in 1978 was still relatively new. Percy was still writing fiction, having just completed *Lancelot* in 1977. In this book, Coles is working out ideas for himself about the world, with the aid of an able writer of essays and fiction. The open, obliging tone of *Walker Percy* seems to imply deference for a working novelist, a man with ideas still to craft, as well as respect for the assistance that Percy had offered Coles.

Walker Percy emphasizes Percy's work as cultural and moral criticism. Along with a few oblique references to events and cultural themes of the 1960s and 1970s, such as the self-help movement that both Percy and

Coles despised, "Philosophical Roots" takes up Percy's "intellectual fore-bears" (*Percy*, 5, 8). As in *Erik H. Erikson*, Coles weaves Percy's philo-sophical and literary temperament with that of Søren Kierkegaard, a major influence on the novelist. Later the essay turns toward the minor existentialist Gabriel Marcel. Constantly moving across disciplinary lines, the chapter alludes to the ideas and lives of many thinkers and writers. "Philosophical Roots" and, to a lesser degree, the subsequent chapter, "The Essays," can be dense with philosophical reasoning. At the same time, in homage to Percy's own witty style, these chapters are written in a direct—even playful—manner, with many sketches of real or imagined everyday life. These sketches allude to movies, Manhattan, and the favelas of Rio de Janeiro. But rather than fictional characters, Coles describes the real people he has observed. He juxtaposes the lives and ideas of noted thinkers with those of ordinary people, like an Amer-ican business executive, a Brazilian mother of 10, and a Brazilian "expert on urban affairs" (41). Their insights play off each other and the philoso-phers' concepts, grounding abstract philosophical terms in the particu-lars of lives that cross the lines of class and education. This technique, more than any other factor, distinguishes *Walker Percy* from earlier stud-ies like *Irony*. In a very real sense, Coles broadens the scope of Percy's existentialism to include poor, often illiterate people from North and South America as well as Percy's privileged middle-class Southerners. Moreover, the condition of the people he interviews is an ironic warning for Coles, Percy, and other elevated commentators on human life to be humble. Coles and his companions are outsiders who cannot actually participate in the lives of slum dwellers. True to its existentialist sources, "Philosophical Roots" is a restless essay not content with its own conclu-sions.

The search is the main theme of *Walker Percy*, and the volume is a major contribution to Coles's thinking about the pilgrim in relation to the artist and the scientist. The first essay proclaims that Percy's philo-sophical articles represent "an American search, an existentialism: a writer's struggle to dig himself and others out of a certain cultural and historical trap—the secular world, with its fast-changing, contradictory pieties, not to mention its unprecedented capacity for self-destruction" (*Percy*, 5). The voyage may be literal or symbolic, attempted consciously or realized only in retrospect to be a journey. The theme is elaborated in the remaining chapters, "The Essays," "The Novels," and the brief "Epi-logue." Psychoanalysis is one type of journey. Percy's heroes undertake other versions of the search: Binx Bolling's excursions through New

Orleans; Bill Barrett's actual travels in the eastern and southern United States; and Lancelot's ruminations, in a bed in a hospital for the criminally insane. *Walker Percy* symbolically places the Louisiana physician, who rarely traveled, among the celebrated wanderers of American literary and cinematic mythology: Walt Whitman, Jack Kerouac, and Bobby Dupea (of the movie *Five Easy Pieces*). "The Loss of the Creature," one of Coles's favorites both for its philosophy and its deft writing (*Percy*, 112), has the controlling metaphor of the explorer and the explorer's discovery. Coles also views Percy's transition from writing essays to writing fiction as the artistic equivalent of an existential voyage: "The departure is from statements, interpretations—the fixed, static, asserted, and defined. The voyage is toward the ambiguous, the imaginary—the concrete, yet metaphorical and 'merely' entertaining or 'only' suggestive" (49). That is, the writer of philosophical essays, no matter how engaging and literary, remains a scientist who must take a risk, embark on a journey toward fiction, that is, art. Melvin J. Friedman, discerning the parallels between the two men, observes that "Coles is as much on an American 'search' as is Percy."[4]

The readings of the novels are close, affectionate, and nuanced. In "The Novels," two of Gabriel Marcel's ideas figure prominently. First, the seeker, *homo viator*, is preferable to the mere observer of life (*Percy*, 164). Second, we are not alone in our search. The term *fidelity* expresses the "commitment of one person to another, out of a shared commitment to a search for life's meaning" (230). In *presence*, "an 'exchange of free acts,' " two persons mutually acknowledge their fidelity, or commitment (171). "The Novels" interprets *The Moviegoer, The Last Gentleman, Love in the Ruins*, and *Lancelot* with great attention to the possibilities for searching and fidelity. In each, the main character is helped in his journey (all the protagonists are male) by another who also commits himself or herself to the shared task. Although Coles generally approves Percy's portrayals of women, in a discussion of *Love in the Ruins,* he debates whether they are stereotyped and sexist (206). Coles is somewhat defensive about this possibility and suggests that the narrow view of women belongs to the flawed male characters, not to Percy.

Walker Percy enables Coles to reconcile science, psychology, and philosophy—the last having a definite spiritual and theological cast. Percy "holds out for the wonderful attentiveness of the experimental, scientific tradition" and also for "the 'self' as transcendent" and real (*Percy*, 110). Most important, "consciousness is something shared: not only obtained from others (the social behaviorists would certainly agree) but something constantly affirmed by others, even when they are not to be seen—for instance when a person all by himself figures out a mathematical equation or works his way through a chemical experiment. Though he is alone, 'voices' from his academic past have made themselves heard" (110). Although he uses an academic example, an experiment in chemistry, this passage is one of Coles's best statements of the relation between psychology and philosophy. Later, in *The Call of Stories*, he would achieve an even more textured formulation. In literary terms, this book refines Coles's ideas on writing and art. However, it does not yet make a clear place for Coles's own art. *Walker Percy* privileges novel writing and thus leaves Coles's documentary writing in an artistic limbo.

A Festering Sweetness and *Rumors of Separate Worlds*

In the late 1970s Coles actively began shaping literary writing to fit his moral vision. He also tried a different sort of shaping—poetry. Robert Coles's two volumes of poems, *A Festering Sweetness: Poems of American People* (1978) and *Rumors of Separate Worlds* (1989), are interesting as much for their existence as for their substance. In a sense they are equivalent to photographs. They stand in relation to his prose as Alex Harris's photographs do: largely independent but parallel, a distinctive means of apprehending reality that is nonetheless explicated by the prose. In creating small poetic objects for readers to experience, Coles at least gestures to the towering figure of Williams, to whose poems the titles of these collections allude.

The poems of *A Festering Sweetness* are based largely on the words of children and adults whom Coles interviewed over two decades. The two parts of the collection divide the eastern from the western United States, paralleling the divide between the first three and the last two volumes of *Children of Crisis*. The first section has political overtones; Coles calls the poems "soldiers" in the fight against segregation and poverty.[5] Against the usual monotone of speakers in *Children of Crisis,* these short lines often re-create the rhythms of speech, as in "Mostly It's Buried," "Let Us Be," and "It Feels Funny," all "found" poems. The second section, with its strong evocation of Southwestern mesas and Alaskan meadows, is more visual and lyrical. The collection was lauded for its "clear, eloquent statements" by the speakers.[6]

By contrast, *Rumors of Separate Worlds* is much more, and more surprisingly, personal, but the revelations are guarded by the ellipses and allusions common to poetry. The first part, "Remembering a World," is chiefly about memories from Coles's private life: his parents and sons, a teacher who expected her students to pray, his own classes, family dogs ("Grady and Aran"), a beloved hospital supervisor ("On Dutch's Death").[7] William Carlos Williams is paired with Bruce Springsteen in "New Jersey Boys." The second part, "Meeting Worlds," recalls *A Festering Sweetness*, updating the voices of children and adults from Coles's travels to the world's trouble spots: Managua, Belfast, and South Africa. It also includes several poems on Ruby Bridges, two of whose drawings are reproduced in color plates. The last section, a sequence of poems written for Christmas, blends private moments with political reflections and fleeting vignettes from these many children around the world. A reviewer suggested that the "humanity of his vision redeems the flatness of his verse."[8] Although these poems will be of minor interest, some, like "A Rooming-House Christmas," have an impelled energy, honing them into stories that do justice to Williams's maxim, "no ideas but in things."

Flannery O'Connor's South

Coles's next literary appreciation has all the hallmarks of his mature works on literature: personal acquaintance with the writer, an abiding concern with religion and philosophy as well as the literary portrayal of everyday life, and the weaving of his own speakers as characters in the exploration of Flannery O'Connor's themes. Like *Walker Percy*, *Flannery O'Connor's South* (1980) mixes biography, literary analysis, and existential response in a Marcelian act of "fidelity" between reader and writer. It draws heavily on Sally Fitzgerald's collection of Flannery O'Connor's letters, *The Habit of Being*, published in 1979. Although the book is mainly a strong, affectionate reading of O'Connor, it adds the experiences of a number of people that Coles and his wife had met in the South, particularly Georgia and South Carolina. Because these voices are prominent enough to shape the whole, the book marks a subtle change in Coles's thinking about documentary literature.

Robert and Jane Hallowell Coles met Flannery O'Connor in 1961 shortly before the writer's death.[9] The catalyst for the meeting was Ruth Ann Jackson, a black woman who was " 'a lay minister of the Gospel' " as well as the daughter of a sharecropper, grandmother of one of the first students to desegregate Atlanta schools, a nurse's aide, and, not incidentally, a former mental patient in the state hospital at Milledgeville, Flannery O'Connor's home town (*O'Connor*, xv). The Coleses grew to respect

Ruth Ann Jackson for her moral courage and ability to show them their own prejudice (xx). Ruth Ann Jackson exemplifies the South that Flannery O'Connor knew. She is not to be dismissed by professionals or intellectuals as an object of study or humor, any more than O'Connor dismissed the people among whom she lived. Her story foreshadows the way that *Flannery O'Connor's South* confronts readers with people they seldom hear or listen to.

Dedicated to a literary critic, Richard Poirier, and a sociologist, David Riesman, *Flannery O'Connor's South* began as the Walter Lynwood Fleming lectures in Southern History given at Louisiana State University in 1979. In *Walker Percy*, Coles notes that O'Connor, Percy, Simone Weil, and Georges Bernanos are "four Catholic travelers of serious purpose indeed" (*Percy*, xvii). O'Connor is treated with gravity as an intellectual and a spiritual seeker; Coles finds many parallels between her thought and that of Simone Weil. Using the fruit of interviews that Robert and Jane conducted for *Women of Crisis*, *O'Connor's South* also acknowledges that women struggle not only individually but also by reason of their gender (*O'Connor*, 99).

The theme of *O'Connor's South* is the devious ways of intellectual pride. The three chapters that compose the book, "The Social Scene," "Hard, Hard Religion," and "A Southern Intellectual," place O'Connor's literary portrayals next to Coles's social observations of the rural and urban South, evangelism, and learning. Each chapter is suffused with the ethical and eschatalogical consequences of pride. Closely allied is the theme of sight and blindness; yet a third motif is the responsibility of the writer to render both microcosm and macrocosm although words themselves may not be sufficient to do so. The book's epigraph, from Revelation 1.17–19, contains a vision of the Apocalypse and God's injunction to John to "Write the things which thou hast seen, and the things which are, and the things which shall be hereafter." Coles invokes these motifs throughout the book, not only in reading O'Connor's work but also in assessing gains in civil rights and other endeavors.

"The Social Scene" contains readings of two short stories, "The Displaced Person" and "Everything That Rises Must Converge." These stories, supplemented by evidence from her letters and essays, demonstrate Flannery O'Connor's stance on a number of social issues, including civil rights. One story is rural, one urban. Both deal with outsiders, racism, and integration. Coles does not think that O'Connor was either racist or sexist (118). To the fictional characters is added a real-life companion, a Georgia black tenant farmer who provides "an echoing voice of sorts"

(*O'Connor*, 5). She politely but firmly consigns the civil rights workers she has met (the year is 1962) to minor status. They are admirable but flawed do-gooders—"prideful," to use a favorite term of both O'Connor and Coles. The technique of the "echoing voice" illuminates the fiction, or, in Marcel's term, "responds" to it. By becoming part of a dialogue of ideas in serious fiction, ordinary people's voices are made public and their thoughts granted the dignity they deserve. These voices also counter the charge that O'Connor's characters are merely "grotesques," others from whom non-Southern readers can remain aloof (6). The echoing voices, a kind of "literary counterpoint," evoke complex reactions (Friedman 122). They speak out of nowhere, as it were, outside of fiction, yet they collaborate with—or even take over—the fictional voices.

The second essay, "Hard, Hard Religion," forms the core of the book. Continuing a theme touched on in *Irony*, "Hard, Hard Religion" explores the infatuation that many Americans have with gnostic ideas. Gnosticism is a set of heresies that generally include being able to know God directly and without the mediation of church or priest, but here it also applies to beliefs in scientific progress and individualism. As a devout Catholic, O'Connor deplored gnosticism, yet was fascinated by its influence on her fellow Georgians, who were mainly Protestant and fundamentalist. The chapter takes its theme from one of her published letters dated September, 1959, which suggests that her characters are dramatically working out their " 'practical heresies' " (*O'Connor*, 59). "Hard, Hard Religion" examines O'Connor's unrelenting, delicious portrayals of certain Southern Protestant evangelicals and fundamentalists. Coles extends this critique to modern science. The essay contrasts O'Connor's Christian, apocalyptic vision of history with various scientific frames of reference. The main part of "Hard, Hard Religion" reads the novella *Wise Blood*. Its themes of vision and blindness are applied symbolically to knowledge, heresy, and fanaticism (82). The apostate Southern preacher Hazel Motes, the main character, is certainly a fanatic, but so are civil rights activists, Coles argues (99). The echoing voice, a north Georgia evangelist (85–86), leads into an analysis of preaching techniques as well as social and theological issues (86). The chapter also contains a reading of the short story "Parker's Back," concentrating on its portrayal of evangelism's vibrant oral storytelling and its Bible literacy that even the poor possess (94). Heretical or not, evangelism demonstrated to O'Connor that " 'When the poor hold sacred history in common, they have ties to the Universal and the holy' " (94).

Above all, she stressed that " 'When you write about backwoods prophets, it is very difficult to get across to the modern reader that you take these people seriously, that you are not making fun of them, but that their concerns are your own and, in your judgment, central to human life' " (94).

Central to Coles's philosophy and his judgment of O'Connor, this statement also provides a key to a gradual change in Coles's aesthetic. In *Walker Percy*, he still privileges novel writing above other forms of literary art, including his own documentary writing. Novel writing and reading are undeniably middle-class preoccupations, but not so telling stories or reading and interpreting sacred stories. Via his reading of Flannery O'Connor, Coles accepts that storytelling cuts across class lines. The echoing voices have appeared in earlier literary appreciations, for example, the Brazilians of *Walker Percy*. *O'Connor's South* provides a name and a justification for those voices.

The third essay turns to a group of characters that Flannery O'Connor's readers outside the South would recognize on a city street: liberal humanists and intellectuals. These include Asbury in "The Enduring Chill," Hulga of "Good Country People," and Julian of "Everything That Rises Must Converge." Treated at greatest length are O'Connor's "psychologist" characters: the psychiatric social worker Sheppard of the short story "The Lame Shall Enter First" and the atheist educational psychologist Rayber of the novella *The Violent Bear It Away*. Although this group represents some of O'Connor's "most memorable, if not completely successful" comic creations (122), they are more important as moral exempla. All of them exhibit the consequences of a troublesome modern gnosticism. The readings of "A Southern Intellectual" examine the many forms of intellectual pride, especially those that wear the masks of empathy and concern.

A further target of "A Southern Intellectual" is the language of social science and experts (129). The tone of the chapter shifts back and forth from anger to sadness because, after all, Coles too is a professional, an intellectual, and a liberal. The echoing voices include an exchange between a young patient—a teenaged criminal—and Coles's own pseudoexpert voice as a psychiatric resident. This exchange anticipates the essay "Stories and Theories" in *The Call of Stories* (133–34). The language of intellectuals like Sheppard leaves no room for themselves, a desperate condition. Sheppard pigeonholes Rufus Johnson, the young Bible-quoting delinquent whom he wants to help, as a patient or a victim of sociological circumstance. However, in existential terms, that system of classification leaves no place for the professionals themselves. In a word, Sheppard is "homeless," that is, in despair (137). The spirit's journey must start from a place, that is, at least a glimmering recognition of one's own suffering condition. It is clear that Coles, like O'Connor, places experts in peril, almost outside human concerns. They are not likely to have adventures, for they have no spiritual home to set out from. The expert's dilemma is resolved by listening to the other as a human being, not as a theorizer.

The last echoing voice of *O'Connor's South* is that of a child evangelist whom Coles and his wife heard in 1961 (145). In one of the luminous passages that Coles's writing sometimes achieves, the girl's sermon on "the exalted sense of self" of those who believe in words and progress becomes an ironic, personal meditation on literature, language, science, religion, and a Mississippi summer night (145). Above all, the passage affirms that self-knowledge comes only in communion with others (147). This girl evangelist closes what Rev. Ruth Ann Jackson began. Both the girl and the woman appear to move smoothly between the worlds of spirit and public action—whether at a hospital, a school-integration meeting, or an outdoor revival. Both can, for a moment, bring others "to themselves."

That Red Wheelbarrow and *Times of Surrender*

Two anthologies demonstrate how pronounced a turn toward the literary Coles's writing was taking. *That Red Wheelbarrow: Selected Literary Essays* (1988) and *Times of Surrender: Selected Essays* (1988) each gather over 40 essays and reviews originally published between 1964 and 1986. Taken together they provide a sample of his voluminous output of short pieces. Each also has significant biographical interest. The former reprints "Shadowing Binx," an important autobiographical statement, while the latter includes a long interview by David Hallerstein entitled "On Medicine and Literature."

That Red Wheelbarrow combines selections from columns in *American Poetry Review* as well as articles and reviews that appeared in *New Republic*, *New Yorker*, and other magazines and scholarly journals. The title comes from a poem by Williams, lightly touching on Williams's imagism and, too, Coles's friendship with the poet.[10] The seven sections into which the essays are sorted mention only historical periods, genres, and favorite authors like Williams and O'Connor, but the essay titles themselves reveal Coles's fascination with the moral and psychological value of literature: "The Virtues of *Middlemarch*," "To Break the Shell of Self," "Painfully Human," "Psychoanalysis and the Poetic Psyche," "The Empty Road," "James Agee's Search."

They also show the fruits of his teaching literature to law and medical students as well as undergraduates. "Charles Dickens and the Law" opens the collection, while the final section gathers seven pieces on Williams as doctor-poet and writer. Familiar themes emerge: the moral character of enduring literature, the limits of social reform and social theory (including legal remedies), the pride and sinfulness of human endeavor. Not least, Coles wrestles with the idea that we break the bonds of self-obsession only through the mediation of someone else who becomes a moral image in our minds. Reflecting on Dickens's *Little Dorrit*, Coles muses: "If we are all prisoners, we are at least able . . . to dream of freedom, to rise to its demands, as Arthur Clennam finally begins to realize with the help of not only what Little Dorrit is but, just as important, what she became for him, what she ended up being in his mind" (*Wheelbarrow*, 29).

He probes the popularity of J. D. Salinger and the enduring appeal of Tillie Olsen, whose lower-class roots strike a chord. The poets include James Wright, "who lives in the wilderness all the time" (272), Muriel Rukeyser, William Stafford, and the physician John Stone. The five essays on O'Connor supplement *Flannery O'Connor's South* and in particular draw out connections between the Georgia writer and the French philosopher Simone Weil. Coles remains interested in Cormac McCarthy's fiction, as shown by three meditations here. His taste for brooding, ironically macabre writers of high moral vision is also apparent in pieces on Franz Kafka, Knut Hamsun, and Jerzy Kosinski.

"James Agee's Search" and "Camera on James Agee" add considerably to Coles's output on this influential writer since his chapter on Agee's fiction in *Irony in the Mind's Life*. (In 1985 Coles penned a narrative to accompany photographs and various writers' reminiscences in *Agee: A Life Remembered*.[11]) "James Agee's Search" poses at length the hard question, Why read *Let Us Now Praise Famous Men*? Eventually the answer emerges: "because it prompts such moral and social questions about the responsibilities of the various observers, investigators, and writers who make their way into this or that community in hopes of discovering something, doing documentary work, finding material for an article, story, or book" (*Wheelbarrow*, 152). The anthology's tone ranges from quizzical to pensive to self-righteous, the last a trait that *That Red Wheelbarrow* shares with *Harvard Diary*, published the following year.

Although one essay alludes parenthetically to "story's eternal purpose" to entertain, there is surprisingly little joy in reading or insight, and when there is, Coles is quick to scrutinize the emotion for signs of his psychological or moral shirking (*Wheelbarrow*, 208). Francis X. Rocca calls Coles's vision of life "rather dismal."[12] In that sense the 1980s essays of *That Red Wheelbarrow* can be called Calvinist.

The companion collection, *Times of Surrender: Selected Essays* (1988), views topics of concern—psychiatry, medicine, religion, politics, minorities, children—through the lens of the humanities, mainly literature. The 41 essays and reviews come from general-interest publications like *The New Yorker* (which accounts for 13 pieces) and also from speeches and articles for journals of medicine, literary criticism, and children's literature. The opening two sections on psychiatry and medicine have an energy and confidence born of great knowledge. The essays, especially those on medicine, often incorporate stories from Coles's own training, his life in the South, his meetings with Robert F. Kennedy, and his teaching—and such stories typically relax his brittle didacticism. For example, "The Wry Dr. Chekhov" manages a level, even jaunty tone despite the poignant subject of a young woman's death. Here and elsewhere the energy makes up for somewhat rambling structure. He punctures the evils of his twin professions, especially the pride of psychologists and the self-centered, destructive competition of physicians in training. These masks keep professionals from knowing themselves and living moral lives. The masks can perhaps be dissolved if professionals allow themselves truly to listen to their patients or clients or research subjects. They must actually be confronted by their own flaws and thus their humanity—that is the "surrender" of the title, a term from checkers borrowed from the war metaphor of chess (*Times*, x). Reading literature—Chekhov, Percy, George Eliot, F. Scott Fitzgerald—can also alert budding professionals to the pitfalls of their vocations. Again literature serves as a warning to be "heeded" (*Times*, 77).

The remaining sections are more diverse but contain many worthwhile items. In the group on children and children's literature, Coles reviews Holocaust literature written for young people and in another piece presents several arresting poems by Ruby Bridges. The essays on religion touch the unexpected as well as themes familiar in Coles's writing. John Kennedy Toole's *A Confederacy of Dunces* is peopled by characters "dim-witted, driven, distended" by satire, the massive protagonist Ignatius "a representation of the Catholic Church itself," trying to comprehend an insane world (*Times*, 121, 124). Three articles on Georges

Bernanos recount the "almost unbearable" response that Coles has to reading this otherwise obscure Frenchman, who wrote the novel *The Diary of a Country Priest* (*Times*, 127). He is particularly fascinated with the priest's conscience-stricken observations and the diary form as a means of solving the problem of the "presence of the author" (*Times*, 134). In a way Coles describes the priest as he might his own narrator's presence from *Children of Crisis* on: "One moment he can be rude, tactless, himself insufferably priggish. Then he turns, catches himself, and speaks in an honest, strong, and clear way that can only be called revelatory" (*Times*, 135).

"Minorities, Art, and Literature" is an eclectic gathering, mainly but not exclusively about black writers and subjects. Included are a review of Alice Walker's *The Third Life of Grange Copeland* and "James Baldwin Back Home," a 1977 interview with the expatriate writer (during a visit to New York) that is more sympathetic than the review of *The Fire Next Time* reprinted in *Farewell to the South*. "Through Conrad's Eyes," also in this section, is a memoir of Robert Kennedy, filtered through brief conversations on literature by and about Africans and African Americans. Most of the political essays date from the 1970s and enlarge an area that Coles has more often than not come at obliquely. Indeed, the volume's two final essays, both from 1983, quickly move from politics to ethics, character, and the ironies of human frailty. Like others of his short pieces written during the 1980s, these essays tend to invoke novelists and essayists as touchstones rather than elucidate the references in any detail.

Like *The Mind's Fate*, these collections demonstrate Coles's wide reading as well as his touchstones. In this variety the reader also detects the prodigious number of book reviews and articles that Coles has written. More important, *That Red Wheelbarrow* and *Times of Surrender* pave the way for an extraordinary statement about the teaching of literature, *The Call of Stories*.

The Call of Stories

For much of his career, Coles has pursued two quite different projects, the first his research and writing about children, and the second his various scholarly readings of the work of intellectuals, chiefly psychologists, fiction writers, and ethicists. He has tried to bring insights from each to bear on the other, so that his research is sprinkled with references to philosophers and fiction writers, whereas his literary studies began to incorporate echoing voices from his research. Over the years the points of intersection have increased. His research explicitly began to examine moral action and the role of imaginative works of art. The end of *Privileged Ones* (1977), the last volume of *Children of Crisis*, suggests that bright, well-educated children need experiences that turn their "moral notice" to people unlike themselves. *The Moral Life of Children* (1986) explores the role of certain films in inspiring children to imagine and work through matters of conscience. On the other hand, Coles's study of writers has produced an aesthetic that can accommodate not only morality and transcendence but also social action and observation.

The Call of Stories: Teaching and the Moral Imagination (1989) integrates his understanding of imaginative literature with his concerns for the whole life of the educated person. This slender, 212-page volume also fuses concepts from Coles's major influences: Erik Erikson's life histories, Anna Freud's direct observation, the dialogic existentialist theology of Gabriel Marcel, William Carlos Williams's "no ideas but in things," James Agee's documentary nonfiction, and the moral fiction of Walker Percy and Flannery O'Connor. Finally, *The Call of Stories* makes teaching the hinge that joins Coles's two major projects, bringing children (or rather adolescents) to new moral experiences through literature and voluntary service. To use terms that Coles himself would avoid, *The Call of Stories* contains his mature aesthetic and epistemology—his theory of literature and moral action.

The subtitle, "Teaching and the Moral Imagination," stresses academic learning. With its lists of selections that Coles teaches in his courses, *The Call of Stories* may seem aimed narrowly at secondary and college teachers, especially English teachers. The chapters may be considered a teacher's anecdotes to gloss these lists. It was warmly received by reviewers, especially in educational publications.[13] Yet because of its integrative nature, the book has broad appeal. *The Call of Stories* has a mellowness, a coming to terms with the intractabilities of life that Coles had previously dealt with more combatively in works like *Migrants*, *Irony*, and *Harvard Diary*. It is retrospective, consciously autobiographical, and highly shaped as art and argument. For all its conceptual sophistication and the intricate texture of its narratives, the style is extraordinarily clean and accessible. For these reasons, as well as its intense look at literature and the lives, training, and work of professional men and women, many readers may find *The Call of Stories* the best introduction to Coles's work.

After the introduction and the first chapter, "Stories and Theories," the book is loosely organized by what used to be known as the "ages of man," from childhood to age. This structure recalls and refines that of his first work on literature, *Irony in the Mind's Life*. Typically each chapter begins by relating an individual's encounter with a literary work or works. These stories are drawn from patients, students, friends, parents, and Coles's own childhood. The words of the readers and storytellers are for the most part edited from transcripts of tape recordings. They are combined with Coles's perceptions. In each essay, the first tale accrues stories from other people, developing new facets that join at the edges of the reader's moral imagination.

The autobiographical introduction traces the genesis of Coles's own response to "the call of stories." The chapter details Coles's discovery of fiction in youth, his pursuit of literary study in college, and the effect of reading fiction on his vocation. The opening vignette portrays a young "Bobby" Coles enamored of radio programs and at odds with his parents, whose evening habit is to read novels aloud to each other. When Coles turns to reading fiction, it is both in harmony and in conflict with the wishes of parents and teachers. Years later, as he teaches literature himself, he better understands his parents. Playing off the authority of youth to decide for itself and the authority of age to confirm and direct youthful choices, Coles recognizes the differing appeals of literature to people at various times of life.

The first essay, "Stories and Theories," is central to Coles's mature understanding of language, art, and literature. It is the one chapter that does not focus on specific literary works. Rather, "Stories and Theories" sets forth an argument about psychological development and education. The conceptual power of "stories" is contrasted with the much less powerful "theories" of the well educated. The argument itself proceeds by means of stories, those narratives of our lives by which we represent our experience to ourselves and make sense of it to ourselves and to others. Coles takes the insight of *Flannery O'Connor's South*, that stories are available to all, as a counterweight to the emphasis in American colleges on theory and analysis. Perhaps because stories are universal, educated people look down on them and those who rely on them. Prestige is involved in acquiring analytical skills. Yet according to "Stories and Theories," so much is lost by ignoring stories for theories that one's intellectual growth, understanding, and moral gravity—the very things one seeks in education—are endangered. The argument develops out of a long narrative from Coles's own psychiatric residency, the story of a woman patient (*Stories*, 1) of his. From the outset there are two storylines, that of the woman's life, locked up inside her and only gradually coaxed out, and Coles's story of learning his job and thereby learning her story.

The essay also develops a contrast between Coles's two supervisors, one who represents the triumph of psychoanalytic "theory" and the other who encourages Coles to pursue the slower, more difficult road of "story." The latter, Dr. Ludwig, tells the young resident: " 'The people who come to see us bring us their stories. They hope they tell them well enough so that we understand the truth of their lives. They hope we know how to interpret their stories correctly' " (7). As Coles listens, the woman's tale reveals her as more interesting, articulate, sensible, and humorous about herself than any formally structured interview could have elicited (12). The essay draws together many conceptions of oral and written story, such as psychiatric case notes (14). By connecting the narrative making of professionals in a "scientific" helping discipline with that of traditional writers and ordinary people, the essay establishes "story" as a flexible and powerful concept.

The remaining seven essays return to the catalyst of literature. In sequence they follow the course of a life, echoing and completing the experiences patterned in the introduction and "Stories and Theories." In the second chapter, "Starting Out," young people of junior high and high school age make personal connections, some of them won at Coles's expense, with classic novels like *Huckleberry Finn* and *The Catcher in the Rye.* In "Finding a Direction," college students speak of the stories that have moved them and those that have not, and why. The fourth chapter, entitled "Interlude: Bringing Poems to Medical School Teaching," interrupts this sequence to relate Coles's friendship with the editor and poet L. E. Sissman, whose illness with cancer was accompanied by writer's block. The interruption draws attention to the commonality of the book's narrators: their wisdom, their quizzical acceptance of their predicaments regardless of age or accomplishment, and their need for literature. "Interlude," which concerns poetry, writing, and the American Southwest, is a ribbon of contrast to the overall focus on fiction, reading, and New England. The essay's title and placement also suggest a secondary structure in the book. The first four essays (counting the introduction) make one group; the last four make a second group. "Interlude" stands in the middle, its subjects forming a change of pace, and its theme of impending death urging a different kind of contemplation.

"Vocational Choices and Hazards," the fifth chapter, turns to the experiences of young professionals and intellectual pride. The essay describes the young Coles accompanying William Carlos Williams on house calls in 1953. The chapter contains an intense and fully realized portrait of Williams as writer and as old-fashioned doctor, as well as the emotionally and intellectually confusing waters into which a doctor is pitched at a patient's bedside (*Stories*, 112). In "The Private Life," the sixth chapter, the fiction of Walker Percy and John Cheever is brought to bear on college students' homelife, which is fraught with the silences and memories of families contending with alcoholism, boredom, and existential despair. The seventh chapter, "Looking Back," opens with a description of a painting, Paul Gauguin's comments on his work "Where Do We Come From? What Are We? Where Are We Going?" The essay's theme is the value of constructing a life in retrospect, what Frank Kermode has called "our deep need for constructing intelligible Ends" to our lives.[14] Literature—the catalyst of others' stories—can be an important part of this retrospection. The essay focuses on but is not limited to the meditations of those severely disabled or near death, as they have been influenced by Tolstoy's short story "The Death of Ivan Ilych."

Like the first essay, the final chapter, "On Moral Conduct," widens the perspective. It asks what literature is ultimately worth, morally and spiritually, in the life of this world—especially the lives of privileged college students and well-educated Americans. In *The Call of Stories* reading and insight go hand in hand with moral action. Discussions of two doctor-writers, Williams and Anton Chekhov, are balanced with young people's stories of how volunteer work has affected their lives. The point of the essay is not the naive observation that literature is really real but rather that the intense imaginative quality of good fiction, together with readers' moral and emotional imagination, can move us not only to reflect but also to act. The moral force of literature has been argued since Horace, but Coles's formulation has urgency as well as contemporary dress. After we answer literature's tantalizing call to read and reflect, the call of stories is finally a call to action. That action includes speaking one's own stories and also seeking out and listening to others' stories. Those persons do not only attend college classes; they live in shelters, on the street, in barrios, even in our own homes. *The Call of Stories* is among Coles's most spiritual works. At one point he speaks of a compelling story being "a gift of grace" (191). Indeed, these essays approach spirituality with the same subtle, profound, but relaxed tone that they take toward art. Although Coles continues to read and teach literature, his works of this period increasingly turn directly to spiritual matters.

This chapter has traced the growth of Coles's aesthetic, a way of shaping literary writing to his moral vision. That vision is the major component of his writing about religion and spirituality.

Chapter Eight

The Pastoral and the Prophetic: Writing about Spiritual Experience

Writers of fiction are often in love with "the commonplace, the routines of millions of lives" (*Weil*, 4) that they describe so well. But the novelists and storytellers whom Coles admires usually aim for more, for religious or spiritual themes. His fascination with the nature of people's stories frequently leads to the ultimate meanings that we give the lives that we tell stories about. From *Children of Crisis* on, Coles has given a place to religion unusual in writers trained in the social sciences. His own spiritual sensibility came into play as he encountered the strong faith of many of his "voices." For example, in the concluding chapter of *The South Goes North*, "The Lord in Our Cities," he struggles to square the persona of "objective" observer with his urge to pray (*South*, 651). The culmination of his work as a social scientist is the 1990 volume *The Spiritual Life of Children*. Coles's book-length explorations of adult faith and spirituality are the subject of this chapter: *The Geography of Faith*, *A Spectacle Unto the World*, *Dorothy Day*, *Simone Weil*, *Harvard Diary*, and *The Call of Service*. The books span 20 years. Three of the volumes concern single individuals, and two of those—*The Geography of Faith* and *Dorothy Day*—are wholly or substantially made up of interviews that Coles conducted.

The Western literary tradition of the spirit has taken many forms, such as the spiritual autobiography, the sermon, and the formal prayer. All of these assume a single or monophonic speaker. Coles's religious writing acknowledges several genres, partaking most of the spiritual autobiography, the soul's search. Bruce A. Ronda's study of Coles, *Intellect and Spirit*, has delved into the spiritual significance of the "autobiographical impulse" in his work (Ronda 1989, 13). But there is an important qualification. Aside from *Harvard Diary*, which is frankly autobiographical, Coles has generally taken a more collaborative approach to matters of the spirit than these traditional genres urge. It is not his own beliefs that hold the center, but those of others. This novel approach casts him as part social scientist, part psychiatrist-confessor, and part humble supplicant of wisdom. Thus to the spiritual pilgrimage Coles adds the tradition of the classical and Christian colloquy, a fictional conversation or dialogue.[1] He also draws on his extensive experiences in social and clinical case study, melding the search of the scientist to that of the soul.

Although Søren Kierkegaard's existential theology underlies much of Coles's writing, two other theologians' versions of existentialism have especially influenced his religious writing. From Paul Tillich, Coles learned to treat spiritual yearnings as aspects of the pastoral and the prophetic modes of existence. The pastoral, characterized by the life of the Christian pastor or shepherd, is a life of caring for others with its "obligations and dangers" as well as its "limits" (*Irony*, 5). The pastoral mode is best seen in the character of the curé in Georges Bernanos's *The Diary of a Country Priest*. The enemy of the pastoral is complacency and lack of self-scrutiny. The prophetic mode is the urge "to comment on things, take the lead in bringing about a new way of thinking or acting" (*Irony*, 5). The prophetic includes intellectual curiosity and also intellectual ambition or pride (*Irony*, 6).

Gabriel Marcel, whose work Coles explicated in *Walker Percy*, has had an even greater influence on the dialogic form of Coles's writing. Although concerned with *homo viator*, the seeker, Marcel nevertheless rejected the simple notion of "finding oneself." Rather, "man only finds himself through solidarity with others, through the 'actualization' of his freedom in several kinds of love: a wife, husband, friends, the person one may meet only briefly, but in a way that is honorable and kind-spirited on both sides—without false or automatic gestures" (*Percy*, 164). This means that "consciousness is something shared: not only obtained from others . . . but something constantly affirmed by others, even when they are not to be seen . . ." (*Percy*, 110). Calling on Martin Buber as well as Marcel, Coles notes: "By an 'exchange of free acts' one person nods to another, the nod is reciprocated, and two 'realities' become joined" (*Percy*, 171). Speaking together can be such an act, a part of the joined search: "[S]peaking is a means by which one joins hands with another" or in Kierkegaard's terms, "takes risks with one's pride, one's integrity, one's 'situation' " (*Percy*, 20). Together companions who are "committed" in Marcel's sense can move closer to God (*Percy*, 230). The primacy of dialogue in Marcel's theology seems reflected in Coles's secular and spiritual writing. One might argue that the dialogic form, the act of reaching out and listening to a committed other, becomes a type of devotion, in itself a spiritual act.

Secondarily, Coles's writings about spirituality are reminiscent of one other quite neglected genre of spiritual instruction, hagiography. Hagiography is the practice of writing about saints to "inspire remembrance and imitation of their lives and deeds."[2] Of course Coles's biographies and biographical essays are not hagiography, but they do explore the moral actions of people that are as exemplary as human lives can be and so perhaps are "a source of encouragement, . . . a means of self-definition, . . . an example of what has been and is still being done" (*Spectacle*, xi). As with hagiography, simply undertaking to write about worthy, devout persons can itself be a moral act and an expression of faith (*Spectacle*, x). It is also an act in keeping with Marcelian fidelity.

Although they are by no means saints, Coles's subjects may fairly be called Christian (and Jewish) ascetics. For example, Simone Weil "exerted so much domination over so many of her impulses or urges that the words *discipline* and *self-control* hardly do justice to the reality of her daily life" (*Weil*, 117; italics Coles's). Yet self-denial is not enough. Tacitly renouncing the monastic and anchorite traditions, in which religious persons dedicate themselves to cloistered or solitary devotion to God, Coles seeks those who try to live in the spiritual and political tradition of the early Christians. These ascetics combine austere, devout lives with radical—although not orthodoxly ideological—politics, sustained good works, and life among ordinary people. If a further distinction can be made, Coles is also especially attracted to those who, as he says, are "drawn to Catholicism as adults rather than born heirs to its traditions and rituals" (*Day*, xix).

There are dangers, of course, in portraying models of human behavior: glorification, sentimentality, the neglect of all-too-human frailties. However, by asking tough psychological as well as spiritual questions of his subjects, Coles reduces the tendency to eulogize individuals. He also recognizes and empathizes with the frailty of every human, including those whom he has elevated to the stature of ethical and spiritual models. Finally, by keeping himself in his studies as a listener and talker about ordinary life, Coles helps to keep his subjects evenly lit. The result of this unique approach to spiritual writing is a curious marriage of old and new. In his insistent queries to others, Coles maps psychoanalytic ideas onto moral questions and dissolves political philosophy into a troubling spiritual quest for both his speakers and himself. The collaboration may be of mutual interest to his speakers, but it is also for Coles's and his readers' benefit. He wants to illumine his speakers' experiences for us, his implied readers, who may be well informed but are also in need of guidance. There is surprisingly little consolation in Coles's religious writing, although he seeks it in others'. Instead, there is always tension in his conception of religion. To avoid sentimentality, to touch the threads in our intricate webs of psychological self-justification and spiritual yearning—these are his goals.

The Geography of Faith

Coles's first book on faith and spirit may seem an unlikely choice, and indeed *The Geography of Faith: Conversations between Daniel Berrigan, when Underground, and Robert Coles* (1971) resulted from an impelled gesture rather than from years of reflection. In July, 1970, Coles had several meetings with Father Daniel Berrigan, a priest, poet, and radical activist who was then in hiding from federal agents for his role in the 1968 burning of draft board files in Catonsville, Maryland. A dissident who opposed the Vietnam war, Berrigan was living "underground" with sympathetic families. After being approached by a group of young doctors (and others), Coles agreed to meet with Berrigan, in part to protest the way that Daniel's brother, Father Philip Berrigan, was being treated in Pennsylvania's Lewisburg Prison.[3] The two men did not know each other. One was a radical Catholic antiwar activist who engaged in acts of civil disobedience that got his name and picture onto the evening news; the other was a self-described agnostic psychiatrist, writer, and "field worker" who had become known to an educated readership as a man of conscience and liberal political views, as well as a friend and associate of civil rights activists. By any standard *The Geography of Faith* is a singular work. Published under the auspices of the Unitarian Universalist Association, this collaboration is like no other by Coles before or since. Berrigan was arrested and imprisoned not long after their meetings, and the troubled Coles hurriedly prepared the edited version of their taped conversations (*Geography*, 22).

The hasty assembling of *Geography* is evident in the somewhat disorganized introduction, which concerns primarily the agonies of deciding what constitutes just political action. With a minimum of context, the opening reprints a host of communications, including letters from the Berrigan brothers, other Catholic activists, and a prison psychiatrist as well as Coles's own letters regarding the Berrigans and excerpts from his interviews with a policeman and a gas station owner, representing the "middle Americans" who were religious but also angered and perplexed by war resisters. These varied statements recall one of the most divisive times in recent American history and, too, one contemporary literary means of dealing with that division: to "lay it all out" presumably as it happened, with as little tampering by the writer as possible. Daniel Berrigan's telegraphic first contact with Coles rings with the slashing, glittering questions and assertions of the New Left, mixed with the terms of radical Christianity. Coles was regarded skeptically by the anti-war activists and in turn was disgusted by their "antics and provocations" (*Geography*, 25). Nonetheless, this introduction shows Coles's determination to be evenhanded, showing a nervous, intense respect for Berrigan as well as the middle Americans whose views, Coles believed, were too often ignored. The ethical and eschatological implications of these meetings are clear, and the introduction ends in a flourish, with Berrigan's quotation of Paul, "I die daily," as theme (32–33).

What common ground could Father Berrigan and Coles find, aside from the goodwill of those who insisted that they should talk? Both had committed themselves to lives of considered moral action. They both admired two Christian writers who undertook political action as acts of conscience: Dietrich Bonhoeffer, a theologian who voluntarily returned to Nazi Germany, joined the Resistance, and was hanged at Auschwitz in 1945; and St. John of the Cross, who was burned at the stake in Spain in 1591 (*Geography*, 31). After the meetings, Coles came to regard passages from these writers (31) as central to the conversations. Years later Coles would again write about Bonhoeffer in *Harvard Diary*. *The Geography of Faith*'s seven chapters, or sections, progress from broadly secular to intensely spiritual perspectives: "Families," "Pride and Violence," "At the Edge," "Compassionate Man and Political Man," "Professional Life," "Inside and Outside the Church," and " 'Twice-Born Men.' " According to the introduction, these groupings made the transcripts coherent while keeping the original sequence "intact" (*Geography*, 21).

The format makes for an intense, sometimes surprising discussion of what could have been abstract political speeches. For example, the first chapter circles the two men's quite different perceptions of families. Berrigan has been drawn into close relationship with a number of liberal middle-class families that risked being charged as accessories to a fugitive. In his research, Coles has grown to know many types of families, mostly poor or lower middle class. At first Coles is content to draw Berrigan out, asking him to clarify his ideas. Gradually, in order to understand how Berrigan's presence in a family gives rise to moral—and political—change, Coles edges out on his own: "In that sense they take a step with you. Your presence among those people compels a kind of self-scrutiny that might not be possible for them were you not there, were your position among them not a given" (*Geography*, 41). However, as Berrigan explores the idea that families and small groups like communes provide hope for a new way of human dealings, Coles demurs, and the conversations become genuine dialogue: "Forgive me, but as one who has his own feeling of despair and who perhaps first believed in original sin, and now believes in the psychoanalytic version of it, which is that there are inevitably tensions and miseries and difficulties in all human relationships, I have to ask you this: what about the more somber or grim side of these communes? Or can it be that there is no such side, . . . ?" (53). Thus Coles broaches the subject of the Left's utopian thinking. Throughout *The Geography of Faith*, Coles repeatedly challenges Berrigan's utopianism as inconsistent with both Christian doctrine and psychoanalytic observation. Although Berrigan, who is trained in theological argument and doctrine, maneuvers away from this charge, the subject of man's perfectibility haunts Coles. A few years later, in *Irony in the Mind's Life* and again in *Flannery O'Connor's South*, he would again explore utopianism as one expression of the gnostic fallacy.

The two proceed through considerations of the antiwar movement's violence and egoism (or pride), the dangers that celebrity poses even to moral leaders (the peril of the prophetic mode), the intertwined nature of political awareness and spiritual transformation, the need to act in the world as part of observing one's faith, the resources that professionals have for ethical action, the possibility of a conscientious stand within an institution like the Catholic Church, and finally, the emergence of individuals, called "Twice-Born Men," who quietly carry on the values and energy of the early Christians. Along with utopianism, the greatest source of their disagreement is the Weathermen, whose violence Coles finds a serious threat to both Christian and democratic values, yet many of whose actions Berrigan finds worthy. On the other hand, for the sake of acting at all in an imperfect world, Berrigan accepts the real possibility that he is wrong, an admission that is harder for Coles to make (*Geography*, 81). And discussing personal religious beliefs is relatively easy for Berrigan, a Jesuit in holy orders for almost 30 years, whereas Coles is reluctant to speak of his private beliefs and practices (135). When Berrigan asks him to explain "what it is to be a Christian in your profession," Coles is willing but indirect, calling on Freud, Weil, Bernanos, and Tillich (134). Through respect as well as challenges, each man makes the other scrutinize a host of actions and attitudes. Each man has been in the middle of violent mobs and has been consulted as a moral expert by persons of conscience and by politicians, so their ponderings are not abstract. Too, each has studied the vagaries of the human heart and understands how poorly his particular calling has equipped him to guide those trying to make the world "more decent" (31).

The title arises from a metaphor that develops in their conversation. Using the common contemporary metaphor for radical action, living "on the edge," Berrigan, with an intensely visual understanding of moral action, expands: "I could not remain at peace at the center, so the issue continues to be spatial—an issue of one's geography, one's place, one's decision to stand here, not there, and for this rather than for that" (82). He describes an ethical life at this moment in history as partaking of "a shared jeopardy" (81). Men like Dietrich Bonhoeffer, Philip Berrigan, and Martin Luther King knew that the pastoral life of being "merely a listener, or a good friend" is not enough (81); one must act and even put oneself at risk, away from the comfortable center of faith and conventional morality. The metaphor embraces the range of topics that the two men traverse in their conversations.

For Coles's work in general and his religious writings in particular, *Geography* is significant. It is an early, readable, often direct statement of his basic views on the moral and spiritual life. Although he hesitates to expand on certain matters of private faith, he is forthright on many issues, a rarity in his work that often presents his views through the screen of his explication of another author's work. Here he folds together what matters to him from psychology, psychoanalysis, sociology, political action, and religion. He makes clear the lines that distinguish his thought not only from Berrigan's but also from that of other thinkers and activists. The conversations are genuine colloquy, in which the circumstances lend urgency to the search for answers. *The Geography of Faith* is also an interesting document of its time and, not least, an intense portrait of two men, each with the confidence, ability, and gentleness to probe the other's deepest-held convictions.

A Spectacle Unto the World

In the same year that his first collaboration with photographer Alex Harris, *The Old Ones of New Mexico*, was published, Coles collaborated with another photographer, Jon Erikson, to pay homage to a profound influence in his life, Dorothy Day. *A Spectacle Unto the World: The Catholic Worker Movement* (1973) celebrates 40 years of publication for *The Catholic Worker* newspaper, which Dorothy Day cofounded in 1933 with

Peter Maurin (*Spectacle*, ix–x). As a photographic collaboration, *Spectacle* falls somewhere between the teamwork of *Old Ones* and the more casual partnership of some of Coles's other documentary books. As a study, it has affinities with many of Coles's other efforts, including his examinations of adults in the margins. These adults, the homeless men and women of the Bowery who come to St. Joseph's House for food, beds, and prayer, are treated directly only through Jon Erikson's photographs. Coles is not so interested in rendering their lives as in rendering the history of the Catholic Workers, which is inextricably bound with the people they serve. The object is to inform young people of this model of activism, the Catholic Workers' special brand of lay spiritual leadership (*Spectacle*, xi). Jon Erikson spent considerable time at St. Joseph's, participating in the daily life of the mission in order to photograph as unobtrusively as possible. As a writer, Coles was able to consult his memory and conduct interviews with Day and other older Workers. As a medical student he had come to know Dorothy Day and had volunteered at the mission. During the period of producing the book, Coles gave a lecture at St. Joseph's (*Spectacle*, xii–xiii).

Dorothy Day: A Radical Devotion

The Catholic Worker movement blends activism and faith in a way that Coles finds most sympathetic. He met Dorothy Day while he was in medical school; he visited her many times after that and for a while volunteered at her Bowery mission. Dorothy Day died before the publication of Coles's biography of her, *Dorothy Day: A Radical Devotion* (1987). This slender work, along with *Simone Weil: A Modern Pilgrimage*, published simultaneously, marked Coles's renewed interest in biography and enlarged his collaborative, inquiring approach to spirituality. Part of the Radcliffe Biography Series, the works probe two formidable women's ideas in relation to their lives. The books are not intended as full-scale biographies. Rather, they examine "certain themes" that run through Weil's and Day's thinking and practice (*Weil*, xix). Read individually, each book serves as a fine introduction to the life and thought of its subject. Although part of an academic series, the books are short and the prose is straightforward, making them accessible to a range of readers. Brief, clear endnotes, a lively bibliographic essay, and an index also guide the reader to discover more about these writers. Coles teaches the works of Dorothy Day and Simone Weil in his courses. These volumes take into account that younger readers may not be familiar with the

Zeitgeist of Day's or Weil's time. For example, *Simone Weil* evokes the wartime circumstances in which the Frenchwoman lived with a gentle but ironic reference to the popular movie *Casablanca* (*Weil*, 14, 16).

As their prefaces indicate, *Dorothy Day* and *Simone Weil* are companion volumes that play off each other. Unrelated as their legacies seem, Dorothy Day and Simone Weil both lived their lives deliberately, conscious of both the political and the religious scope of their acts. Insofar as any human is able to, they sought to enact their beliefs. For Coles, they fused intense—and unremitting—self-scrutiny with political and social action. They reflected, wrote, and desired to lead others in the prophetic mode. Yet they also acted directly to help others, without thought for creating legacies or fame for themselves, in the pastoral mode. In Coles's eyes, those who would live thoughtfully must consider the questions that Weil and Day sought to answer.

There are other important likenesses between the two. Dorothy Day, an American born in 1897, and Simone Weil, a Frenchwoman born in 1909, were young adults when the political horrors of fascism rocked Europe. Both were educated women (Weil formidably so), daughters of families of some means and expectations in life. Early on, both showed signs of social conscience that led them outside a comfortable middle-class life. Neither took up for long an orthodox role for women. Both developed radical political philosophies. Contemporaries of George Orwell, both women observed at close hand the grinding lives of ordinary people and expressed their observations in writing. Like many other writers, artists, and intellectuals of the time, both were shaped by their strong reactions to the Spanish civil war in the 1930s, followed soon after by the rise of Hitler and Mussolini. Both opposed fascism and tyranny of all types, although in different ways. Day was a lifelong pacifist, and Weil, who had been a pacifist, briefly saw military action. Unlike most of their peers, both came to view their personal political experience and philosophy in spiritual terms. As adults both were strongly attracted to Catholicism, despite the deterrents presented by their upbringing and class. Day was baptized in the Catholic faith; Weil was not. Yet conventional religion did not by itself assuage their spiritual thirst. Throughout their maturity, both Day and Weil were solitary searchers. Day titled her autobiography *The Long Loneliness*. Coles remarks the existential nature of that loneliness (*Day*, 64) and also applies Day's phrase to Weil ("Mystery," 320). It is the quality of their loneliness that Coles explores in these companion volumes.

In the seven chapters of *Dorothy Day: A Radical Devotion*, Coles follows not only the shape of a life but also the shape of a vision. He begins with a biographical summary, "A Life Remembered," then expands Day's life and thought in chapters on her exacting, well-examined idealism, her conversion to Catholicism, her points of difference with the Church, her "localist politics," her daily life of prayer and service within a house of hospitality, and her "spiritual kin." The "life remembered" is chiefly Coles's recollection but also Day's own, often stated in her own words from her autobiographical works or from Coles's taped conversations with her. Coles knew Day for over 25 years (from 1952 until her death in 1980).

Dorothy Day weaves the intricate search for love and God that led Day to a unique blend of activism and faith. Like other of Coles's favorite subjects, for a long time she drifted, joining suffragettes and unionists and taking odd jobs. She was briefly married and from another relationship bore a daughter. Her child's baptism precipitated Day's own entrance into the Catholic Church. Then, with Peter Maurin, a Catholic lay brother, Day launched *The Catholic Worker* newspaper and the houses of hospitality where she strove to be " 'poor, chaste, and obedient' " (*Day*, 50). (A portrait of Peter Maurin is given in *A Spectacle Unto the World*.) Her conversion and what followed put an end to the " 'drifting on water' " that so vividly marked her earlier life (*Day*, 7). For nearly half a century, from 1933 to 1980, Dorothy Day lived and worked among the poorest, most destitute of Americans. At the same time she wrote articles for and published *The Catholic Worker*, a monthly socialist newspaper. Despite success, Day and the Catholic Worker movement remained modest and single-minded in their works. To her the Catholic Workers were best described by Paul's words, "fools for Christ's sake" (I Corinthians 4:10). Her political and religious views isolated her from other activists and her Church, from which she sought no official support. Although she could have had fame as a journalist and writer, she regarded service to the poor as her true vocation. That work, as she repeatedly reminds Coles, is for her own soul's sake, not for the sake of the needy. For Coles, Day's combination of radical politics and traditional faith represents the pastoral mode of existence at its best, as actually lived by one woman. Only Georges Bernanos's fictional country curé compares with Dorothy Day. She also had daily struggles with her own pride, the constant temptations to give up the work or (equally treacherous) to accept fame, and a thousand other insidious distractions—which struggles demonstrate to Coles that she also maintained the self-scrutiny necessary to keep the pastoral mode of service from becoming an empty routine.

There is a homeliness to *Dorothy Day* that is largely a result of the interplay between Coles, who appears as narrator and interlocutor, and his subject. This quality is the more remarkable because Day died in 1980, seven years before the book was published. The book re-creates conversations that had taken place over some years. The simplicity of the prose calls to mind Day's own journalism. There is little outright description, but the location forms a subtle backdrop. The two talk in St. Joseph's House in New York City, where the life of preparing soup, serving and talking with the guests, interacting with volunteers and full-time Catholic Workers, praying, and reading are ever in mind. Day's reflections, plus her readings from favorite passages of the Bible, novels, or even her own books, make up a good portion of the volume. Her ideas are deceptively simple. *Dorothy Day* elaborates them to give the reader background, then returns to her practical application, which embodies those ideas in everyday actions. For example, the chapter "Her Spiritual Kin" illustrates Day's sense of "comradeship" with the Catholic writer Ignazio Silone and likens her focus on love and community in *From Union Square to Rome* with Silone's novel *Bread and Wine* (*Day*, 146–47). Coles then turns back to Day's modest activities: "Companionship in its literal meaning is 'the sharing of bread,' and several times, as she contemplated a lunch scene at St. Joseph's House—people offering and receiving bread (and soup and coffee)—she mentioned *Bread and Wine* . . ." (147). The perspectives on "companionship" reverberate within this plain scene and recall how deeply the imagery of Christianity touches basic physical and emotional needs.

Coles is interested in the accommodations that any human being, and one who has clearly led a stormy life, makes to live a life of service and voluntary poverty. In Day he finds no pleasure in self-denial but instead gratitude for the ability to serve, which he associates with her being a convert rather than born in the faith (*Day*, xix). At the time of these interviews, Day was over 70, and she sees her life in retrospect—especially her early bohemian years. As a narrator with a presence in the text, Coles is very gentle with her, although at times slightly exasperated. For her part, Day is quick to note Coles's impatience or misguided attention. She turns him away from psychology back to matters of eternity—and the present, everyday matters of common concern, such as students that he has brought to work at Hampton House in Boston.

Small gestures, such as Day's hands holding or putting down a cup of tea, punctuate the dialogue. Indeed, the homely rituals of tea drinking mark shifts in the mood of both speakers. The focus on Day, with Coles as interlocutor, highlights the existential loneliness that he senses even as she speaks repeatedly of the community that defines her life—and indeed, is all about them. The intimacy of their conversations leaves that loneliness, and some of her mystery, untouched.

Simone Weil: A Modern Pilgrimage

The companion to *Dorothy Day* poses a very different problem of approach. Coles had obviously never met Simone Weil, who died in 1943. In fact, until *Simone Weil: A Modern Pilgrimage* (1987), Coles had not written a full-length work on a figure whom he did not personally know. However, as an undergraduate at Harvard he had become familiar with her work, which was still being discovered and translated, and in 1984 he published in *Yale Review* an essay titled "Simone Weil: The Mystery of Her Life." Like other readers who have found Weil an inspiring but difficult writer, whose thought and life are full of vexatious contradictions, Coles has a complex attitude toward Weil. At one time he felt "unstinting" admiration for her and nonetheless shame at her failings; later his veneration turned to "ironic affection" (*Weil*, xvii, xviii). The terms in which Coles describes his attitude toward Weil are both intimate and mythical. For Coles the writing of *Simone Weil* is "a chance to affirm an old love and take on a few genuine demons" (xviii). Indeed, his relationship with this ghostly personage is something like a man with a demon lover. He has loved—and been shamed and angered—by her for being like himself, better than he is, and worse. He freely acknowledges her great power, her very great frailty, indeed her ordinariness, yet he is still amazed at his inability to quite understand her.

In a subdued way, Coles's struggle with Weil's life and ideas permeates *Simone Weil*. The result has an intimacy something like that achieved in *Dorothy Day*, while recognizing the distance between the contemporary view of Weil and what she might have known and felt. Like *Dorothy Day*, *Simone Weil* contains seven chapters. The first summarizes Weil's life, and with characteristic irony, begins with her much-remarked-on death. Into this outline are woven the major moral, political, and spiritual questions of her thought as well as some historical and cultural background. The middle chapters directly confront thorny issues of Weil's life. The chapter titles reflect this confrontation and emphasize Weil's singularity: "Her Hunger," "Her Jewishness," "Her Political Life," and "Her Moral Loneliness." The final chapter, "Idolatry and the Intellectuals," is reminiscent of the conclusion of *Flannery O'Connor's South*.

During the 1930s and early 1940s, Simone Weil, a Frenchwoman, a brilliant student of philosophy and later a teacher, worked in factories and on farms, joining a number of radical causes. At first a pacifist, she joined the communists in the Spanish civil war and for a short time was at the front. She traveled in Europe and briefly to the United States. From her observations she wrote forcefully on political theory (especially the tyranny of modern states, as cited in *The Political Life of Children*) and moral action; later she wrote as well on her religious experiences. Yet during her lifetime these writings were mainly unpublished, gathered in letters and her private notebooks. They had their impact only after Weil's puzzling death at the age of 34, of tuberculosis compounded by her refusal of food.

The biographical sketch stresses that Weil was neither saint nor victim. It emphasizes how much she saw of life—and how much more she tried to see despite the risks. Weil is characterized as "forever on the move, morally and spiritually and politically and culturally" (*Weil*, 5), making a lifelong, restless pilgrimage. As a teacher in the French national system, she was transferred from school to school because of her activism. In 1940 she found that because she was Jewish, the anti-Semitic Vichy government barred her from teaching. Her family emigrated in 1942, and Weil never returned to France, although she tried. With her family she spent two weeks in a Libyan refugee camp. She lived for several months in the United States, left her family to sail to London, and spent her last months as a tuberculosis patient there, still trying to join the Resistance.

Quotations from Weil's writing help to personalize the work, but another strategy, uniquely Coles's, affords an even more immediate sense of dialogue in the book. Weil is dead, but he can speak with others about her. These are two of Weil's contemporaries, her brother André Weil, whom Coles had met, and most important, Coles's mentor and friend, the psychoanalyst Anna Freud. The brother's remarks, although limited, make for a quiet sense of the "real" Simone Weil. Anna Freud, who never met Weil, is nonetheless a significant presence in the book. Miss Freud becomes a living voice from the times that Weil endured and the necessary other with whom Coles can try to resolve some of the questions he has about Weil. As in *Dorothy Day*, Coles is a presence, and in dialogue with Anna Freud, he creates colloquy, the encounter through which the spiritual searching and questioning occur.

Anna Freud's knowledge of the state of the psychoanalytic art in the 1940s allows for many interesting exchanges on the "vexing" problems of Weil's self-starvation, her death, and her anti-Semitism ("Mystery," 318). However, Miss Freud's presence is not simply as psychiatric expert. She is introduced at once, setting in motion an intricate skein of themes and implied comparisons. Born in Austria, Anna Freud was older than Weil by 14 years, but a European and a near contemporary. Miss Freud was also a well-educated professional woman, of Jewish but secular parents. Both women lived in exile in England during World War II. Their lives did not touch. In her brief, heart-wrenching memories of 1943, the year that Weil died, Miss Freud gives a sense of what London was then like, what a European woman of Weil's background, intellect, and emotional strength might experience in the political and social turmoil of the 1930s and 1940s (*Weil*, 5). Emotionally, Miss Freud's words not only evoke the dark days of Hitler but also suggest that persons of immense talent and achievement, including the doctors who treated Weil, were helpless in their supposed expertise. People drew into themselves. To be honest with oneself was to recognize one's limits to act, despite one's stated ethics. In such circumstances Weil strove with her illness, her beliefs, and her doctors in a London hospital. Through Anna Freud's general description of the war, Weil's decision to assist her own death is given a horrific context. In later exchanges, they debate but generally agree, although Miss Freud is more pragmatic than Coles, and more secular. Above all, the conversations between Miss Freud and Coles give *Simone Weil* some of the dramatic quality that *Dorothy Day* has.

"Her Hunger" and "Her Jewishness" take up two important issues that have been demons for Coles when students ask him about Weil: Why did she refuse food when she was ill? Was she an anorexic suicide, as the death-certificate given by her London doctors reads? And why did Weil write the Vichy authorities to repudiate her Jewishness, when she patently despised that government and the Nazis who installed it? "Her Hunger" is a serious exploration of the facts of Weil's death and the facets of her life—her morality, political sympathies, religious beliefs, and not least, her lifelong attitudes toward food—that bear on her death. The essay treats matters of faith and morality together with psychological tendencies. In concluding that Weil was not subject to *anorexia nervosa*, Coles draws on his own clinical observations, the vast experience of Anna Freud, and even nineteenth-century literature (*Weil*, 27). The discussion is earnest but lightened by some humor. Weil's death retains some of its mystery, but Coles gives it perspective.

"Her Jewishness" is the second demon Coles faces. Sadly, Weil, who had always held her Jewish heritage in light regard, crassly and without coercion renounced it to public authorities. For Coles, her renunciation seems to contradict her usual ability to fathom complex moral questions and her customary willingness to risk her livelihood and life for the sake of ethical action. Those failures have angered, not to say mortified, countless readers of Weil, and the essay explores them in detail. In his fieldwork, Coles has seen many other instances of self-hatred, of racism towards one's own race. He compares Weil's self-justifying stance at length with that of Jimmy, a gifted black Boston schoolchild. Jimmy lived to recognize his youthful self-hatred; Weil did not (*Weil*, 52–57). His own conflicted religious and cultural background, Christian and Jewish, makes Coles a credible analyst of Weil. The essay sketches what Weil, a student of many cultures, seemed to know, understand, and perhaps misunderstand about Judaism.

Weil's racism is complicated by the nature of her spirituality. Her self-denial and her insistence on the possibility of seeing and knowing God are consistent with Christian doctrine but less so with Judaism. "Her Jewishness" warmly describes the worldly and family-based spirituality that Judaism embraces, anticipating similar discussions in *The Spiritual Life of Children* (*Weil*, 59). Weil rejected this aspect of her religious heritage; Coles speculates that she knew that she could not fulfill Jewish religious obligations that included marriage and family and that Judaism could not satisfy her own highly individual spiritual nature: ". . . [S]he may have known full well that Judaism is a religion *of this earth*, a religion which takes open and honest stock of the here and now and urges its adherents to engage themselves in that here and now fully and vigorously, as honorably as their ability allows them to. Judaism is not a penitential religion or an immediately messianic one; it dedicates itself to each day's, each year's personal and ethical responsibilities" (*Weil*, 59).

"Her Political Life" and "Her Moral Loneliness" subject her political writing and acts to balanced scrutiny, noting her weaknesses—a certain utopian tendency, for example—as well as her strengths, such as the documentary, activist purpose for keeping records of her millwork and soldiering (68). It is important for Coles that Weil saw cruelty and injustice among radical groups as well as state bureaucrats. These views, which Weil shared with Orwell, Agee, and other early twentieth-century documentary writers, also distinguish Coles from many later progressives and liberals. He once borrowed a phrase from Irving Howe to describe this isolated political and moral existence: "She, too, belonged to the 'homeless left,'. . ." ("Mystery," 320). Coles also regards himself as a member of the homeless left.

"A Radical Grace" examines Weil's religious writings, known today as the collections entitled *Waiting for God* and *Gravity and Grace*. The essay focuses on Weil's strong will and her dramatic experiences of faith during the last five years of her life. To elucidate these mystical and at times sensual or violent accounts, Coles examines factors like her migraine headaches, her chastity, and her theory of "decreation." As in *Flannery O'Connor's South*, he enlists the aid of an echoing voice, a former prostitute of Rio de Janeiro (*Weil*, 126–29). Weil and the *favelado* woman, who is dying of cancer, both conceive of Jesus in erotic terms, a common theme for Christian mystics like St. John of the Cross. Coles thinks Weil "fell in love with Jesus" (119). The final chapter, "Idolatry and the Intellectuals," places Weil "squarely in a certain tradition, that of intellectual anti-intellectualism," with O'Connor, William Carlos Williams, Agee, and Orwell (139). Putting this chapter last, rather than the more spiritual "A Radical Grace," brings Weil's legacy up to our time and back to this world. The end of "Idolatry and the Intellectuals" shifts disarmingly from this mysterious Frenchwoman to a real figure in Coles's life, an American with thoroughly secular values, his father Philip Coles. A chemical engineer, Coles's father believed in science and progress, only to see the promises shattered (152). Simone Weil is simply offered as a forerunner, one who has gone before on this "modern pilgrimage": "[H]er journey is ours" (152). The conclusion, lushly phrased but plain in imagery, paints Weil as a restless figure "glad to be hurrying home" to God (153). Through an odd, homely connection with his father, Weil's strangeness becomes familiar and human.

Harvard Diary

Coles's next book-length work on religion departs from the collaborative approach altogether. The 50-odd essays in *Harvard Diary: Reflections on the Sacred and the Secular* (1989) were originally published between 1981 and 1988 as columns in *New Oxford Review*, a neoconservative Catholic magazine (Rocca 40; *Diary*, 4). In his previous writing on religion, Coles has presented himself as a questioner with certain types of knowledge, or a supplicant, not a moral authority. Here, maintaining the autobiographical impulse, Coles names the column a "diary." He sees it in the tradition of George Orwell's "London Letters" in *Partisan Review* as well as part of a family tradition of reflective letter writing (*Diary*, 1–2). The subjects of these columns, as well as Coles's speaking about his beliefs in his own voice, recall *The Geography of Faith*. But *Harvard Diary* is somewhat more at ease in publicly expressing aspects of faith than was *Geography*. In these short essays Coles speaks as one of the flock, castigating what is outside the fold. The theme is that we live in a "grimly secular society" (*Diary*, 84). In particular, social science is "a pagan faith," whose instruments he once "venerated," but no longer (5).

The essays are arranged chronologically, as they originally appeared in *New Oxford Review*. These are sometimes loosely grouped, often indicated by like titles. For example, an early column, "Spiritual Kinship," concerns students (and others) in whom Coles has discovered this kind of companionship. The essay begins a series on other spiritual kin: Simone Weil, Dietrich Bonhoeffer, a New Mexican grandmother, children in Belfast, Georges Bernanos, Joshua Travis (an Alabama tenant farmer), Dorothy Day, and several others. The volume is interesting for its essays on controversial social questions like abortion, teenage pregnancy, homosexuality, women's rights, and pornography. Many pieces cross the territory between religion, sociology, politics, and moral action. For example, there are discussions of liberation theology, Latin American politics, and the international fieldwork that would become *The Moral Life of Children*, *The Political Life of Children*, and *The Spiritual Life of Children*. Ample energy is spent on one special problem within this shared territory, psychiatry. There are also essays on traditional religious subjects like sin, grace, forgiveness, and aspects of the life of Christ, as well as contemporary issues like voluntary poverty.

Coles's favorite religious and literary writers are sketched, with an emphasis on matters of faith. He deals with writers whose faith was prominent in their lives, such as Tolstoy, and also with those who had a less obvious "religious sensibility," like Agee, or who scoffed at religion, like William Carlos Williams. A number of essays examine figures that Coles has treated only glancingly in other books, like Edith Stein, Thomas Merton, Ignazio Silone, Reinhold Niebuhr, and Paul Tillich. Whenever possible, Coles draws on the experiences and voices of people that he has known: children, mothers, rich people and poor. Another prominent set of voices is those of college students. Like *The Call of Stories*, *Harvard Diary* is situated in Coles's everyday life as a teacher at

Harvard College. Some of the ethical discussions arise from a seemingly casual meeting with a student over a paper or an incident that she or he wishes to discuss. These carry him into areas like sexual harassment as well as the greed that seemed to characterize the 1980s.

The opinions expressed in these diary "entries" vary along the political and religious spectrum, but many of them are thoroughly conservative. Coles sees himself as a political liberal but a cultural conservative (*Times*, 72; *Diary*, 200). His fieldwork has led him to hold a strong notion of family, which may be the sole earthly good for many people. All of his writing expresses a strong reverence for human life. These essays add a traditional religious perspective to social issues, many of them revolving around sexual behavior. According to *Harvard Diary*, the life of the spirit is clouded or impeded by the very real needs of the body. For example, Coles relays his "mixed feelings" about abortion, but his experiences as a doctor and psychiatrist, along with his personal beliefs, cause him to deplore it and its widespread availability: "Abortion, then, is an aspect of our utter sinfulness toward ourselves, toward others."[4] Coles takes a tolerant view of homosexuality, which is not a matter of "will," as some conservatives would have it, but an existential condition and as far as we know a psychological fact. Having argued for understanding homosexuals, he has moral reservations about some kinds of sexual behavior and no sympathy for gay activism (*Diary*, 83).

Politically, he explores the tangled history of the United States and Nicaragua to show the inconsistencies, if not outright lies, in connecting a rich nation's foreign policy with the promotion of Christianity. When he and two of his sons visited, poor Nicaraguans spoke forcefully about their contradictory loyalties to both the Sandinistas and the Church. In hewing his own line between traditional faith and democratic social reform, Coles looks to those he has most admired, especially Simone Weil, Georges Bernanos, and François Mauriac. He invokes them directly in an autobiographical piece, "On Politics," near the conclusion of *Harvard Diary* (200).

Language is another major theme. From the start the collection professes "a preference for a biblical rather than sociological language" ("Remembering Dorothy Day," *Diary*, 5). Thus many ordinary words are put into quotation marks to emphasize them or call their meanings into question. This technique is often a feature of Coles's style, but the brief essays make it prominent in *Harvard Diary*, where it becomes the theme of several columns. For example, "Psychiatric Stations of the Cross" deplores the use of psychological terms as substitutes for the traditional language of Christian faith. In Coles's eyes, the American clergy has granted psychiatry an "intellectual, and yes, moral authority" to the detriment of the Church's sacramental vision (11). The same theme surfaces in other essays, as the jargon of pastoral counseling is labeled "the junk talk of the social sciences" (200). In addition to words used as words, the style makes heavy use of parentheses and punctuation for ironic effect, which results in a somewhat mannered style. In particular, the opening of "Orwell's Decency" and portions of "James Agee's Religious Sensibility" show this tendency.

Occasionally, the religious language can be awkward and sentimental. At one point death is mentioned twice, as if the reader will not get the point: "after he left us (was called from us)" (*Diary*, 56). The dual reference underscores the euphemisms rather than the spiritual journey (56). Other essays show a preacherly mastery of rhyme and puns. For example, in "Mystery and Flannery O'Connor," Coles explains O'Connor's attitude toward new knowledge: "She only wanted us to understand where the water's edge begins—at what point we are not exploring, but rather, imploring in our own name" (15). Like *Irony in the Mind's Life*, *Walker Percy*, and *Flannery O'Connor's South*, *Harvard Diary* has its share of miniature sermons. The earlier essays occasionally have a strident, defensive tone that fades in the later columns, which nonetheless maintain a relentless solemnity. Overall, *Harvard Diary* is more hortatory than exploratory, more prophesying than pastoral. In tone the collection is "largely a jeremiad" (Rocca 40). The monologic voice and the brevity of the essays are mainly to blame. Thomas Molnar has noted that the "three-page tributes are too short to allow any real probing."[5] At times Coles re-creates the dialogic voice that he is more at ease with. Some of the essays, whether created "with" the voice of a student or a Managuan woman or Paul Tillich or Ruby Bridges or one of Coles's sons, tell simple but intricate stories of morality and faith battling with psychology. Coles can be a good preacher, and *Harvard Diary*, although sometimes brittle and doctrinaire, tries to maintain the perspective of his other works.

The Call of Service

At first glance *The Call of Service: A Witness to Idealism* (1993) seems like anything other than what it is. It certainly seems to be an extension of *The Call of Stories*, a way to keep that energy going—or a way to do for voluntary service what *The Call of Stories* did more successfully for literature, reclaiming social action as a foundation of liberal thought. It is also yet another rumination over Coles's favorite themes and writers, with service perhaps just floated to the top of the mixture. (The book's footnotes refer mainly to Coles's own works, as Robert A. Sirico has noted.)[6] It is oral history, even more desultory and laxly structured than others of Coles's books—and on occasion boring. But *The Call of Service* is at bottom none of these. What it is is a kind of promise kept to Dorothy Day, to whom the book is dedicated. Nor is it too much to call it an act of devotion.

Its eight chapters, punctuated by two "interludes," adapt the structure of *The Call of Stories*. The book, which documents "the subjectivity, the phenomenology of service" (*Service*, xxiv), defines what service is, what people get out of it, what problems they encounter, and what in a larger psychological and social sense service represents. Much of the volume draws on Coles's teaching of a course called "Community Service" and his mentoring (the word and concept are carefully discussed in one chapter) of students who have chosen to work with children. However, the service of older citizens—in schools, hospitals, shelters, and even a prison—is integral. With its marrying of readings to "doing" service, it can and should serve as a textbook for those who are engaged in or want to begin volunteering. The early chapters, especially "Kinds of Service," "Satisfactions," and "Hazards," suffer from being organized into happenstance catalogues. For example, "Kinds of Service" concludes with military service, whereas the rest of the book concerns mainly voluntary, unpaid community work. It is as if, in presenting a kind of textbook about service, Coles feels an obligation to acknowledge forms that he cannot easily endorse. The strength of *The Call of Service* is not in its structure but in individuals' stories, which gradually body forth a complex set of psychological, philosophical, and religious ideas about good works.

These stories are told as oral histories, slowly recounted in the (edited) words of various speakers. The form stays close to conversation and indeed tends to downplay drama. Drama there is, as one speaker, Alice, tells a humorous but startling tale of being jailed for her civil rights work; as another civil rights worker, Alan, reflects on his conversations with a tenant farmer about the man's horse; as Alex, a student of Coles's, tells of a young man dying of a gunshot wound in a Boston emergency room; as Frank Donovan, a Catholic Worker, singles out the story of one man at the hospitality house. Dorothy Day's crusty, somewhat enigmatic presence is close by, in Coles's and Donovan's reminiscences of her. Coles tells many other personal stories. The examples of young people's teaching and mentoring must be accompanied by some analysis, since Coles is often in the position of assisting those mentoring, but they too are full of a quiet drama. Great emotion is held in check by the matter-of-fact monologues and the no-nonsense brusqueness of several of the speakers, especially the older ones. More than his other works, *The Call of Service* deals with urban poverty, gangs, abuse, alcoholism, addiction, and homelessness. Schools and hospitals are a mainstay, although some areas remain untouched; for example, none of these speakers works with Acquired Immune Deficiency Syndrome (AIDS) patients.

The Call of Service gathers strength as it proceeds. Inevitably Coles asks himself why people do voluntary service. The stories and the extremely gentle analyses begin to coalesce in the first interlude, "Mentoring," which explores that concept in the form of a conversation with Anna Freud. By the second interlude, "What They Mean to Us," several answers have surfaced, all complex, none definitive, but a persuasive cluster. Miss Freud's " 'altruistic surrender' " and Coles's notion of "moral provocateur" are teased out of several stories, as adults reflect on possible key events or mentors of their youth and in turn recount complicated stories of working with children on their own (*Service*, 202, 253). The images are homely but profound: hands, companions at table, in one instance a telescope that enables a boy and his young mentor to " 'get a bigger view of life' " (113). *The Call of Service* succeeds in suggesting how, person by person, generations pass on their hopes and in turn learn from the new: "Mentoring as one person handing another along until the moment that allows both of them together to envision possibilities hitherto out of sight" (114). It gives a rare glimpse at the ideal society that Coles, with Day, can envision, a society that takes equality before God to heart. That is expressed not in any mass view of humanity, but in one-to-one conversation, in mundane activities like breaking bread and simple talk in which two people can occasionally forget themselves and reach toward each other (242). Encouraging well-off citizens to engage in voluntary service is one means for them to treat other citizens on something like an equal footing, although there are many variations on that encounter. Finally, service is an act of faith, in which the "call toward others" is also "a call inward, a call toward oneself, a call that is a reminder: 'Watchman, what of the night?' " (284). The homely talk of *The Call of Service* is like that of *Dorothy Day*, and for the same reason. In form as well as substance it foregrounds the pastoral mode of faith prized by the "older idealism" of Day and others (231).

Many readers will find that *The Call of Service* teeters on the brink of sentimentality or maybe even tumbles into that chasm. "Cloying and frustrating" is Francine du Plessix Gray's judgment.[7] Others will be refreshed by its plain treatment of ordinary life and sadness. Elliot Robins asserts that Coles "eschews sentimentality" and rightly "avoids presenting a grand theory of service."[8] I myself first tried to read *The Call of Service* during long hours in a hospital's intensive care unit waiting room. As hours turned to days, I gave up trying to read; the following year, I was finally turning the pages of the "Epilogue," only to be drawn away to the telephone to hear that my partner's father had died. Read in such circumstances, the narratives of *The Call of Service* seem bracing.

Conclusion

Rather than look directly inward, the narrator in these works on spirituality and religion usually engages another person in discursive reflection or colloquy. Coles and his spiritual confidant each speak at length and take direction from the other. *The Geography of Faith* is literally composed of conversations between Berrigan and Coles. In *Dorothy Day* and *Simone Weil* collaborative forms are devised from traditional biographical materials. One has only to compare the more conventional essay about Dorothy Day in *A Spectacle Unto the World* to see how different the later "collaborative" portrait is. In *Harvard Diary*, the lack of another voice makes for occasional sermonizing, although sometimes Coles re-creates dialogue. The parallel in purpose and method with his research is clear, and indeed the final volume of Coles's decades of fieldwork, *Spiritual Life* (1990), culminates this dialogue. *The Call of Service* returns to the collaborative mode. The works on religion also highlight the spiritual jeopardy of the solitary mind. Coles's own meditations, if left unchecked, gnaw at his own failures and amount to another kind of self-absorption, as Rocca has noticed (41). As a spiritual help, the interlocutor's words on faith and morality urge Coles not so much to talk as to experience a moment of self-awareness. Through this Marcelian act of fidelity, a shared commitment with another speaker, Coles and his readers can come closer to God. Coles's writing about spirituality is most persuasive when he mines the special form of colloquy that he has invented for his biographies as well as his research, a form that suits his understanding of the quest for transcendence as an encounter between two beings.

Conclusion

In a sense, judging Robert Coles simply by his writing misses the point. Writing is a means to an end, to making changes in oneself and the world. Since the 1970s, Coles's teaching of the humanities, art, and community service has carried on beside and beyond his research and publications. Bruce A. Ronda has evaluated Coles's writing as the expression of his life as an analyst and activist as well as a writer. But Coles has generated an immense body of writing, including books, book reviews, articles, and prefaces to others' books. He and Jane Hallowell Coles have chosen to give many primary materials—notes, tape transcripts, and children's drawings—to the University of North Carolina at Chapel Hill. Coles is undeniably a writer.

I have described two main projects: his research with children and adults plus an intellectual inquiry into the means by which to judge his research. The second project, which distinguishes him from writers like Studs Terkel and Oscar Lewis, has been Coles's exploration of the tensions among the claims of the scientist, the artist, and the pilgrim. Despite his disdain for intellectual specialists, Coles's writing from *Erik H. Erikson* and *Irony in the Mind's Life* onward shows him keenly aware of others' thought and also forging his own intellectual contribution across the bounds of social science, literature, and moral philosophy. Within these works is also a sense of legacy, so that future readers can understand his work. Certainly since 1977, when *Privileged Ones* was published, Coles has devoted himself to teaching new generations, mainly students at elite colleges, aiming to give them his ethical, personal awareness of class and race.

Coles gradually pulled the strands of his thinking together into a unique, increasingly literary form. Around 1980, with the publication of *Flannery O'Connor's South*, the technique of counterpointing famous writers' words with the echoing voices of poor or marginalized speakers reached maturity. The mid-1980s saw the publication of his first "colloquy" biographies—of Dorothy Day and Simone Weil. Both of these approaches—literary versions of the Marcelian encounter—have ethical implications. The first crosses class lines, violating the usually undisturbed voices of the famous and intellectually powerful. The second— the colloquy or "collaborative" biography—treats the writer not only as part of the subject but also as exposed or subject to moral influence by the biographee. *The Call of Stories*, one of Coles's most personal works, integrates storytelling and storylistening, which are Coles's extrapolations from Marcel. In a sense storytelling and storylistening are a literary demonstration of the mutuality of influence that Marcel sought in committed encounters.

The mid-twentieth century moral documentary tradition with which Coles allies himself probably offers the most points of comparison. Like George Orwell, who made being a factotum of the British Empire into an opportunity to study political language, Coles has made being an American specialist a lifelong opportunity to deplore the jargon and moral inadequacy of well-meaning professionals. Coles has the social conscience of Orwell and James Agee as well as their modernist sense of a core self and the writer's moral authority. Part of Agee's and Orwell's authority derives from their witness to human experience that otherwise would not be told. Although they knew the ironies of the observer's role, their witness still takes its value from the assumption that no one speaks for the poor or oppressed. Coles has seen that bias uncovered. Poor children will always need an adult voice; however, some poor people and members of marginalized cultures can and increasingly do speak for themselves. In many ways, like the technique of the echoing voices, Coles has striven to confront such assumptions. Realizing how description can imply judgment, he increases his distance from his speakers. But he cannot escape the fact that he interprets what his speakers tell him. In another way, his turn toward the inward call may be a response to the contradictions of being a privileged observer.

The reader who expects to find the concrete detail of an Orwell, Agee, or William Carlos Williams may be surprised at Coles's prose. His writing seems irrevocably marked by his psychoanalytic training, with its model of the clinical encounter and certain (but not all) methods of oral history. He focuses on speech, that is, the report of the subject (or patient or, ideally, interlocutor) as the key to reality. Reality consists of the mind plus its interactions with its circumstances and with other minds. People are described in their own terms, with very little physical depiction except of landscapes. For a writer so taken with documentary photography and art history, this omission may seem odd. However, what Coles seeks to document is not the physical reality but the qualities of mind he encounters. Thus his writing describes children's art, which is akin to their speech: Both portray their worlds as they see them. Only late in his career has he been able to pull these drawings away from his method, away from their mediating status and into focus as things themselves.

Future studies might well examine Coles's writing in terms of medical writing and case study or as influenced by particular philosophers and novelists such as Walker Percy. They might look at the confluence of his one-on-one psychoanalytic training with the oral heritage of sermons and storytelling, the stuff of his years of listening. While I have joined with other commentators like Bruce Ronda in viewing Coles in the light of Christian tradition, I also think that he has been more than a little influenced by Judaism, especially in his honoring of parents and mentors and his implicit recognition of the duty of the righteous man. There is much to consider in his particular blending of both traditions. Ronda has already called for a feminist critique (Ronda 1989, 140). Even after *Women of Crisis* and several biographies about celebrated women, Coles's writing seems to have a curious, not to say traditional, division of labor between genders that bears more scrutiny. Too, he should be considered alongside other late-twentieth-century social critics, especially liberal critics of education.

Scholars might also regard his work as a way to challenge current characterizations of nonfiction, which tend to divide into specialist scholarship, popularizations or literary treatments of that scholarship, and journalism. Each of these broad categories abdicates the high modernist tradition in which the artist and scientist comprehend and interpret culture. But rather than allude to an older modernism—the circumstances of which cannot be reproduced in the late days of the twentieth century—we should examine the fissures and contradictions that Coles's work points out. It would be wrong to reduce Coles's writing to the activities of a literarily talented psychiatric specialist who embraces an outmoded or naive intellectual tradition. The tension in Coles's writing embodies the contradictions: The scientist is suspect precisely because of his specialization, and the artist can likewise become a mere aesthetic specialist. It is the pilgrim, the seeker, who (with the insights of the other two) has any hope of traversing the mental but often literally physical boundaries of academic privilege and literary genre, although she too is subject to living on a private intellectual reserve. There is a romantic nostalgia in Coles for a wholeness of intellectual and moral life, but he has not shirked the task of reporting the fissures; devising thoughtful, unfaddish ways to instill moral awareness; and insisting on an open conduit between writing and action, that is, between the prophetic and the pastoral modes of life.

Readers who wish to become familiar with Coles may be intimidated by the sheer number and length of his books. However, most of Coles's writing is very accessible. In general the new reader should be aware that works published after 1977 tend to be shorter and thus somewhat more inviting than the earlier research. They also benefit from the literary experimentation that resulted from Coles's study of Native Americans and his collaboration with photographer Alex Harris. *The Call of Stories* is in my view the best overall introduction to Robert Coles's work. Compact, graceful, and beautifully structured, it thoroughly integrates his research with his literary and ethical passions. It is also his major statement of "antitheory theory" and marks the apotheosis of his bumbling researcher's persona. This more relaxed but dynamic persona attains the humor of wisdom, with the ability to leave his ambivalence alone and not to moralize his failures.

With their third-person point of view and life-stories that develop over years, the volumes that Jane Hallowell Coles coauthored, *Women of Crisis I* and *Women of Crisis II*, most closely resemble fiction. *Eskimos, Chicanos, Indians* also has a fictional sensibility, though in a more diffuse format. The volumes in the Radcliffe Biography Series, such as *Dorothy Day*, are eminently accessible and offer Coles's uniquely collaborative approach to biography. Although *Children of Crisis* is massive, readers who dip into the narratives of any of the five volumes will find riveting stories and subtle insights. I recommend the second volume, *Migrants, Sharecroppers, Mountaineers*. A quarter century after its original publication, it remains as startling as ever, and it is in many instances as true today as it was in 1971. *Courage and Fear* also retains its drama and relevance. There is no better way to understand the heroism of Ruby Bridges and the impact of desegregation or the way that small details construct racism than to read Section Two of the first volume of *Children of Crisis*. The staccato reportage of *Farewell to the South* also recreates those times.

In another vein, the chapters "Comfortable, Comfortable Places" and "Entitlement" plus the individual narratives of *Privileged Ones* offer a fascinating, often chilling portrait of the life that is held up as an ideal in American society. *The Political Life of Children* combines an unusually sharp focus with psychological and sociological insight. In addition to the sometimes dramatic stories of children's perceptions of political strife, the chapter "Homeland" demonstrates Coles at his best, weaving direct observation into an easily grasped concept of socialization. *The Spiritual Life of Children* is the culmination of Coles's research with children as well as a polished treatment of his religious interests. It also brings his interpretation of children's drawings to a new level of insight, and for many it will be the logical choice after *The Call of Stories*. Readers drawn to literary criticism might look at *Flannery O'Connor's South* whereas those with an interest in photography should certainly read Coles's biographical essay in *Dorothea Lange*. Collections such as *A Robert Coles Omnibus* (which includes *Times of Surrender* and *That Red Wheelbarrow*) offer an attractive way to approach Coles through short essays.[1] However, for me Coles's best writing requires ample space. His themes slowly bubble up through what seem to be desultory, even rambling, conversations with children and adults.

For 30 years Coles has plied the same themes. Like the dyer's hand, his writing has deepened its hues so that its sources are now clearer than ever. He treats "a respect for narrative as everyone's rock-bottom capacity, but also as the universal gift, to be shared with others" (*Stories*, 30). For him the reciprocal telling of and listening to stories is one of humanity's main sources of spiritual renewal.

Notes and References

Chapter One

1. Robert Coles, *The South Goes North*, vol. 3 of *Children of Crisis* (Boston: Atlantic-Little, Brown, 1971), 38; hereafter cited in the text as *South*.

2. Robert Coles, *The Mind's Fate: Ways of Seeing Psychiatry and Psycho-analysis* (Boston: Atlantic-Little, Brown, 1975), 135; hereafter cited in the text as *Fate*.

3. "Sketches of the Winners of the 57th Pulitzer Prizes in Journalism and the Arts," *New York Times*, 8 May 1973, 32; Anne Janette Johnson, "Coles, Robert (Martin) 1929 –," *Contemporary Authors*, New Revision Series, vol. 32 (Detroit: Gale Research, 1991), 89 –91; hereafter cited in the text as *Authors*.

4. Bruce A. Ronda, *Intellect and Spirit: The Life and Work of Robert Coles* (New York: Continuum, 1989), 21; hereafter cited in the text. Also see Robert Coles, "The End of the Affair," *Katallagete* 4 (1972): 47 –49; hereafter cited in the text as "End." Also see *South*, 43 –44.

5. Jay Woodruff, "Robert Coles: Don't Worry, Dad," in *A Piece of Work: Five Writers Discuss Their Revisions*, ed. Jay Woodruff (Iowa City: University of Iowa Press, 1993), 123; hereafter cited in the text.

6. Robert Coles, *The Call of Stories: Teaching and the Moral Imagination* (Boston: Houghton Mifflin, Peter Davison, 1989), xiv; hereafter cited in the text as *Stories*.

7. Robert Coles, *Irony in the Mind's Life: Essays on Novels by James Agee, Elizabeth Bowen, and George Eliot* (Charlottesville: University Press of Virginia, 1974), vii; hereafter cited in the text as *Irony*. See also the following: Woodruff, 122; and Jay Woodruff and Sarah Carew Woodruff, eds., *Conversations with Robert Coles* (Jackson: University Press of Mississippi, 1992), xvii; hereafter cited in the text as Woodruff and Woodruff.

8. "Shadowing Binx," in *That Red Wheelbarrow: Selected Literary Essays by Robert Coles* (Iowa City: University of Iowa Press, 1988), 100; hereafter cited in the text as "Binx."

9. Erik H. Erikson, *Childhood and Society*, 2d ed. (New York: W. W. Norton, 1963), 262– 63.

10. Robert Coles, *Dorothy Day: A Radical Devotion* (Reading, Mass.: Addison-Wesley, 1987), xv, xviii; hereafter cited in the text as *Day*.

11. Robert Coles, "Remembering Reinhold Niebuhr," in *Harvard Diary: Reflections on the Sacred and the Secular* (New York: Crossroad, 1989), 152; here-after cited in the text as "Niebuhr" and *Diary*.

12.   Robert Coles, *William Carlos Williams: The Knack of Survival in America* (New Brunswick, N.J.: Rutgers University Press, 1975), xiv; hereafter cited in the text as *Williams*. Also see "Binx," 101.

13.   Robert Coles, *Children of Crisis: A Study of Courage and Fear*, vol. 1 of *Children of Crisis* (Boston: Atlantic-Little, Brown, 1967), vii; hereafter cited in the text as *Courage*. See also "Binx," 154.

14.   Robert Coles, *Walker Percy: An American Search* (Boston: Atlantic-Little, Brown, 1978), xi; hereafter cited in the text as *Percy*.

15.   "Simone Weil: The Mystery of Her Life," *Yale Review* 73 (Autumn 1984): 309–15; hereafter cited in the text as "Mystery." See also *Percy*, xi.

16.   Robert Coles, *Farewell to the South* (Boston: Atlantic-Little, Brown, 1972), 365; hereafter cited in the text as *Farewell*.

17.   Robert Coles, "The Inexplicable Prayers of Ruby Bridges," *Christianity Today* (9 August 1985): 17–18 (17–20); Kim Hubbard, "After 30 Years Plumbing Children's Hearts and Minds, Robert Coles Writes an End to His Life's Greatest Chapters," *People Weekly* (24 December 1990): 86; hereafter cited in the text.

18.   Robert Coles, *The Political Life of Children* (Boston: Houghton Mifflin, 1986), 10; hereafter cited in the text as *Political Life*.

19.   Robert Coles, with Jon Erikson, photographer, *A Spectacle Unto the World: The Catholic Worker Movement* (New York: Viking, 1973), 69; hereafter cited in the text as *Spectacle*.

20.   Robert Coles, *Erik H. Erikson: The Growth of His Work* (Boston: Atlantic-Little, Brown, 1970), xv; hereafter cited in the text as *Erikson*.

21.   The essay, "Serpents and Doves: Nonviolent Youth in the South," is reprinted in *Farewell*.

22.   Robert Coles, *Eskimos, Chicanos, Indians*, vol. 4 of *Children of Crisis* (Boston: Little, Brown, 1977), xi; hereafter cited in the text as *Eskimos*; *Farewell*, 95.

23.   Daniel Berrigan and Robert Coles, *The Geography of Faith: Conversations between Daniel Berrigan, when Underground, and Robert Coles* (Boston: Beacon Press, 1971), 18, 21, 23; hereafter cited in the text as *Geography*; *New York Times*, 28 June 1970, sec. 6, and 12 August 1970, sec. 1, p. 1.

24.   Robert Coles, *Privileged Ones: The Well-off and the Rich in America*, vol. 5 of *Children of Crisis* (Boston: Atlantic-Little, Brown, 1977), 48; hereafter cited in the text as *Privileged*.

25.   *New York Times*, 25 March 1966, 4, and 7 June 1966, 1.

26.   Robert Coles, *The Moral Life of Children* (Boston: Houghton Mifflin, 1986), 11; hereafter cited in the text as *Moral Life*; Robert Coles, *The Spiritual Life of Children* (Boston: Houghton Mifflin, Peter Davison, 1990), xiii; hereafter cited in the text as *Spiritual Life*.

27.   Ellen K. Coughlin, "Scholars Use Film, Family Albums, and Oral History to Document the Lives of Ordinary People," *Chronicle of Higher Education* (21 February 1990): A6–7,12.

28.   David Hellerstein, "On Medicine and Literature: An Interview with Robert Coles," in Robert Coles, *Times of Surrender: Selected Essays* (Iowa City: University of Iowa Press, 1988), 60; hereafter cited in the text.

29.   I have omitted from discussion Coles's books for children, his coauthored books on child development, and his many articles and reviews; see the bibliography.

30.   Michael Wyschogrod, "Buber, Martin," in vol. 1 of *The Encyclopedia of Philosophy*, ed. Paul Edwards (New York: Macmillan and Free Press, 1967), 410; hereafter cited in the text.

31.   *Merriam Webster's Collegiate Dictionary*, 10th ed. (Springfield, Mass.: Merriam-Webster, 1993).

32.   Samuel McMurray Keen, "Marcel, Gabriel," in vol. 4 of *The Encyclopedia of Philosophy*, ed. Paul Edwards (New York: Macmillan and Free Press, 1967), 154; hereafter cited in the text.

33.   Robert Coles, *Anna Freud: The Dream of Psychoanalysis* (Reading, Mass.: Addison-Wesley, 1992), 68; hereafter cited in the text as *Anna Freud*.

34.   Robert Coles, *Simone Weil: A Modern Pilgrimage* (Reading, Mass.: Addison-Wesley, 1987), xix; hereafter cited in the text as *Weil*.

35.   Lynne V. Cheney, "A Conversation with Robert Coles," in Woodruff and Woodruff, 220; hereafter cited in the text.

36.   Robert Coles, *The Call of Service: A Witness to Idealism* (Boston: Houghton Mifflin, 1993), 33–67; hereafter cited in the text as *Service*.

Chapter Two

1.   George Eliot, *Middlemarch*, ed. Gordon S. Haight (Boston: Houghton Mifflin, Riverside Press, 1956), 607; quoted in *Irony*, xii.

2.   George Abbott White, "Clinical Approaches to Biography: The High Price of Mixed Truth," review of *The Mind's Fate* and *Irony in the Mind's Life*, *Sewanee Review* (Spring 1977): 331; hereafter cited in the text.

3.   David Elkind, review of *Erik H. Erikson*, *Saturday Review* (16 January 1971): 52; hereafter cited in the text.

4.   Ronda, 1989, 100–101; John Leonard, "Young (Old) Man Erikson," review of *Erik H. Erikson*, *New York Times*, 24 November 1970, 39; Marvin K. Opler, review of *Erik H. Erikson*, *American Anthropologist* (December 1972): 1366–67; review of *Erik H. Erikson*, *Virginia Quarterly Review* (Spring 1971): lxxii.

5.   See, for example, "The Letter Killeth," *Mind's Fate*, 36–37; and *Erikson*, 65–66.

6.   See, for example, Margaret Gean, review of *Anna Freud*, *New England Journal of Medicine*, vol. 327, no. 24 (10 December 1992): 1765.

7.   Virginia C. Hoch, review of *Anna Freud*, *Christian Century* (26 August 1992): 784; hereafter cited in the text.

8.   Elizabeth Hegeman, review of *Anna Freud*, *New York Times Book Review* (10 May 1992): 16; hereafter cited in the text.

Chapter Three

1. *Irony*, 7; James Agee and Walker Evans, *Let Us Now Praise Famous Men: Three Tenant Families* (1941; reprint, Boston: Riverside Press, Houghton Mifflin, 1960), xvi (hereafter cited in the text as Agee and Evans).

2. Maxine Greene, "The Humanity of Desegregation," review of *Courage and Fear*, *Saturday Review* (17 June 1967): 67; hereafter cited in the text.

3. For example, Alvin F. Poussaint, review of *Courage and Fear*, *Harvard Educational Review* (Spring 1968): 373; hereafter cited in the text; Walker Percy, "The Doctor Listened," review of *Courage and Fear*, *New York Times Book Review* (25 June 1967): 7. Coles told Jay Woodruff that the latter review gave him "the biggest thrill" of his early writing career; he wrote Percy to thank him (Woodruff and Woodruff, 233).

4. Robert Coles, *Migrants, Sharecroppers, Mountaineers*, vol. 2 of *Children of Crisis* (Boston: Atlantic-Little, Brown, 1971), 25; hereafter cited in the text as *Migrants*.

5. Adele V. Silver, "What the Light of Social Science Obscures," review of *Migrants, Sharecroppers, Mountaineers* and *The South Goes North*, *Nation* (24 July 1972): 53; hereafter cited in the text.

6. Paul Starr, "Rich Child, Poor Child," review of *Eskimos, Chicanos, Indians* and *Privileged Ones*, *New York Times Book Review* (22 January 1978): 1; hereafter cited in the text.

7. Henry Caudill, "Victims," review of *Migrants, Sharecroppers, Mountaineers* and *The South Goes North*, *New York Review of Books* (9 March 1972): 21; hereafter cited in the text.

8. Marge Piercy, review of *Migrants, Sharecroppers, Mountaineers* and *The South Goes North*, *New York Times Book Review* (13 February 1972): 20; hereafter cited in the text.

9. Peter S. Prescott, "Learning from Children," review of *Eskimos, Chicanos, Indians* and *Privileged Ones*, *Newsweek* (16 January 1978): 75; hereafter cited in the text.

10. Revelation 22:1–5, used as epigraph, *Privileged*, viii.

11. Christopher Lasch, "To Be Young, Rich, and Entitled," review of *Privileged Ones*, *Psychology Today* (March 1978): 124; hereafter cited in the text.

12. Gore Vidal, "Rich Kids," review of *Privileged Ones*, *New York Review of Books* (9 February 1978): 10; hereafter cited in the text.

13. K. L. Woodward, in "Books: Critics' Choices for Christmas," *Commonweal* (8 December 1972): 238.

14. Joseph Epstein, "Dr. Coles Among the Poor," *Commentary* (August 1972): 62; hereafter cited in the text.

15. Edgar Z. Friedenberg, "Love in a Cold Climate," review of *Courage and Fear*, *New York Review of Books* (28 September 1967): 28; hereafter cited in the text.

16. See, for example, Oscar Handlin, review of *Courage and Fear*, *Atlantic Monthly* (June 1967): 129; Christopher Lehmann-Haupt, "What Is Robert Coles Saying?" review of *Migrants, Sharecroppers, Mountaineers* and *The South Goes North*, *New York Times*, 18 February 1972, 33; also Epstein, 62, and Starr, 32.

17. Starr, 33; Mary Ellman, "Psychiatry and Prejudice," review of *Courage and Fear*, *Commentary* (November 1967): 92; hereafter cited in the text.

18. Eliot Fremont-Smith, "People of the South in the Stress of Change," review of *Courage and Fear*, *New York Times*, 5 June 1967, 41.

Chapter Four

1. Although Coles had read Winnicott early on, the object relations or Kleinian school of psychoanalytic thought was the major rival of the ego psychologists, led by Anna Freud. For a summary of the two schools' ideas, see "Freudianism: Later Developments," *The Oxford Companion to the Mind*, ed. Richard L. Gregory (Oxford: Oxford University Press, 1987), 270–75.

2. *Spiritual Life*, 8–9; see also the discussion of *Walker Percy*.

3. Mary Gordon, "What They Think about God," review of *The Spiritual Life of Children*, *New York Times Book Review* (25 November 1990): 28; hereafter cited in the text.

4. Donald H. Heinrich, review of *The Spiritual Life of Children*, *Commonweal* (8 March 1991): 173–74; hereafter cited in the text.

5. Chester E. Finn Jr., "Children and God," review of *The Spiritual Life of Children*, *Commentary* (June 1991): 64; hereafter cited in the text.

Chapter Five

1. Robert Coles, *The Middle Americans: Proud and Uncertain*, with Jon Erikson, photographer (Boston: Little, Brown, 1971), vii; hereafter cited in the text as *Middle Americans*.

2. Jonathan Yardley, review of *Farewell to the South*, *New York Times Book Review* (6 August 1972): 3; hereafter cited in the text.

3. Robert Coles, *The Last and First Eskimos*, with Alex Harris, photographer (Boston: New York Graphic Society, 1978), 9; hereafter cited in the text as *Last*.

4. Robert Coles, *The Old Ones of New Mexico*, with Alex Harris, photographer (Albuquerque: University of New Mexico Press, 1973), xv; hereafter cited in the text as *Old Ones*.

5. "Robert Coles," in *Photography within the Humanities*, ed. Eugenia Parry Janis and Wendy MacNeil (Danbury: Addison House, 1977), 151; hereafter cited in the text as *Photography*.

6. Robert Coles and Jane Hallowell Coles, *Women of Crisis: Lives of Struggle and Hope*, Radcliffe Biography Series, ed. Merloyd Lawrence (Reading, Mass.: Addison-Wesley, 1978), 6; hereafter cited in the text as *Women*.

7.   Robert Coles and Jane Hallowell Coles, *Women of Crisis II: Lives of Work and Dreams*, Radcliffe Biography Series, ed. Merloyd Lawrence (New York: Delacorte, 1980), 14; hereafter cited in the text as *Women II*.

Chapter Six

1.   Robert Coles, *Still Hungry in America*, with Al Clayton, photographer (New York: New American Library-World, 1969), 84; hereafter cited in the text as *Hungry*.
2.   William Stott, *Documentary Expression and Thirties America* (New York: Oxford University Press, 1973), 20–21; hereafter cited in the text.
3.   Robert Coles, *Dorothea Lange: Photographs of a Lifetime* (Millerton, N.Y.: Aperture-Viking, 1982), 36; hereafter cited in the text as *Lange*.
4.   Gerald Walker, review of *Still Hungry in America*, *New York Times Book Review* (13 April 1969): 24.
5.   Robert Coles, *The Image Is You*, ed. Donald Erceg (Boston: Houghton Mifflin, 1969), 58; hereafter cited in the text as *Image*.
6.   Steven Weiland, "Prose for Pictures: Documentary Style and the Example of Robert Coles," *Kansas Quarterly* 11, no. 4 (1979): 138; hereafter cited in the text.
7.   Robert Coles, *The Darkness and the Light: Photographs*, with Doris Ulmann, photographer (Millerton, N.Y.: Aperture, 1974), 82; hereafter cited in the text as *Darkness*.
8.   Robert Coles, "Looking and Listening," *Aperture* 19, no. 4 (1975): 4; hereafter cited in the text as "Looking."
9.   *Lange*, 15; Coles's italics, citing Willard Van Dyke's 1934 statement about Lange.
10.   Shaun McNiff, "Art, Artists and Psychotherapy: A Conversation with Robert Coles," *Art Psychotherapy* 3 (1976): 118–19; hereafter cited in the text.
11.   Robert Coles, "Children as Visionaries," in Helen Levitt, *In the Street: Chalk Drawings and Messages, New York City, 1938–1948*, ed. Alex Harris and Marvin Hoshino (Durham: Duke University Press, 1987), 6; hereafter cited in the text as *Street*.
12.   Robert Coles, *Their Eyes Meeting the World: The Drawings and Paintings of Children*, ed. Margaret Sartor (Boston: Houghton Mifflin, 1992), ix; hereafter cited in the text as *Eyes*.

Chapter Seven

1.   Dulcy Brainard, "Robert Coles," *Publishers Weekly* (16 November 1990): 42; reprinted in Woodruff and Woodruff, 181.
2.   Coles has also written six books for children, with the most recent published in 1995, but regards himself as "not a really accomplished writer of

children's books," being too inclined to "preachiness." Critics have generally agreed. See Marion E. Bodian, "Robert Coles on Activism," *Harvard Crimson* (29 May 1968): 1–4; reprinted in Woodruff and Woodruff, 9–10.

3. Bruce A. Ronda, "Robert Coles: Psychiatry and the Life of the Spirit," review of *The Moral Life of Children* and *The Political Life of Children*, *Christian Century* (18–25 June 1986): 583.

4. Melvin J. Friedman, "Robert Coles's South and Other Approaches to Flannery O'Connor," review of *Flannery O'Connor's South*, *Southern Literary Journal* 15 (1982): 121; hereafter cited in the text.

5. Robert Coles, *A Festering Sweetness: Poems of American People* (Pittsburgh: University of Pittsburgh Press, 1978), 2; hereafter cited in the text as *Sweetness*.

6. Review of *A Festering Sweetness*, *Publisher's Weekly* (6 March 1978): 90.

7. Robert Coles and Jane Hallowell Coles, *Rumors of Separate Worlds: Poems by Robert Coles* (Iowa City: University of Iowa Press, 1989); hereafter cited in the text as *Rumors*.

8. Review of *Rumors of Separate Worlds*, *Publisher's Weekly* (15 September 1989): 112.

9. Robert Coles, *Flannery O'Connor's South* (Baton Rouge: Louisiana State University Press, 1980), xvii; hereafter cited in the text as *O'Connor*.

10. Robert Coles, *That Red Wheelbarrow: Selected Literary Essays* (Iowa City: University of Iowa Press, 1988), xiv; hereafter cited in the text as *Wheelbarrow*.

11. Robert Coles, *Agee: His Life Remembered*, ed. Ross Spears and Jude Cassidy (New York: Holt, Rinehart, 1985), 3–13, 79–102, 125–33, 181–84; hereafter cited in the text as *Agee*.

12. Francis X. Rocca, review of *Harvard Diary: Reflections on the Sacred and the Secular* and *That Red Wheelbarrow: Selected Literary Essays*, *American Spectator* (March 1989): 41; hereafter cited in the text.

13. See, for example, Helen Bevington, "You Tell Me Yours, I'll Tell You Mine," review of *The Call of Stories*, *New York Times Book Review* (26 February 1989): 38; Ellen K. Coughlin, review of *The Call of Stories*, *Chronicle of Higher Education* (8 March 1989): A10; Sanford Pinsker, " 'After Such Knowledge, What Forgiveness?': The Rise of Ethical Criticism," review of *The Call of Stories*, *Georgia Review* (Summer 1989): 404; Gordon Pradl, "Separate but Not Equal: Robert Coles' *Call of Stories*," *English Journal* (April 1990): 103; Kieran Egan, review of *The Call of Stories*, *Teachers College Record* (Fall 1990): 128; Lana S. Leonard, review of *The Call of Stories*, *Social Education* (January 1991): 61; Samuel Totten, review of *The Call of Stories*, *Educational Studies* (Spring 1991): 46.

14. Frank Kermode, *The Sense of an Ending: Studies in the Theory of Fiction* (New York: Oxford University Press, 1967), 8.

Chapter Eight

1. "Colloquy," in William Flint Thrall and Addison Hibbard, *A Handbook to Literature*, rev. C. Hugh Holman (New York: Odyssey, 1960), 94.

2. See "Hagiography," in *Encyclopedia of Early Christianity*, ed. Everett Ferguson (New York: Garland, 1990), 408.

3. *Geography*, 1; Woodruff and Woodruff report that the meetings took place in the Coleses' Concord home (xx–xxi).

4. *Diary*, 68. Although Coles states that he has not previously written on these topics (*Diary*, 65), Ronda points out that "Who's to Be Born?" *New Republic* (10 June 1967): 10–12, does support liberalized abortion laws, although not without ambivalence (Ronda, 1989, 134, 196).

5. Thomas Molnar, review of *Harvard Diary: Reflections on the Sacred and the Secular*, *National Review* (2 June 1989): 62.

6. Robert A. Sirico, "A Tribute to Altruism," review of *The Call of Service: A Witness to Idealism*, *Wall Street Journal*, 15 November 1993, A10; hereafter cited in the text.

7. Francine du Plessix Gray, "When We Are Good We Are Very, Very Good," review of *The Call of Service*, *New York Times Book Review* (21 November 1993): 9; hereafter cited in the text.

8. Elliot Robins, review of *The Call of Service*, *Antioch Review* (Spring 1994): 368.

Conclusion

1. Robert Coles, *A Robert Coles Omnibus* (Iowa City: University of Iowa Press, 1993), also gathers twenty essays originally published between 1987 and 1992.

Selected Bibliography

PRIMARY SOURCES

Nonfiction

Children of Crisis: A Study of Courage and Fear. Vol. 1 of *Children of Crisis*, Boston: Atlantic-Little, Brown, 1967.

The Image is You. Ed. Donald Erceg. Boston: Houghton Mifflin, 1969.

Still Hungry in America. With Al Clayton, photographer. New York: World, 1969.

Wages of Neglect. With Maria Piers, coauthor; Stephen L. Feldman, photographer. Chicago: Quadrangle Books, 1969.

Drugs and Youth: Medical, Psychiatric, and Legal Facts. With Joseph H. Brenner and Dermot Meagher. New York: Liveright, 1970.

Erik H. Erikson: The Growth of His Work. Boston: Atlantic-Little, Brown, 1970.

Teachers and the Children of Poverty. Washington: Potomac Institute, 1970.

Uprooted Children: The Early Life of Migrant Farm Workers. Pittsburgh: University of Pittsburgh Press, 1970.

The Geography of Faith: Conversations between Daniel Berrigan, when Underground, and Robert Coles. With Daniel Berrigan. Boston: Beacon Press, 1971.

The Middle Americans: Proud and Uncertain. With Jon Erikson, photographer. Boston: Little, Brown, 1971.

Migrants, Sharecroppers, Mountaineers. Vol. 2 of *Children of Crisis*. Boston: Little, Brown, 1971.

The South Goes North. Vol. 3 of *Children of Crisis*. Boston: Atlantic-Little, Brown, 1971.

Twelve to Sixteen: Early Adolescence. Ed. with Jerome Kagan. New York: W. W. Norton, 1972.

The Old Ones of New Mexico. With Alex Harris, photographer. Albuquerque: University of New Mexico Press, 1973.

A Spectacle unto the World: The Catholic Worker Movement. With Jon Erikson, photographer. New York: Viking Press, 1973.

The Buses Roll. With Carol Baldwin. [New York]: W. W. Norton, 1974.

The Darkness and the Light: Photographs. With Doris Ulmann, photographer. Millerton, N.Y.: Aperture, 1974.

Irony in the Mind's Life: Essays on Novels by James Agee, Elizabeth Bowen, and George Eliot. Charlottesville: University Press of Virginia, 1974.

William Carlos Williams: The Knack of Survival in America. New Brunswick: Rutgers University Press, 1975.

Eskimos, Chicanos, Indians. Vol. 4 of *Children of Crisis.* Boston: Little, Brown, 1977.

Privileged Ones: The Well-off and the Rich in America. Vol. 5 of *Children of Crisis.* Boston: Atlantic-Little, Brown, 1977.

A Festering Sweetness: Poems of American People. Pittsburgh: University of Pittsburgh Press, 1978.

The Last and First Eskimos. With Alex Harris, photographer. Boston: New York Graphic Society, 1978.

Walker Percy: An American Search. Boston: Atlantic-Little, Brown, 1978.

Women of Crisis: Lives of Struggle and Hope. With Jane Hallowell Coles, coauthor. Radcliffe Biography Series. Reading, Mass.: Addison-Wesley, 1978.

Flannery O'Connor's South. Baton Rouge: Louisiana State University Press, 1980.

Women of Crisis II: Lives of Work and Dreams. With Jane Hallowell Coles. Radcliffe Biography Series. New York: Delacorte, 1980.

Dorothea Lange: Photographs of a Lifetime. Millerton, N.Y.: Viking-Penguin for Aperture, 1982.

The Doctor Stories of William Carlos Williams. New York: New Directions, 1984.

Agee: His Life Remembered. Ed. Ross Spears and Jude Cassidy. New York: Holt, Rinehart, 1985.

Sex and the American Teenager. With Geoffrey Stokes. New York: Harper & Row, Harper Colophon-Rolling Stone, 1985.

The Moral Life of Children. Boston: Houghton Mifflin, 1986.

The Political Life of Children. Boston: Houghton Mifflin, 1986.

Dorothy Day: A Radical Devotion. Radcliffe Biography Series. Reading, Mass.: Addison-Wesley, 1987.

In the Street: Chalk Drawings and Messages, New York City, 1938–1948. Compiled by Helen Levitt; ed. Alex Harris and Marvin Hoshino. Durham: Duke University Press, 1987.

Simone Weil: A Modern Pilgrimage. Radcliffe Biography Series, ed. Merloyd Lawrence. Reading, Mass.: Addison-Wesley, 1987.

The Call of Stories: Teaching and the Moral Imagination. Boston: Houghton Mifflin, 1989.

The Child in Our Times: Studies in the Development of Resiliency. Ed. with Timothy Dugan. N.p.: Brunner/Mazel, 1989.

Harvard Diary: Reflections on the Sacred and the Secular. New York: Crossroad, 1989.

Rumors of Separate Worlds: Poems by Robert Coles. Iowa City: University of Iowa Press, 1989.

The Spiritual Life of Children. Boston: Houghton Mifflin, 1990.

Anna Freud: The Dream of Psychoanalysis. Radcliffe Biography Series. Reading, Mass.: Addison-Wesley, 1992.

Their Eyes Meeting the World: The Drawings and Paintings of Children. Ed. Margaret Sartor. Boston: Houghton Mifflin, 1992.

The Call of Service: A Witness to Idealism. Boston: Houghton Mifflin, 1993.

The Ongoing Journey: Awakening Spiritual Life in At-Risk Youth. Boys Town, Nebr.: Boys Town Press, 1995 (coauthored with others).
The Moral Intelligence of Children. New York: Random House, 1997.
The Youngest Parents. Jocelyn Lee and John Moses, photographers. New York: W. W. Norton, 1997.

Essay Collections

Farewell to the South. Boston: Atlantic-Little, Brown, 1972.
The Mind's Fate: Ways of Seeing Psychiatry and Psychoanalysis. Boston: Atlantic-Little, Brown, 1975.
That Red Wheelbarrow: Selected Literary Essays by Robert Coles. Iowa City: University of Iowa Press, 1988.
Times of Surrender: Selected Essays by Robert Coles. Iowa City: University of Iowa Press, 1988.
A Robert Coles Omnibus. Iowa City: University of Iowa Press, 1993.

Books for Children

Dead End School. Boston: Little, Brown, 1968.
The Grass Pipe. Boston: Little, Brown, 1969.
Saving Face. Illustrated by Robert Lowe. Boston: Little, Brown, 1972.
Riding Free. Boston: Little, Brown, 1973.
Headsparks. Boston: Little, Brown, 1975.
The Story of Ruby Bridges. Illustrated by George Ford. N.p.: Scholastic, 1995.
Coles, Robert, ed. *In God's House: Drawings by Children at Risk.* Grand Rapids, Mich.: William B. Eerdmans Publishing, 1996.

Interviews

McNiff, Shaun. "Art, Artists and Psychotherapy: A Conversation with Robert Coles." *Art Psychotherapy* 3 (1976): 115–33. A treatment of Coles's methods in relationship to art, especially the field of art therapy; many biographical insights.
Janis, Eugenia Parry, and Wendy MacNeil, eds. "Robert Coles." In *Photography within the Humanities*, 138–52. Danbury: Addison House, 1977. Important for Coles's views on photography and photographers and the relationship of photography to his own writing.
Hellerstein, David. "On Medicine and Literature: An Interview with Robert Coles." In Robert Coles, *Times of Surrender: Selected Essays*, 59–76. Iowa City: University of Iowa Press, 1988. Originally appeared in *North American Review* (June 1980).
Woodruff, Jay, and Sarah Carew Woodruff, eds. *Conversations with Robert Coles.* Literary Conversations Series. Jackson: University Press of Mississippi, 1992. Important collection of 23 previously published interviews with Coles, 1968–1991. Includes a detailed chronology of Coles's life.

Woodruff, Jay. "Robert Coles: Don't Worry, Dad." In *A Piece of Work: Five Writers Discuss Their Revisions*, ed. Jay Woodruff, 99–148. Iowa City: University of Iowa Press, 1993. Interview plus reproduction of Coles's original handwritten draft of a short 1986 essay.

Other

"Robert Coles: An Intimate Biographical Interview." Produced by Bruce Baird-Middleton. 60 min. Cambridge, Mass.: Film Study Center-Harvard University Press, n.d. Conducted at Adams House, Harvard University, July 10, 1986, by one of Coles's graduate teaching assistants. Video-recording.

"Listening to Children: A Moral Journey with Robert Coles." Produced by Buddy Squires et al. Television broadcast. 90 min. Social Media Productions-Center for Documentary Studies, PBS, September 22, 1995. Examines the moral lives of six children; an absorbing video extension of Coles's interviewing method.

"Robert Coles: Teacher." 57 min. Social Media Productions, n.d. Excerpts from Coles's lectures on "The Literature of Social Reflection." Videorecording.

SECONDARY SOURCES

Book

Ronda, Bruce A. *Intellect and Spirit: The Life and Work of Robert Coles*. New York: Continuum, 1989. Treats Coles as a literary translator of lives, focusing on his moral and religious sensibility. A scholar of American studies and a writer for *Christian Century*, Ronda traces the influence on Coles of Augustine, Kierkegaard, and the American Transcendentalists as well as that of other philosophers, social thinkers, and fiction writers. An introduction and seven chapters, organized by topic, cover Coles's major works up to 1987 and apply contemporary literary theory to his complex intellectual project.

Articles and Reviews

Avitabile, Alex. Review of *A Spectacle Unto the World: The Catholic Worker Movement*. *America*, 4 August 1973, 70. Commends both Coles and Erikson for capturing the spirit of the Catholic Worker movement. Asserts that Coles's "intricate" text shows religious understanding as well as factual knowledge of the Workers' mission. Recommends *Spectacle* as "an excellent introduction to the movement."

Bamforth, Iain. "Clinical Humanities." Review of *Times of Surrender*. *Times Literary Supplement*, 7 July 1989, 752. Asserts that although the anthology focuses on only a few writers, it gives the profession of medicine an example of edifying literary lives.

Barnes, Henry. Review of *The Spiritual Life of Children. Parabola* (May 1991): 106. Dubs the volume "an explorer's notebook, conscientiously and sensitively recorded, on a journey into the realm where children are actually at home."

Belenky, Robert. "Heroes of a Bad Time." Review of *Courage and Fear. Nation*, 4 September 1967, 188–89. Identifies *Courage and Fear* as an important work of social documentary.

Bell, Marty G. Review of *Harvard Diary: Reflections on the Sacred and the Secular. Religious Studies Review* (October 1989): 373. Praises the collection and calls Coles "one of the most engaging writers on contemporary issues of religion and society."

Bevington, Helen. "You Tell Me Yours, I'll Tell You Mine." Review of *The Call of Stories: Teaching and the Moral Imagination. New York Times Book Review*, 26 February 1989, 38. Reads in this volume Coles's own career. Like William Carlos Williams, she asserts, he is a storyteller and a scourge of intellectuals, though less truculent and angry. Notes Coles's belief in the universal value of stories.

Briggs, Jean L. "The Inner Eskimo." Review of *The Last and First Eskimos. Natural History* (December 1978): 80. Although this volume succeeds in showing Eskimos' aesthetic sophistication, Briggs, an anthropologist, suggests that the evocative style of *Eskimos* is due more to Coles than to the informants. Praises Alex Harris's photographs as embodying the volume's stated purpose, documenting a time of transition.

Caudill, Henry. "Victims." Review of *Migrants, Sharecroppers, Mountaineers* and *The South Goes North. New York Review of Books*, 9 March 1972, 21–23. Assesses the national significance of *Children of Crisis* and sensitively characterizes the immensity of Coles's project in volumes 2 and 3.

Chaddock, Gail Russell. "Helping Others, Helping Ourselves." Review of *The Call of Service. Christian Science Monitor*, 9 December 1993, 17. Notes that the volume looks frankly at burnout, anger, and cynicism among volunteers.

Chappell, Fred. Review of *Irony in the Mind's Life. South Atlantic Quarterly* (Autumn 1975): 517–18. Applauds Coles's bold reading of literature but puzzles over the unevenness and psychological interpretations of the argument. Praises the analysis of *Middlemarch* but finds that the opening chapter fails because it attempts too much.

Conarroe, Joel. Review of *Flannery O'Connor's South. American Literature* (March 1981): 138–40. Regards the work as unsophisticated because it regards literary characters as case studies and stories as "tracts." Praises the presentation of Coles's own interviews.

Cook, Timothy E. Review of *The Political Life of Children* and *The Moral Life of Children. American Political Science Review* (March 1987): 257–59. Finds

Moral Life's main points accessible but considers *Political Life* more original. Critically examines Coles's treatment of nationalism.

Coughlin, Ellen K. Review of *The Call of Stories: Teaching and the Moral Imagination*. *Chronicle of Higher Education*, 8 March 1989, A10. Emphasizes that Coles regards the power of stories as reciprocal, that the telling or reading elicits important tales from the listener and reader.

Dietrich, Jeff. "Simone Fasted, Dorothy Fed." Review of *Dorothy Day: A Radical Devotion* and *Simone Weil: A Modern Pilgrimage*. *Los Angeles Times Book Review*, 13 September 1987, 23. Dietrich, himself a writer for *Catholic Worker*, perceptively evaluates *Dorothy Day* as a contribution to studies of the Catholic Worker movement and its founder. Approves Coles's ability to describe Day's more sensuous side. Observes that Weil is a difficult subject and assesses Coles's negotiation of her many contradictions. Judges the two volumes as important statements on the lives of "*two modern saints*" (Dietrich's italics).

du Plessix Gray, Francine. "When We Are Good We Are Very, Very Good." Review of *The Call of Service*. *New York Times Book Review*, 21 November 1993, 9. Dryly appraises the volume as sentimental and as oblivious to the less noble side of altruism.

Egan, Kieran. Review of *The Call of Stories: Teaching and the Moral Imagination*. *Teachers College Record* (Fall 1990): 128. Thoughtfully characterizes *Stories* as "an affecting book about affecting books" as well as a "book that practices what it preaches," demonstrating that literature is not merely a leisure pursuit but helps us make sense of our lives. Also offers the salient point that Coles speaks mainly to the well-educated, so that his ideas are a "challenge to current schooling practices" (Egan, 128).

Elkind, David. Review of *Erik H. Erikson*. *Saturday Review*, 16 January 1971, 51–55. Admiring but probing analysis of the biography's prose and assumptions. Laments the work's repetition and ambiguity and its failure to trace how Erikson's ideas related to his environment. Cites the bad fit between Erikson's ideas and classical psychoanalysis, observing that Coles does not really deal with this anomaly. Notes that Coles's unwavering admiration actually obscures his subject. Compliments the deft descriptions of Erikson's boyhood and the Viennese psychoanalytic circle.

Ellman, Mary. "Psychiatry and Prejudice." Review of *Courage and Fear*. *Commentary* (November 1967): 91–92, 94. Points out "the inadequacy of the psychiatric mode" to describe either racism or the people affected by and responding to it; thus, Coles's subject may ultimately have to be understood in ethical terms (92).

Epstein, Joseph. "Dr. Coles Among the Poor." *Commentary* (August 1972): 60–63. A jaundiced but often perceptive assessment of *Children of Crisis*'s methods and author. Indicts Coles's liberal social scientific aspirations, notes the volumes' lack of "an organizing sensibility" and sees Agee as a pernicious influence on Coles's prose.

————. *Plausible Prejudices*. New York: W. W. Norton, 1985. Mentions in passing Coles's propensity to review many books uncritically (50).

Findley, Cecil. "Puncturing Balloons." *Religion and Intellectual Life* (Fall 1985): 35–39. Reports on Coles's address to a conference at Andover Newton Theological School.

Fink, Barbara. "Lange's Luminous Icons." Review of *Dorothea Lange: Photographs of a Lifetime*. *Christian Science Monitor*, 3 December 1982, B6. Regards this "stunning, eloquent" volume as a fitting tribute to Lange's work and philosophy.

Fremont-Smith, Eliot. "People of the South in the Stress of Change." Review of *Courage and Fear*. *New York Times*, 5 June 1967, 41. Stresses Coles's role as an advocate and a propagandist as well as a physician and scientist.

Friedenberg, Edgar Z . Review of *The Moral Life of Children* and *The Political Life of Children*. *Educational Studies* (Winter 1987): 598–602. Observes that the companion volumes explicate children's perceptions of reality with "unbearable clarity" but that neither offers "a unifying political or economic view of the way the world works" (601). *Moral Life* seems a mere collection of essays without an overall conclusion whereas *Political Life* is more coherent.

————. "Love in a Cold Climate." Review of *Courage and Fear*. *New York Review of Books*, 28 September 1967, 28–31. Assesses volume 1 of *Children of Crisis* with other works of psychology and social criticism. Compares the work with Truman Capote's nonfiction novel *In Cold Blood*. Comments that Coles's writing is deceptively simple but shows sophisticated methodology.

Friedman, Melvin J. "Robert Coles's South and Other Approaches to Flannery O'Connor." Review of *Flannery O'Connor's South*. *Southern Literary Journal* 15 (1982): 120–29. Warmly appraises *O'Connor's South* in a review essay on O'Connor criticism. Sees Coles's readings as influenced by Hawthorne and Emerson; indeed, Coles brings "an Emersonian brightness and optimism" to O'Connor's admiration of darker-minded Hawthorne (121).

Fuller, Edmund. "A Fine Study of a Remarkable Writer." Review of *Flannery O'Connor's South*. *Wall Street Journal*, 2 June 1980, 24. Reckons Coles an astute writer of literary appreciation, especially in grasping O'Connor's Catholicism.

————. "A Thinker Who Turns Ideas into Art." Review of *Walker Percy: An American Search*. *Wall Street Journal*, 11 June 1979, 14. Lauds the commentary on the novels and believes that the chapters on Percy's philosophical essays will be difficult for those unfamiliar with existentialism.

Fussell, Paul. "William Carlos Williams and His Problems." Review of *William Carlos Williams*. *Virginia Quarterly Review* (Summer 1976): 509–15. Respects Williams's prose fiction and this effort to call attention to it but faults Coles's appreciation as poorly written, sentimental, and overly influenced by "immersion in the assumptions of the therapeutic and welfare culture" (515).

Galligan, Edward L. Review of *The Call of Stories: Teaching and the Moral Imagination, That Red Wheelbarrow: Selected Literary Essays*, and *Times of Surrender: Selected Essays. Sewanee Review* (October 1989): cxxiv. Regards both *That Red Wheelbarrow* and *Times of Surrender* as worthwhile for their literary insights as well as their critique of social scientific jargon. Recommends *Stories* "for every graduate student in English in the country," citing its artistry that persuades people actually to read or reread literature (cxxiv).

Gardner, Peter. Review of *Women of Crisis II: Lives of Work and Dreams. Psychology Today* (June 1980): 122, 127. Faults *Women II* as having the lax organization of oral history but finds that the work skillfully shapes two decades of material on "pre-women's liberation survivors." Commends the handling of larger themes that emerge, including the "flashes of self-understanding" that the women experience (127).

Gean, Margaret. Review of *Anna Freud. New England Journal of Medicine*, vol. 327, no. 24, 10 December 1992: 1765. Notes that the volume combines biography and Coles's autobiography. Although not as comprehensive as other recent biographies of this figure, *Anna Freud* serves readers interested in "psychoanalysis, women's issues, the development of children, and the history of the twentieth century" (1765).

Geltman, Max "Who Speaks for America?" Review of *The Middle Americans: Proud and Uncertain. National Review*, 10 August 1971, 879–80. Although suspicious of the project and Coles's claims to objectivity as a liberal whom politicians read, asserts that the volume is a cautionary tale for both liberals and conservatives. Remarks that the people portrayed seem generic, although a few stories, like that of the couple grieving for their fallen son, achieve poignancy. Dismisses Jon Erikson's photographs as cold.

Gordon, Mary. "What They Think About God." Review of *The Spiritual Life of Children. New York Times Book Review*, 25 November 1990, 1, 28–29. Regards *Spiritual Life* as a moving, artful corrective to adults' misreadings of children's religious life. Although not always clearly structured, the volume generally coheres while remaining a series of narratives. The most powerful sections dramatize children's confrontations with sorrow and injustice. Criticizes the work for avoiding religion's darker side, specifically some children's intense anxiety at trying to live up to strict standards of conduct and faith. Nor does it deal with fear of damnation or intolerance. Notes that no child in the volume sees God as female.

Graber, David. "Poor Women, Prehumans, and the Specter of Mood Control." Review of *Women of Crisis: Lives of Struggle and Hope. Human Behavior* (December 1978): 73. Finds ample merit in *Women of Crisis*, with its deft editing to bring out common themes among these diverse women, whose lives would ordinarily be overlooked. Points out the women's "deep and subtle" consciousness and their unwillingness to be victims (73).

Gray, Richard. Review of *Flannery O'Connor's South*. *Journal of American Studies* (August 1981): 299. Dislikes O'Connor and hence this volume, although Coles's experiences in the South provide some illumination.

Greeley, Andrew. Review of *The Middle Americans: Proud and Uncertain*. *Critic* (November-December 1971): 77. Lauds Coles's unwillingness to accept media labels for these Americans and his search for the complexity of their lives.

Greene, Maxine. "The Humanity of Desegregation." Review of *Courage and Fear*. *Saturday Review*, 17 June 1967, 66–67. Locates the power of *Courage and Fear* in its humane artistry that depicts how racism and national crisis affect individual lives.

Greenfield, Jeff. Review of *Women of Crisis II: Lives of Work and Dreams*. *New York Times Book Review*, 6 July 1980, 10. Finds these portraits moving and remarks the subjects' memory of "turning points in their lives" (10).

Hegeman, Elizabeth. Review of *Anna Freud*. *New York Times Book Review*, 10 May 1992, 16. Finds that *Anna Freud* lacks the psychological insight of Coles's earlier biographies but successfully presents Miss Freud's public face. Regards the discussion of the feud with Melanie Klein to be fairly balanced, although brief, whereas other conflicts, such as Anna Freud's control of her father's archives and her narrow sense of the role of psychoanalysis, receive too little attention.

Heinrich, Donald H. Review of *The Spiritual Life of Children*. *Commonweal*, 8 March 1991, 174. Rev. Donald H. Heinrich praises *Spiritual Life* for showing how children are more sophisticated, indeed theological, in their reflections on the spirit than most adults have believed.

Heller, David. "A Vision of Children." Review of *The Moral Life of Children* and *The Political Life of Children*. *Psychology Today* (June 1986): 73–75. Positive evaluation by a former student of Coles. Heller is interested in the concept of vulnerability, which is identified as a major premise in Coles's construction of morality. Maintains that *Political Life* "reads a bit more smoothly than the morality volume" (74).

Henderson, Keith. "Being and Meaning for Children." Review of *The Spiritual Life of Children*. *Christian Science Monitor*, 12 February 1991, 13. Assesses the "almost invariably intriguing, often startling" dialogues in *Spiritual Life*, briefly questioning how typical the speakers are. Observes that the children's insights become "epiphanies of sorts for Coles." Finds the obligatory sections on Coles's research methods unnecessary but the narratives worthwhile.

Hoch, Virginia C. Review of *Anna Freud*. *Christian Century*, 26 August 1992, 784. Faults the biography for its uneven writing and coverage as well as admiring tone but recommends the last 50 pages for a sense of Anna

Freud's weaknesses that balance the eulogizing. Approves the inclusion of new primary materials, including interviews and unpublished letters.

Humphries, Sharon, Heidi Ravven, and Stephenson Brooks. "A Team Response." *Religion and Intellectual Life* (Fall 1985): 40–46. A philosophical critique of Coles's anti-intellectual stance.

"Kitchen Matches in the Dark." Review of *The Middle Americans: Proud and Uncertain*. *Time*, 28 June 1971, 78. Judges the book successful in detailing its subjects' "remarkable breadth and subtlety" of opinions in prose that is occasionally quite powerful.

Lamon, Lester C. Review of *Farewell to the South*. *Journal of Southern History* (August 1973): 422–23. Observes that in this volume the South emerges as "a region of people rather than a theoretical enigma" (422). Does not favor comparing Coles with the great historians of the South but acknowledges Coles's power to dramatize everyday racism. Notes the autobiographical cast, repetition in the civil rights section, and the particular rewards of the last section of essays.

Langer, Elinor. "Unsung Heroines." Review of *Women of Crisis: Lives of Struggle and Hope*. *New York Times Book Review*, 11 June 1978, 7, 40. Movingly analyzes *Women I* in terms of its narratives that evoke the "grand themes of life and literature." Asserts that although literary scholars, feminists, and "radicals" may all have their various reservations, the book's strength is that it defies classification (40). Prefers more elaboration of the Coleses' role as interviewers and participants.

Lasch, Christopher. "To Be Young, Rich, and Entitled." Review of *Privileged Ones*. *Psychology Today* (March 1978): 124–26. Asserts that *Privileged Ones* makes a unique, compassionate but not sentimental contribution to psychology as well as to social commentary. Notes Coles's dedication to leftist ideals but "rejection of leftist jargon and cant" (124).

Leary, Lewis. Review of *Walker Percy: An American Search*. *American Literature* (January 1980): 580. Praises the chapter on Percy's fiction but finds the early chapters "hard going."

Lee, John. "Mysteries." Review of *The Moral Life of Children*. *Time*, 17 March 1986, 81. Generally negative review summarizes the concerns of other contemporary reviewers. Although conceding Coles's intelligence and commitment to ethics, reproaches *Moral Life* for its pat conclusions about morality, its anti-intellectual stance, and its naive attitude toward the children, the last of which causes Lee to question Coles's abilities as an interviewer.

Lehmann-Haupt, Christopher. "What Is Robert Coles Saying?" Review of *Migrants, Sharecroppers, Mountaineers* and *The South Goes North*. *New York Times*, 18 February 1972, 33. An early criticism of Coles's lack of interest in theory and structure. Judges the books to have "moments of great satisfaction" but concludes they have wasted the opportunity to unite those moments.

————. "Making People Stereotypes." Review of *The Middle Americans: Proud and Uncertain. New York Times*, 28 June 1971, 78. Finds that Coles has stereotyped ordinary Americans from the outset, thereby making his project to discover their complexity moot. Questions why the speakers are not even identified by geographic region and judges the prose generally bad.

Leonard, John. "Young (Old) Man Erikson." Review of *Erik H. Erikson. New York Times*, 24 November 1970, 39. Calls *Erikson* a combination of biography and homage in which Coles "brilliantly summarizes" the works of the older psychoanalyst and researcher. Also finds parallels between the two men in that both "choose to integrate instead of isolate" and both eschew academic gamesmanship.

Lipman, Matthew. "On Morality as 'Life Put to the Test." Review of *The Political Life of Children* and *The Moral Life of Children. Journal of Education* 168 (1986): 104–9. A favorable review of *Moral Life* that stresses the eloquence of the young speakers and the uniqueness of the subject.

Lomas, Peter. Review of *Erik H. Erikson. New York Times Book Review*, 22 November 1970, 1. A balanced review by a fellow psychoanalyst. Praises the biography's account of Erikson's early life, its style, and its exposition of Erikson's thought while faulting its uncritical admiration of its subject and its failure to show how much Erikson departed from classical psychoanalytical theory. Also prefers a greater accounting of existentialist insight into Erikson's work.

Mandell, Arnold J. Review of *The Mind's Fate. Psychology Today* (November 1975): 21–22. Finds that the collection is thoughtful and well written, with "stimulating" portraits of psychologists and other figures. Applauds Coles's project of direct observation but is least impressed with the fourth section, in which Freud is absurdly characterized.

Marty, Martin E. "What They Believe: Robert Coles Listens Carefully to the Spiritual Ideas of Children." Review of *The Spiritual Life of Children. Tribune Books (Chicago Tribune)*, 23 December 1990, 1. Disagrees that *Spiritual Life* avoids the hard questions and asserts that the volume might rescue the term *spiritual* from misuse. Praises the attention to specific faiths although "Some of the exchanges sound like catechism class."

Meltzer, Milton. Review of *Dorothea Lange: Photographs of a Lifetime. Library Journal*, 1 December 1982, 2251. Observes that "As a visionary artist, Lange makes rewarding demands on the special talents of Coles."

Merchant, Preston. "Man of Letters, Man of Action." Review of *A Robert Coles Omnibus. Sewanee Review* (Spring 1995): xlv–xlviii. Declares that the subject of these essays is people as they read and are represented in literature. Stresses Coles's union of literary study with moral education and attaches his project to the broad goals of multiculturalism. Finds that Coles does not overplay the moralist and considers him to be "at his best in the longer essays" like "James Agee's Search" (xlvii).

Molnar, Thomas. Review of *Harvard Diary: Reflections on the Sacred and the Secular*. *National Review*, 2 June 1989, 62. Welcomes the collection but judges it "finally disappointing" since the times do not permit "a literature of piety" and Coles is not a writer or philosopher of sufficient stature to overcome the times (62).

Mudrick, Marvin. "Mad Dogs and Anglo Shrinks." Review of *The Mind's Fate*. *Hudson Review* (Autumn 1976): 471. Criticizes the anthology for its jargon, illogic, and uncritical stance. Compares Coles with the psychoanalyst Thomas Szasz.

Nachman, Larry D. "Soul-Gazer." Review of *The Moral Life of Children* and *The Political Life of Children*. *Commentary* (May 1986): 72–74. A detailed critique of these volumes focusing on their lack of argument and their philosophical assumptions. Asserts that *Moral Life* relies on Christian pietism rather than analysis of ethical consequences. Uncovers *Political Life*'s assumptions of "universalism," which downplays the role of culture in socialization and posits an autonomous self.

Opler, Marvin K. Review of *Erik H. Erikson*. *American Anthropologist* (December 1972): 1366. Sensitively examines the biography, its subject, and its writer but disagrees with some of Erikson's and Coles's theoretical stands on the role of social identity.

Ornstein, Robert E. "Aging with Dignity." Review of *The Old Ones of New Mexico*. *Psychology Today* (September 1974): 14. Considers this work to be a corrective to modern views of "getting old as a sorrowful occasion." Praises the text and photographs for their directness: "The photographs are extraordinary, and the text . . . is almost perfectly written" (14).

Paul, Sherman. Review of *William Carlos Williams*. *Journal of English and Germanic Philology* (October 1976): 617. Lauds the volume for calling attention to Williams's fiction but finds it otherwise unremarkable.

Percy, Walker. "The Doctor Listened." Review of *Children of Crisis: A Study of Courage and Fear*. *New York Times Book Review*, 25 June 1967, 7. Considers the work a successful balance "between theorizing and novelizing" and praises Coles's values as a "physician, and a wise and gentle one." This review prompted Coles to write Percy and thus begin their long association.

Piehl, Mel. Review of *Dorothy Day: A Radical Devotion*. *Journal of American History* (December 1988): 999. Labels the biography "an analytical report and interpretation" of Coles's conversations with Day, concerned only with certain themes and thus not a comprehensive biography. Nonetheless, recommends it to historians and others interested in American religious idealism for the insights contained in the exchanges.

Piercy, Marge. Review of *Migrants, Sharecroppers, Mountaineers* and *The South Goes North*. *New York Times Book Review*, 13 February 1972, 1, 20, 22. Exposes problems with Coles's approach while remaining sympathetic to his purposes. Exceptionally detailed and wide-ranging review of volumes 2 and

3 of *Children of Crisis* assesses their liberal social and moral consciousness, describes the genre as an artistic blend of subjects' monologues and Coles's comments, and praises the clarity of the prose. Notes Coles's quizzical persona, his "uptightness about sex," his lack of sympathy for women outside traditional roles, his discomfort with his speakers' anger, and his seeming approval of a passive stoicism rather than political activism (22).

Pinsker, Sanford. " 'After Such Knowledge, What Forgiveness?': The Rise of Ethical Criticism." Review of *The Call of Stories: Teaching and the Moral Imagination. Georgia Review* (Summer 1989): 395–405. A review essay on ethical criticism that treats *Stories* as an important contribution to the field. States that although the volume lacks theory, it challenges educators and students "to tackle tougher ethical questions" (405). Designates *Stories* an "altogether human and humanizing book" by "one of our consummate teachers of literature" (404).

Postman, Neil. "A Singer of Their Tales." Review of *The Moral Life of Children* and *The Political Life of Children. New York Times Book Review*, 19 January 1986, 1, 28. Dubs Coles a modern Homer whose speakers are in a sense characters. Treats the two volumes as essentially one, eliding the moral into the political as "inseparable" (28). Thinks Coles's position against nationalism could be stronger but still regards *Political Life* as "a major contribution" (28).

Poussaint, Alvin F. Review of *Courage and Fear. Harvard Educational Review* (Spring 1968): 373–74. Important review of Coles's first book by a sociologist and a participant in the civil rights movement. Although faulting Coles's method and the lack of valid scientific results, the review honors the psychiatrist's civil rights credentials and acknowledges the power of individual histories, which have "immortalized" the people portrayed (373). The reader feels "vicarious participation in the joys and struggles of the characters" (373).

Pradl, Gordon. "Separate but Not Equal: Robert Coles' *Call of Stories.*" *English Journal* (April 1990): 103–4. Important for its placing of *Stories* in the development of Coles's thinking of the mind, as Pradl puts it, as "a narrative organ" (104). Points to *Stories* as the basis for "a new and integrative story (theory)" for the teaching of English (104).

Prescott, Peter. "Learning from Children." Review of *Eskimos, Chicanos, Indians* and *Privileged Ones. Newsweek*, 16 January 1978, 75–76. Notes that Coles seeks "the truth of the spirit" like that of art or fiction (75). Speculates that artistry like Coles's is needed in social documentary; otherwise, no one would read it.

Review of *Dorothea Lange: Photographs of a Lifetime. Booklist*, 15 February 1983, 759. Singles out the volume as outstanding in part for Coles's sensitivity to documentary field research.

Review of *Dorothea Lange: Photographs of a Lifetime*. *Wilson Library Bulletin* (December 1982): 353–54. Observes that the introduction addresses the question of whether Lange's work was propaganda.

Review of *Erik H. Erikson*. *Virginia Quarterly Review* (Spring 1971): lxxii. Regards the biography as most worthwhile, noting the connections it makes between existentialism and Erikson's psychoanalytic work. Calls the work "the documentation of a love affair between two psychiatrists."

Review of *Farewell to the South*. *Saturday Review*, 21 October 1972, 80. Regards the volume as a coherent collection of "moving human documents."

Review of *Flannery O'Connor's South*. *Modern Fiction Studies* (August 1982): 516–17. Commends the work as useful and necessary for nonspecialists. Asserts that "Hard, Hard Religion" in particular offers insights into migrant preachers that can be applied to O'Connor's fiction, while the reading of the character of the social psychologist in "Greenleaf" is especially good.

Review of *Flannery O'Connor's South*. *Virginia Quarterly Review* (Autumn 1980): 127. Notes that the central structure of *O'Connor's South* juxtaposes real-life accounts with O'Connor's characters.

Review of *Rumors of Separate Worlds*. *Publisher's Weekly*, 15 September 1989, 112. Approves Coles's vision but not his verse.

Review of *That Red Wheelbarrow: Selected Literary Essays*. *Virginia Quarterly Review* (Spring 1989): 48. Praises the collection's prose and its humane treatment of literature's role in moral life.

Review of *The Geography of Faith*. *Commonweal*, 8 December 1972, 239. States that the volume is remarkable for a set of taped conversations and concludes that the two men's conversations may at times be better than their writing.

Review of *The Old Ones of New Mexico*. *New Yorker*, 14 January 1974, 98–99. Notes the beautiful photography; remarks the subjects' "incredibly active, unembittered lives" and disdain for Anglo culture.

Review of *Walker Percy: An American Search*. *Virginia Quarterly Review* (Summer 1980): 89. Asserts that the material from Coles's research affords "a kind of counterpoint" to Percy's characters and themes while the analysis cogently explicates an "often enigmatic" writer.

Robins, Elliot. Review of *The Call of Service*. *Antioch Review* (Spring 1994): 368. Recommends the work for community volunteers and calls Coles a "raconteur."

Rocca, Francis X. Review of *Harvard Diary: Reflections on the Sacred and the Secular* and *That Red Wheelbarrow: Selected Literary Essays*. *American Spectator* (March 1989): 40–41. Devoted mainly to *Harvard Diary*, this full review first claims Coles as a conservative "with a vague sense of obligation to liberalism" (40). Also remarks the hagiographic cast of *Harvard Diary*. That tendency is not as troublesome as Coles's humorless self-doubting, which Rocca sees as a "corruption" of Augustine (41).

Ronda, Bruce A. "Robert Coles: Psychiatry and the Life of the Spirit." Review of *The Moral Life of Children* and *The Political Life of Children*. *Christian Century*, 18–25 June 1986, 583–87. Characterizes Coles as Coles once characterized William Carlos Williams. Extends Coles's definition of moral as the "intersection of the private and the public," placing it in the context of national crises.

Schwartz, Albert. "Single Humanity." Review of *The Old Ones of New Mexico*. *New Republic*, 29 June 1974, 28. Elaborates the volume's exquisite relationship between the verbal and the visual.

Schwartz, Judith D. Review of *Their Eyes Meeting the World: The Drawings and Paintings of Children*. *New York Times Book Review*, 13 December 1992, 18. Remarks that the text is thoughtful and "poetic."

Silver, Adele V. "What the Light of Social Science Obscures." Review of *Migrants, Sharecroppers, Mountaineers* and *The South Goes North*. *Nation*, 24 July, 1972, 53–55. A brief but comprehensive assessment of *Children of Crisis*, volumes 2–3, plus an early exploration of Coles's religious sensibility.

Sirico, Robert A. "A Tribute to Altruism." Review of *The Call of Service: A Witness to Idealism*. *Wall Street Journal*, 15 November 1993, A10. Charges that *Service* is, despite the "many anecdotal gems," merely politically correct. Asserts that standards of conduct are required to give its ideals meaning.

Sorrentino, Gilbert. "America, America." Review of *William Carlos Williams*. *Partisan Review* (Fall 1975): 463–67. Regards Coles's treatment of Williams as "first-rate," recommending it as "one of the most valuable additions" to studies of Williams (466).

Springsted, Eric O. "Condemned to Moral Loneliness." Review of *Simone Weil: A Modern Pilgrimage*. *Commonweal*, 6 November 1987, 638–39. Dispassionate analysis of *Simone Weil*, citing the depth of Coles's insight while also weighing it against other evidence of Weil's life. Finds Coles's explanation for her obsession with not eating as spiritually plausible. Approves the treatment of Weil as "a committed moralist" rather than as a mystic (638).

Starr, Paul. "Rich Child, Poor Child." Review of *Eskimos, Chicanos, Indians* and *Privileged Ones*. *New York Times Book Review*, 22 January 1978, 1, 32–33. An important summary of Coles's achievement in *Children of Crisis* that also reviews the last two volumes. Judges *Privileged Ones* to be "the more original contribution" of the two (33) and sees it in light of recent psychiatric literature on narcissism and preoccupation with the self. Volume 4, with its depiction of Indian and Eskimo cultures, is proof that psychology is ultimately too limited to encompass Coles's subject. The series is a "prodigious achievement" and Coles "a splendidly accomplished writer" even when his writing is diffuse (32).

Storr, Anthony. Review of *The Mind's Fate*. *New York Times Book Review*, 28 September 1975, 8. Generally astute review of this anthology but also a summary of Coles's habitual strengths and weaknesses. Agrees with Coles's attack on psychobiography but thinks it does not go far enough. Points out Coles's reluctance to write about traditional psychoanalytic subjects like the id, repression, and the ego's defense mechanisms and his preference for religious or philosophical explanations of human frailty and motivation. Praises the essay on Anna Freud and judges the last two essays, case studies of children, as most typical of Coles's writing.

Stuckey, W. J. Review of *Walker Percy: An American Search*. *Modern Fiction Studies* (Winter 1979–80): 738–40. Finds *Walker Percy* to be a sound, readable work on a demanding subject, more so than Martin Luschei's *The Sovereign Wayfarer*. Notes that Percy's fiction is "not so much explicated as retold so as to reveal Percy's underlying philosophical argument" (739).

Van Herik, Judith. Review of *Harvard Diary: Reflections on the Sacred and the Secular. Journal of Religion* (April 1990): 293. Calls *Harvard Diary* "moving and challenging." Explores how Coles confronts the central theme, the clash between Christianity and the secular/scientific, in himself. Highly regards the essays on children's spiritual lives.

———. Review of *Simone Weil: A Modern Pilgrimage. Journal of Religion* (January 1989): 151. Views the work as more a collection of "loosely organized thematic essays" than a scholarly biography but grants that Coles is a very good interpreter of Weil for the general reader.

Vidal, Gore. "Rich Kids." Review of *Privileged Ones*. *New York Review of Books*, 9 February 1978, 9–12, 14. Not ordinarily a fan of Coles, his prose, or his methods, Vidal approvingly notes *Privileged Ones*'s portrayal of the ways of the rich and the subtleties of class in children's upbringing. Terms Coles a "moralist" and his purposes "essentially polemical" (14).

Walker, Gerald. Review of *Still Hungry in America*. *New York Times Book Review*, 13 April 1969, 24. Praises this collaboration of writer and photographer.

Weiland, Steven. "Prose for Pictures: Documentary Style and the Example of Robert Coles." *Kansas Quarterly* 11, no. 4 (1979): 133–43. Important for its treatment of Coles's writing that accompanies photography. Analyzes seven of Coles's collaborations and calls *Old Ones of New Mexico* "a near perfect match" of text and photographs.

White, George Abbott. "Clinical Approaches to Biography: The High Price of Mixed Truth." Review of *The Mind's Fate* and *Irony in the Mind's Life. Sewanee Review* (Spring 1977): 326–37. In this review essay on psychoanalytic approaches to literary biography, White praises Coles's respect for literature and agrees wholeheartedly with his cautious, ethical approach to psychoanalytical biography. Compares Coles with John E. Mack, a psychoanalyst and biographer of T. E. Lawrence.

Wieder, Alan. "Robert Coles Reconsidered: A Critique of the Portrayal of Blacks as Culturally Deprived." *Journal of Negro Education* (Fall 1981): 381–88. Argues that Coles's studies counter the myth of a culture of poverty among Black Americans.

Witonski, Peter P. "Trendy Revolution." Review of *The Geography of Faith*. *National Review*, 3 December 1971, 1361–62. Dismisses the volume as leftist nonsense.

Woodward, Kenneth. "Two Paradoxical Saints." Review of *Dorothy Day* and *Simone Weil*. *New York Times Book Review*, 6 September 1987, 10–11. This forthright review of the two biographies notes that both are less biographies than collections of "themes and passions," a fact that does not diminish them. Observes that on the whole *Day* is more successful because of its use of primary sources, a treatment that highlights her unique spirituality. Finds Coles's analysis of Weil's suicide persuasive and the biography worthwhile, but Weil ultimately eludes Coles, as she has other biographers. Compares Weil with another Coles favorite, Kierkegaard.

Yagoda, Ben. "A Lucid, Sympathetic Study of Walker Percy." Review of *Walker Percy: An American Search*. *Chronicle of Higher Education*, 5 March 1979, 11–12. Views this study of Percy with sympathy but also finds faults. Praises the biographical material and the readings of the essays but regards the opening chapter on philosophical roots as "irrelevant" (12).

Yardley, Jonathan. "Reader's Response." Review of *Walker Percy: An American Search*. *New York Times Book Review*, 28 January 1979, 10–11. Commends the volume but rates the chapters on Christian existentialism, although often perceptive, as too difficult for most readers.

————. Review of *Farewell to the South*. *New York Times Book Review*, 6 August 1972, 3, 23. Points out the importance of Coles's "discovery of the relationship between literature and his own psychological work," a discovery that informs this anthology (3).

Index

The Author

Susan Hilligoss is assistant professor of English at Clemson University and teaches in Clemson's program in professional communication. She has coedited *Literacy and Computers: The Complications of Teaching and Learning with Technology* (1994). Her teaching and research interests include nonfiction prose, the writing of science, and visual communication.

The Editor

Frank Day is a professor of English and head of the English Department at Clemson University. He is the author of *Sir William Empson: An Annotated Bibliography* (1984) and *Arthur Koestler: A Guide to Research* (1985). He was a Fulbright lecturer in American literature in Romania (1980–1981) and in Bangladesh (1986–1987).